EMBEDDED

EMBEDDED

A Marine Corps Adviser
Inside the Iraqi Army

BY WESLEY R. GRAY

NAVAL INSTITUTE PRESS
Annapolis, Maryland

Naval Institute Press
201 Wood Road
Annapolis, MD 21402

Library of Congress Cataloging-in-Publication Data

Gray, Wesley R.
  Embedded : a Marine Corps advisor inside the Iraqi army / Wesley R. Gray.
    p. cm.
  Includes bibliographical references and index.
  ISBN 978-1-59114-340-6 (alk. paper)
  1. Military assistance, American—Iraq. 2. Iraq—Armed Forces—Training of.
  3. Internal security—Iraq. 4. Iraq War, 2003—Personal narratives, American.
  5. Gray, Wesley R. 6. United States. Marine Corps—Officers—Biography. 7.
  United States. Marine Corps—Iraq. I. Title.
  DS79.769.G73 2009
  956.7044'34—dc22
  [B]

                                                              2008055201

Printed in the United States of America on acid-free paper

14 13 12 11 10 09   9 8 7 6 5 4 3 2
First Printing

All photos are from the author's personal collection.

To the soldiers of the Iraqi army,
who taught me that winning isn't everything,
but friends, family, and honor are.

CONTENTS

ACKNOWLEDGMENTS

Maj. Tom Ross once mentioned to me that his success as a Marine officer could be visualized as a turtle sitting on top of a fencepost—it was obvious he didn't get there alone. For this project, I felt like a blue whale sitting atop Mount Everest—without massive amounts of help, I would still be stuck on the bottom of the ocean.

First, I would like to thank the United States Marine Corps for giving me an opportunity to serve with an elite group of warrior citizens who are second to none. Specifically, I want to thank my advising teammates, who taught me about life, leadership, and how to be a better Marine (in no particular order): Doc, Nuts, V, Slip, Legger, Cpl. Sal, Mac, Moto McCoy, Wonder Twin #2, the Boss, D, Superhero, and Mighty Morgan—oohrah! And thanks to Eric Earnhardt for teaching me how to be a motivated Devil Dog.

The folks at the Graduate School of Business at the University of Chicago went beyond the call of duty in supporting me during my "sabbatical," for which I am extremely grateful. Thank you also to the many friends and family, too numerous to list here, who supported me during my deployment. My biggest fans were (and always have been) my parents, Bill and Jill Gray. Thanks for the unwavering support.

Many friends and family also gave me insightful feedback and razor-sharp editing on early drafts of this book. Mike Beimer, Mike Bennett, Cliff Gray, Mike Hollander, Anne and Craig Jorgensen, Ben Katz, Andy Kern, Gabe Klehr, Sandy Li, Ronica Licciardello, James McGinnis, Maurice Medland, Scott Miller, and Dave Woodworth were all extremely helpful. Of course, Rick Russell and Elizabeth Bauman of the Naval Institute Press have been with me through every step in the publishing process and have really made me feel at home as an author with their organization. Special thanks to Karin Kaufman for her superb copyediting services.

Finally, my sincerest thanks go to my wife, Katie, my lead editor and best friend for life.

Part 1

BECOMING AN EMBEDDED
MILITARY ADVISER

Chapter 1

Guess What? You Are Going to Iraq

February–March 2006

"Gray, nice fuckin' brief. You wanna volunteer for some time in Iraq and train some Iraqis?" Caught off guard after completing an important intelligence brief to Brig. Gen. Mastin Robeson and a room full of Marine and Japanese military officers, I replied out of instinct, "Sir, hell yeah. When would I leave?" The granite-hard Col. Steven Manning, a legend in the Marine Corps intelligence community, peered into my eyes. "July time frame," he said. "We'll talk about it later this evening. Oohrah!"

We never did get a chance to talk about it that evening. Over the next few weeks that February, I participated in the bilateral Japanese and U.S. military Yama Sukura war game in Kumamoto, Japan. At the conclusion of the exercise, Colonel Manning directed me to participate in a joint military operation with the Filipino army in the Philippines until mid-March. After spending almost two months traveling around Asia, Iraq was the last thing on my mind. But this all changed when I returned to my home base in Okinawa, Japan.

On March 14 I strolled into the intelligence offices at the 3rd Marine Division Headquarters at Camp Courtney, a small Marine Corps base in the center of the island of Okinawa. I had had the time of my life in the Philippines participating in real-world operations, working with the Filipino army, and meeting new people. Life was good. I hollered to Lt. Nate Krissoff, who came stumbling into the office. "Krissoff, dude, I can't believe those chicks you got in the Philippines. You are da man!" Krissoff, my best bud in the Marines, had partied too much while in the Philippines and was still feeling the aftereffects. He smirked and said, "Gray, hey brother, what happened in the Philippines . . . stays in the Philippines!" I laughed. "Nate, my lips are sealed—until I need something from you."

I sat at my computer and opened my e-mail box. I had 150 unanswered e-mails, only one of which seemed interesting. The subject line was "RE: MiTT members from Okinawa coming in on March 19th." I opened the e-mail out of curiosity, thinking it must have been addressed to the wrong Second Lieutenant Gray. But it was addressed correctly and would change my life.

At first I could make no sense of the e-mail. According to it I was supposed to be in Hawaii in five days to start training for a "MiTT"—whatever the heck that was. I sprinted to Colonel Manning's office, believing he would know what was happening. Manning examined the e-mail's contents. "Hrmm. Gray, it looks as though you will be going on a MiTT about four months sooner than I anticipated. Congratulations. Head to the operations shop upstairs and tell them Colonel Manning sent you. Tell them you need priority to get the hell off of Okinawa and into the fight." I answered, "Roger that, Sir." But I had one remaining inquiry for Manning. "One question for you, Sir. What exactly does MiTT stand for?" He laughed. "Gray, for an Ivy League graduate you aren't that bright, are you?" He paused then said, "MiTT stands for military transition team. You are going to be America's main effort. I wish I were in your position, you lucky bastard!"

I rushed upstairs and spoke with Master Sergeant Hampton, always the man to turn to in an urgent situation. He calmed my nerves. "Sir," he said, "don't worry about a thing. You are now on my priority list. This Sunday you will arrive in Hawaii, conduct your predeployment training with the MiTT, and by mid-July you will be enjoying the Iraqi sunshine." Crap, I thought to myself, how am I going to tell my wife?

Master Sergeant Hampton was not lying. On March 19 I arrived in beautiful Honolulu, Hawaii, with my military gear, an M-9 service pistol, an M-4 assault rifle, and not a friggin' clue as to what was going to happen next. I knew I was now on a military transition team heading to Iraq. I knew I had to train my ass off. And I knew this was a special duty assignment hooked up through Colonel Manning. I was afraid, but I was excited to get things rolling. I was heading to war.

Chapter 2

Culture Shock

July 2006

I t was 0800—show time. As the intelligence officer for the MiTT team, I was about to give the predeployment enemy situation brief at the 3rd Marine Regiment classified material vault. I took my job seriously, but those in attendance would rather have been surfing or tanning on the beaches of Hawaii. I started the brief with a shallow warning, which at the time I found witty. "Gentlemen," I said, "the biggest threat has gone from a mild sunburn on Waikiki Beach to bullet wounds. Let me tell you how the enemy plans to kill you."

My intention was to get the MiTT members into a combat mindset. My efforts fell flat. The Marines in front of me were "salty dogs," a Marine term for experienced combat veterans. Many of the Marines on the MiTT had spent ten to fifteen years in the Corps and had experienced multiple combat tours. One thing I had learned in my short two years in the Marines was that although the salty dogs bring a lot of wisdom and experience to the table, they also bring a certain amount of complacency and laziness. I now know the value of eager and motivated second lieutenants for the military: they make up for the apathy of the salty dogs.

Of course not all second lieutenants are created equal. A last-minute addition to the MiTT, 2nd Lt. Marco Le Gette, had an "alarm clock malfunction" before the meeting and managed to show up halfway through my brief. Great, I thought, another sign the MiTT team is not taking the upcoming combat deployment seriously.

I continued despite Le Gette's interruption. My brief covered a recent attack in our future area of operations near an Iraqi town called Dulab, which is south of the Haditha Triad, the population areas surrounding Haditha, a small town of about forty thousand residents in Al Anbar Province (see map 1). Insurgents had conducted a coordinated attack on a Marine combat outpost. During the assault a truck approached the checkpoint from the north and fired rocket-propelled grenades (RPGs). Immediately from the south, another group of insurgents pulled up with guns blazing, sending a hail of 7.62-mm lead toward the Marines. The Marines were able to regroup and pour massive firepower onto the two enemy positions. In the end, the game was settled: Marines with eight kills, insurgents with zero.

Remarkably, two of the insurgents killed in the attack were rogue Iraqi police (IP) from Hit, a small town along the Euphrates approximately thirty minutes from the scene of the attack. It did not take a genius to realize that these two insurgents could have easily been Iraqi army (IA) soldiers, the same soldiers we would live with for the duration of our tour in Iraq. By the end of my brief I had the group's attention. The team understood that our forthcoming duties as embedded military advisers would be unlike any experience any of us had gone through, even for the saltiest among us.

After my intelligence brief I rushed to finish packing. The Marine Corps likes to give Marines lists—many lists. In certain contexts (cooking is a good example), lists are great; in others they are a major pain in the ass. For our situation it was a pain in the ass. Major Pyle (a pseudonym) had us pack every item on the four-page predeployment gear list.

The supply officer for our MiTT, 1st Lt. Rob Adams, and I were not about to drag all the trash on our gear list halfway around the world (e.g., keep our normal sleeping bag and stash our bag rated for minus forty below zero). Immediately after our gear inspection Adams and I drove to his on-base home to dump a large chunk of the gear we were certainly not going to need. As Adams and I were loading our extra gear into his garage, his entire family— three young girls, a baby boy, and his beautiful wife—came out to greet us. Adams's youngest daughter rushed up to her father and said, "Daddy, Daddy, how was work? What did you do?" Adams responded, "Oh honey, not much. Lieutenant Gray gave us an intel [intelligence] brief on what we will see in Iraq—nothing exciting, really."

Adams's daughter looked at me with suspicious eyes. "Lieutenant Gray," she said, "what's it like over there? Is my Daddy going to be safe?" Sam,

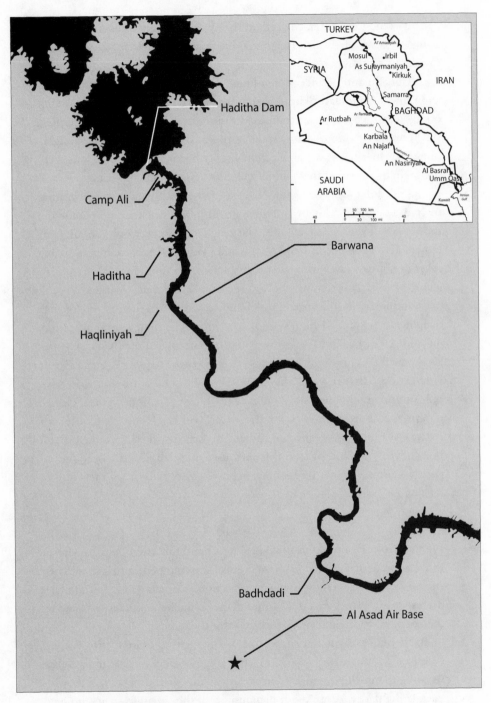

Map 1. The Haditha Triad in Al Anbar Province.

Adams's oldest daughter, chimed in. "Is my dad going to die? Are you guys going to get shot? Will I ever see my dad again?" I felt as if I was in the middle of a firefight.

All my infantry officer schooling, Marine Corps leadership training, and Officer Candidate School hazing should have taught me how to think on my feet. I was supposed to make decisions in the face of intense combat, yet I couldn't figure out how to keep these young girls at bay. Although I knew that the area in which we would serve had become the most dangerous in Iraq, I decided that a little white lie was my only option.

"Girls, don't worry," I said. "I've researched the region we're visiting in Iraq. There are a lot of bad guys in the place, but they have—for the most part—been killed by the Marines. I wouldn't worry about your father. He will be safe in Iraq." Adams and I saw his family members' visible relief as I spoke my words of encouragement. I continued, "Don't worry about your father; neither the insurgents nor the Iraqi soldiers we will be working with will hurt him. I promise." Sam and the rest of Adams's daughters surrounded him, with tears forming in their eyes. They cried, "Thank God, Daddy! We know you'll be safe over there. Call us every single day!" Adams's wife, Virginia, was not reassured. As a Marine Corps wife for over sixteen years, she knew the realities of war better than anyone. Virginia whispered into Adams's ear, "I love you, honey. Be safe."

On the short ride back to the MiTT office, I said to Lieutenant Adams, "God, I was full of shit, man." Adams smirked. "Yeah, well, all intel officers are full of shit. But seriously dude, thanks for keeping my family calm. The last thing they need to worry about is me coming home in a casket."

Kuwait

We flew from Honolulu to Los Angeles to Frankfurt and finally to Kuwait International Airport. The first two flights were cramped. Perhaps Lufthansa and United Airlines enjoy giving Marines non aisle, nonwindow seats. That makes sense, right? Let's put Marines in the scrunched middles seats and let the anorexic-looking teenage girls relax in the aisle.

In the end we got our justice on the flight from Frankfurt to Kuwait when a few of us were bumped to first class. Hot dog! As I sat in first class, enjoying the in-flight wireless Internet, drinking wine, and being fed by attractive flight attendants, the ridiculousness of the situation struck home. I was on my way to a combat zone.

We landed in Kuwait International Airport about 2230 and felt the culture shock immediately. Kuwaiti soldiers were returning from a tour of duty along the Kuwaiti border and the entire airport was celebrating. Women were making an awful yodeling sound that was a mix between a coyote's cry and a cockatoo recently slapped in the head. Meanwhile, the men, in full traditional Arab dress, were dancing and hollering for their heroes. The airport was filled with excitement. This was a hero's welcome done Kuwaiti style. This was a hero's welcome we wanted to see in seven months.

We waded through the crowds of Arabs to find the lounge. We all looked forward to settling into the posh Kellogg Brown and Root (KBR) lounge. The company's lounge rooms are what a Department of Defense (DoD) employee needs after flying around the world. They come complete with a fifty-inch flat screen television playing the latest DVDs and rows of luscious leather lounge chairs.

Just as we were sinking into our lounge chairs, Major Pyle walked in. "Gentlemen, we have a 0500 flight to Baghdad International Airport tomorrow. Buses are heading here now to take us to the Kuwait transient camp. When they get here, grab your trash, and get ready to move." Unmotivated, we all acknowledged the boss with "Roger."

Hell is hot . . . Kuwait is even hotter. Up until this point we hadn't left an air-conditioned space in Kuwait. As Adams and I went rushing outside of the KBR lounge to get on the bus, the heat slammed us in the face. Even in the middle of the night, it felt as if someone was blowing a hair dryer into our faces. "Good God," I murmured under my breath as heat blanketed my body. I have been in some scorching areas of the United States, yet nothing compares to Kuwait. In America, you can witness 120-degree heat in the Southwest, but it will be a "dry heat." In Florida, it can reach 100 degrees and it will be a "humid heat." Well, in Kuwait, it is 140 degrees and it is a "fucking hot heat."

When people ask me about Kuwait when I return home, I thought, my response will be that Kuwait is Kuwait. A large, flat desert with oil refineries and oil operations as far as the eye can see, tons of immigrant labor, and some world-class heat. I hoped that the only other time I would visit Kuwait in my lifetime would be during the return trip out of Iraq.

Iraq

We landed at Baghdad International Airport, commonly called BIOP (I'm not sure why the U.S. Army decided to use the acronym BIOP and not

BIAP). The aircrew lowered the rear cargo door on the C-130 and the brilliant light of Iraq pierced the cabin. We immediately woke up and untangled ourselves from the netting of the C-130 that was acting as our seats.

Watching the cargo door fall to the ground, I wondered if rounds would start flying past us. Before this my only memorable images of Iraq involved bullets and explosions. As a first timer into a combat zone, my visions of Iraq were based more on the movie *Terminator 2: Judgment Day* than reality. Fortunately, we were on the most secure base on the planet—Camp Victory.

Camp Victory is the U.S. Army's crowning achievement in base construction. The base exemplifies the Army's ability to fortify an enormous piece of earth and, at the same time, convince the Iraqi people beyond any doubt that we are here to stay for a long time. One step into the camp and it was hard for me to imagine we would be leaving Iraq any time in the next century, let alone the next few years. Not only was it huge, but it was surprisingly posh. Even the tents in the transient field quarters had outstanding amenities: air-conditioning, a floor-cleaning service, and wireless Internet. In addition to the stellar amenities in the tents, there were KBR chow halls with delicious food and enormous exercise facilities everywhere. I did not feel as though I was in Iraq. In truth I felt as if the C-130 had taken a wrong turn and landed at a Club Med in the middle of the desert somewhere. Things were looking up.

Despite the surprising comforts of Camp Victory, the place took the wind out of my sails. When I landed in Iraq, I was prepared to walk in the footsteps of the combat Marines who fought famous battles in Belleau Wood, Guadalcanal, Iwo Jima, and Okinawa. But in the midst of Camp Victory luxury, my epic vision of being a hard-charging, leather-tough combat Marine vanished.

Camp Victory had a few telltale signs that reminded me we were in Iraq. First, large blimps flew above the camp—the same airships you see flying above NFL stadiums on Sundays. Not surprisingly these aircraft have a different purpose in Iraq. The blimps over Camp Victory were there to pinpoint enemy mortar locations when terrorists decided to launch them into the base.

Another sign we were in Iraq: everyone at Camp Victory carried loaded weapons. After witnessing the caliber of the people who carried the weapons—typically overweight U.S. Army, National Guard, and U.S. Air Force personnel—my biggest fear was not dealing with a terrorist who managed to get through twenty-five layers of camp security but an Air Force airman who negligently discharged his weapon.

The most surprising detail I noticed around Camp Victory was that the place was filled with civilians. It seemed like Halliburton had taken over Iraq. I had been under the impression I would be surrounded by military personnel, but it seemed there were more civilians there. I wanted to kick myself for not buying Halliburton stock and the stock of other defense contractors at the beginning of the war. That trade would have been like taking candy from a baby.

Transient tent life was good. I met many interesting folks. People say Disneyland is a great place for people watching; I would argue that the transient tents at Camp Victory provide the best people watching in the world. There are hardened combat vets on their way out of Iraq (half of whom are mentally warped), "fresh meat" coming into Iraq, Filipino and Nepalese housekeepers who keep the place clean, and an assortment of civilian contractors who do a range of things from cleaning shitters to managing multimillion dollar engineering projects.

From what I observed in the transient tents, there was a high correlation between motivation level and time spent in Iraq. As one would expect, those who had just arrived in Iraq were full of piss and vinegar, whereas those who had been there for a long time were typically pissed and smelled like vinegar. An Army sergeant put it best when I asked him about life around camp. "Sir," he said, "when I got here I was excited about the additional combat pay. Now that I've been here eight and half months, been in numerous IED [improvised explosive device] attacks, and haven't had sex in a long time, I can't wait to get the fuck out of this place."

The evening after we landed we got our first small taste of the difference between camping at Yellowstone and camping at Camp Victory—mortar attacks. The attacks were nowhere near our tents, but I could still hear the rumble and feel the small earthquakes beneath me as the shockwaves moved across the ground. What I learned about mortar attacks is that you can't worry about them because you can't do anything to stop them.

I did some simple calculations to figure out how improbable it was to get whacked by a mortar on Camp Victory. My back-of-the-envelope calculations were based on the camp being six square miles, the mortar attacks being randomly distributed around the camp, and there being concrete barriers and sandbags everywhere. First, a six-by-six-mile area is roughly one billion square feet. Next, let us assume one of the average mortars the insurgents fling into the camp has a kill radius of about a thousand square feet, after we take into account all blast protection measures in place around camp. When you use this simple model you end up with literally a one-in-a-million chance $(1000/1,000,000,000 \approx 1/1,000,000)$ of having a mortar land close enough to kill you at Camp Victory.

Is a one-in-a-million chance a big deal? I remember reading a statistic somewhere that every year a nontrivial percentage of Americans are injured while trying bizarre sexual positions. I liked my chances with the mortars. If I died from a mortar attack at Camp Victory, I reasoned, at least my wife would get four hundred thousand dollars from the military's life insurance fund, I would be buried in Arlington Cemetery, and I would be awarded a Purple Heart. This all sounded better than the alternative: "Kama Sutra gone extremely wrong."

If the mortars reminded me that I was in Iraq, touring Saddam Hussein's Al Faw Palace reminded me of the injustice during Saddam's rein. The palace is stunning and truly ostentatious. Imagine one of the Arab palaces in the Disney movie *Aladdin*. Now put a lake around the palace and fill it with exotic fish species, tended to at all times by a small army of immigrant labor. Next add fifty acres of personal hunting grounds, stocked with nonnative exotic wildlife shipped in from all corners of the globe. Finally add on a few satellite palaces for all of your sons and some additional "recreational" palaces to house your indoor swimming pools. This is the basic setup for Al Faw Palace.

The inside of the sixty-two bedroom, twenty-nine bathroom palace is even more stunning. As you approach the palace there is an elaborate thirty-foot front door made of the most precious metals and woods on earth. Once you enter the palace door, a crystal chandelier the size of a Honda Civic hovers above your head. If you move another twenty feet inside the palace, on your right you will see a gold-plated emperor's throne Yasser Arafat gave Saddam as a gift (see photo 1). In addition the entire interior of the palace, save the thrones and chandeliers, which are made of gold, crystal, and other precious materials, is made of hand-carved marble stones. There is even a bathroom made of pure gold inside the palace. I must admit oil-rich dictators who have a knack for stealing from the United Nations' Oil for Food program really know how to live.

The next day we took a sixty-mile flight from Camp Victory to Camp Taji, which is twenty miles north of Baghdad. We didn't exactly travel in style. We managed to stuff around twenty bags of equipment and six passengers into the Black Hawk helicopter, maxing out the payload in the process.

The helicopter flight over Baghdad was exhilarating. The entire time

I felt as though I was an action hero in a movie. The Black Hawk pilots fly anywhere from one hundred to three hundred meters off the deck at around two hundred miles per hour. The purpose of flying at low altitude and high speeds is to make it difficult for insurgents to attack the aircraft. Of course, the speed is nice for dodging dangers on the ground, but when you have the Black Hawk filled to the brim with twenty bags and half your body is hanging outside the helicopter, the hairs on your neck start to stand on end.

The sights of Baghdad fascinated me. The views made me forget the danger. The Baghdad area is stunning when you put aside the daily car bombs and bristly people. Our path followed the Euphrates River, which slices straight through the heart of the city. I have never seen such lush green vegetation and palm trees in my life. This is saying something, considering I have lived in Hawaii.

From the air the disparity between rich and poor is illuminated. Certain homes in Baghdad are truly royal, complete with gargantuan private swimming pools, Euphrates riverfront views, mansion-sized dimensions, amazing architecture, lush gardens, and extravagant landscaping. Meanwhile only half a mile farther along the Euphrates, people live in extreme poverty. The slum areas of Baghdad make the nastiest parts of South Side Chicago or West Philadelphia look like a Beverly Hills gated community: trash is everywhere, sewage is flowing through the streets, people are muddling about, scrap metal collection piles are on the corners of the roads, and feral animals run rampant.

Despite the drastic differences in circumstances throughout Baghdad, there is one equalizing feature for all inhabitants in the area—the mighty Euphrates River. It is the region's lifeblood. From above Baghdad it looks as though God decided to put an aorta in the center of the city. I had never realized how important water is to this region of the world: without water in this region, there is no civilization.

The helicopter crew chief yelled in our direction, breaking my gaze on the landscape. "Gents, the bird is landing in five minutes. Prepare your gear." SSgt. Jonathan Chesnutt ("Nuts") yelled, "Camp Taji, here . . . we . . . come. Yeehaw!"

Chapter 3

Preparing for Combat Adviser Duty

July–Early August 2006

We settled into Camp Taji, where we would live and train for the next few days. The camp is a joint base, one section designated for Americans and one section designated for the Iraqi army. The American side of camp is gigantic, with all of the over-the-top amenities found at Camp Victory. The base is another shining example of the U.S. Army's finer attempts at fortifying the hell out of a piece of earth.

Camp Taji

Unfortunately, there were no fancy amenities for us; we would be living on the IA side of Camp Taji. The IA side of the camp was more spartan, but despite its lack of comforts, it had a huge advantage: we were immersed in Iraqi culture and language. Alas, a coin has two sides. A negative of the IA camp was that the U.S. Army ran the show because of the IA's incompetence. Usually, the U.S. Army is a decent outfit and the Marines get along nicely with them; however, this time things were different. The Army had decided to put a manly female first sergeant, nicknamed the "Behemoth," in charge of the IA camp. We had to follow the Behemoth's rules at all times.

The Behemoth introduced herself then ranted, "Let me put a few things up front to you gentlemen. This is my camp and you will follow my rules." She paused and started on her laundry list of rules. "My first rule is that you must be in full PT [physical training] gear, to include tennis shoes, and have your weapon with you when traveling to the heads." Our team's

Navy corpsman, James "Doc" McGinnis, protested. "Are you telling me I have to wear my tennis shoes to the shower and bring my weapon? That would imply that I have to walk over to the shower in my tennis shoes, take my tennis shoes off, put my shower shoes on, get out of the shower, put my soggy feet into my tennis shoes, and then travel back to the barracks—and the barracks are thirty feet away! And to compound things, you want me to somehow watch my weapon while I'm cleaning my balls and have soap in my eyes?" Everyone on the MiTT laughed. The Behemoth replied defiantly, "Yes, exactly. Have a nice day gentlemen." She squeezed her large rear through the door to our barracks and exited the room. That woman was scary.

After our encounter with the Behemoth, I put on my full PT gear—with tennis shoes—and scurried to the restroom. As I entered the head I saw a janitor. He greeted me in flawless English. "Hello, how are you doing today?" Figuring I had an Iraqi who was fluent in both English and Arabic, I attempted to ask him some questions. I rattled off Arabic phrases for a good thirty seconds, caught my breath, and waited for a response. Confused, the man again said, "Hello, how are you doing today?"

Perplexed, I spent another minute trying to engage the janitor. He was as interactive as a pet rock. Finally he responded with something I could understand: "I Filipino." I realized I was not dealing with an Iraqi at all. I was dealing with a Filipino laborer who did not understand Arabic or English. He only knew one line in English and he knew it well. Phew, I had been worried my Arabic was no good.

We killed time watching back-to-back episodes of the TV series *24* for a couple days until finally the U.S. Army's Camp Taji Military Adviser Course started. Major Gill, a supermotivated U.S. Army officer, taught our first class on the ins and outs of the PRC-148 radio, a personal handheld radio with which we would communicate. Our next class, on how to operate a personal locator beacon (PLB), a device that sends signals to friendly forces if activated, was terrible.

Everyone on the MiTT thought the PLB was a perfect example of the waste, fraud, and abuse in Iraq that stabs the pocketbook of the American taxpayer, and a sign that whoever was purchasing gear for the military hadn't spent much time in the field carrying these items on their back. The PLB is a device about the size of a large baked potato that all embedded advisers are required to wear at all times. It is bad enough we were required to wear additional gear (I guess eighty-plus pounds was not enough); however, the PLB was especially rotten because it was a neon yellow color that blended in perfectly with a banana tree.

To make matters even worse, the concept behind the device is a joke. Apparently, when taken prisoner by the insurgents, we were somehow supposed to take this potato-sized, neon yellow device from its pouch, set it right side up (in any other position it does not receive a signal), extend the antennae skyward, and press two buttons simultaneously for five seconds. Great. I was sure the insurgents would give me a timeout to get my PLB up and running.

Following our PLB class a U.S. Army officer gave us an intelligence and operations update on the team we were replacing in Haditha. The news was not good. The day before the team had hit a pressure-plate IED, which totaled a Humvee, killed two Iraqis, and seriously wounded two others. Moreover, overall attacks in the Triad area had spiked from fifteen events the week before to almost forty. It was amazing how hanging out on the enormous, stalwart U.S. Army bases could give a person the perception that things were not that bad in Iraq. The reality was that we expected to run into a buzz saw when we arrived in Haditha.

I started training with the Joint IED Defeat Task Force (JIEDD TF). The JIEDD TF is the Department of Defense's well-funded ($1.23 billion for the 2005–6 funding cycle) solution to solving how they can keep a bunch of fifth-grade-level-educated, twenty-something Arabs from making hamburger meat out of service members. Thus far, their success had been poor. There had been an enormous increase in IED attacks and IED lethality over the past couple of years. I hoped the JIEDD TF was like fine wine and would get better with time.

Our class was taught by two former U.S. Army Special Forces Delta operators who spoke to us about winning the fight against IEDs and the various enemy techniques, tactics, and procedures (TTPs) that we may face in Al Anbar Province. The class was lame, as we had been through numerous similar courses in predeployment training. What I did find interesting was that this was my first chance to witness some men who were in the fabled Delta Force.

Delta Force operators are supposed to be the baddest of the bad, the guys who kill you with their stare and have lighting bolts fly from their asses at their discretion. I cannot remember the names of the instructors, but I am going to guess they were Max and Stone Cold. The main speaker, Max, talked about how he had not killed many people face to face but had killed hundreds of people with the radio (either with indirect fire, air support, or calling in a quick reaction force). He suggested we follow suit and ensure our communication procedures are tight. Max summarized his advice: "The radio helps you figure out who is coming to help out if you are stuck in an ambush, who is calling for fire, who is calling in the MEDEVAC [medical evacuation], who is calling EOD [Explosive Ordnance Disposal] teams, and so forth. Without proper radio procedures, you are fish bait for the insurgents."

As a follow-on to the JIED TF classes we were given a brief on a brand-new piece of gear the Marines were fielding in Al Anbar called the Chameleon. By the time we hit the deck in the Triad we were supposed to have Chameleons on all of our Humvees. We had heard rumors of the device before the deployment, and the word on the street was that it came straight from the hands of God. It is an electronic countermeasure (ECM) device that sets the gold standard for stopping radio-controlled IED attacks. The specifics are classified, however. The U.S. Navy lieutenant junior grade teaching the class confided to everyone, "I can't get into the details, but I can tell you that the Chameleon will block any radio-controlled device the insurgents currently have and anything they will have in the foreseeable future."

Hearing the lieutenant junior grade's news was outstanding. I was glad we would have large force fields around our Humvees, blocking all the IEDs in Al Anbar Province. There had to be a catch, right? Well, the catch was that the Chameleon blocks all radio-controlled IEDs—the IEDs triggered by cell phones, garage door openers, wireless telephones, and so forth. Sadly, the Wile E. Coyote method of connecting a group of explosives to a long copper wire with a trigger device attached to the end worked like a charm.

I came away with four pieces of advice from the IED classes. First, if you do not hear the IED, do not worry about it because you will be heading to heaven soon. Second, if you do hear the IED, praise God, because you are alive and still have a chance to kill the bastard who tried to blow you up. Third, if you see wires on the side of the road, odd shapes in the form of an artillery shell, people loitering around batteries, or other suspicious happenings, get as far away from the site as possible. Finally, before you go on a Sunday drive in Al Anbar Province, turn on your Chameleon. Pretty simple stuff, really.

After IED lectures I engaged in my second important endeavor of the day, which was to sit through a brief by Gen. George Casey, the commander of all forces in Iraq. I was humbled as I sat through the presentation. Despite his diminutive stature (five feet six inches tall) and placid temperament, it was exhilarating to hear the powerful words come out of his mouth. General Casey was an impressive man. All the same, one thing disturbed me as I listened to him during the question and answer session. A soldier asked, "General, are the Iraqis in a civil war?" Casey replied, "No." He paused, letting his words sink in, and continued. "We are moving away from an insurgency fight against coalition forces in Iraq to an internal sectarian fight in Iraq where the Sunnis are fighting for control over what they believe to be a Shia-led government." The small crowd of fifty advisers laughed at the response. It was obvious the general did not want to be tagged as being the one who said Iraq was in a civil war.

Sensing the crowd's distaste with the general's response, Major General Everson, General Casey's deputy, commented, "Gents, seriously, if a civil war was upon us, would we ever be able to call a spade a spade without getting in trouble with our bosses?" The crowd chuckled as Casey gave Everson a disapproving look.

At the end of the question and answer session, I was vexed by what General Casey had said. He was so political in his response that he seemed disingenuous. We were not CNN or the *New York Times*; we were his troops and looking for honesty and straight answers, not some crap we would expect from a politician.

I am not sure why the "civil war" term is such an issue. According to the *Merriam-Webster Dictionary*, a civil war is "a war between opposing groups of citizens of the same country." What I saw in Iraq were Sunnis and Shias, citizens of the same country, who were violently fighting each other for political control of Iraq. To me it seemed cut and dried that a civil war was happening in Iraq. I wished someone would call it that and not beat around the bush.

The next day I showed up twenty minutes early to class. This was not my MO because twenty minutes wasting away in the classroom was twenty minutes I could be learning Arabic, doing PT, or sleeping; however, I was glad I showed up early since I had a unique opportunity to talk with a U.S. Army reservist lieutenant colonel who would be leading an adviser team north of Baghdad.

I quickly discovered that U.S. Army adviser teams did not have many of the advantages our MiTT team had prior to deployment. All the soldiers on their teams were meeting one another for the first time at Camp Taji. Moreover, their predeployment training consisted of two weeks at the camp. That was it. This was a scary proposition. Before my conversation with the lieutenant colonel, I felt the Marine Corps was short changing me by only giving me five months to prepare for the same mission for which Special Forces spend two to three years training. Guess I was wrong.

In addition to having no substantial training and no time to create unit cohesion, the U.S. Army personnel sounded naïve about the embedded adviser mission. For example, when I was speaking with the reservist lieutenant colonel, he said, "I am excited about going to the 4th Motor Transport Army Brigade to help support the Iraqi army." As he explained the concept of what he thought he was doing as a MiTT team leader, I concluded that the lieutenant colonel was lost in the sauce. He thought the Army had assigned him to a U.S. Army unit that would be supporting the Iraqi army versus assigning him to embed as an adviser with the Iraqi army.

I addressed the lieutenant colonel with confidence and tact. "Sir, you know your mission is to be embedded with the Iraqi army as an adviser, right? The 4th Motor Transport Army Brigade is an Iraqi unit. You will be living with the unit and training with the unit. You won't be working within a U.S. Army unit that is supporting an Iraqi unit from afar." The silver-haired lieutenant colonel addressed me as a grandfather would a grandson, "Young lieutenant, I think you are sadly mistaken. I am sure I know what unit the Army assigned me. I doubt the U.S. Army would be stupid enough to put me in an Iraqi unit. However, thanks for your concern." At the conclusion of his lecture I suggested, "Sir, seriously, I would ask one of the instructors to double check for you." He obliged and found out the truth. His silver hair turned white.

Staff Sergeant Buff taught a class on maintaining personal health in Iraq. Buff was Chris Rock in camouflage: skinny, short, and hilarious. He had served in the U.S. Army for seventeen years and over the years he had developed a unique teaching style. He enjoyed bringing up shocking examples of what not to do in a particular situation and then assumed we had enough common sense to know what to do in a particular situation.

Buff started his class with an example of what not to do in Iraq. "Gentlemen, I know some of you may think it is a good idea, but having scorpion fights or sand spider competitions is probably not the brightest idea in the world. Marines are especially keen on doing this . . . don't do it!" He smirked at the Marine-filled corner of the small classroom and continued. "If you don't believe me, talk to my Marine buddy who got bit by both of the competitors the last time he tried to host a scorpion fight competition—pure genius, that friend of mine."

Buff then tackled the problem of Iraqi "close-talkers." Close-talkers are people who speak at a distance so close that the person listening can feel the warmth of their breath. Unfortunately, Iraq is filled with close-talkers. In Buff's words, "Embedded advisers and close-talker Iraqis do not mix. Iraqis have mouths filled with airborne diseases that none of y'all have been exposed to. This can lead to serious health issues while you are in Iraq. Now listen up."

Buff had a solution. He joked, "Gents, instead of smelling Iraqi bad breath and eating their saliva as they speak with you, I suggest that you perform my 'perpendicular, circular walk technique.' Basically, as an Iraqi is talking to you, walk in a circle around him with your head perpendicular to theirs. This will keep you from exposing yourself to their diseases. Now, of course, this is going to seem odd to your Iraqi counterparts. Don't worry—I have a solution. Tell the Iraqis you have a lazy eye or that you cannot hear out of your left ear and that you need to point your ear toward them in order to maximize what you can hear. It works every time!" The class burst in laughter, partly because what he said was funny, but mainly because we knew this was a technique Buff used in practice. His anti-close-talker technique may work for a U.S. Army medic, I thought, but it is not going to work for an adviser who needs to earn the trust and confidence of his Iraqi counterparts.

Buff's final point was on the threat of hepatitis in Iraq. In his eloquent and unique fashion, he explained, "Gentlemen, I have a beautiful poem for you: Flies that frolic in your feces today, will be joining you for dinner tomorrow." He paused after receiving some confused looks then continued. "Gents, what I am talking about here is hepatitis. Hepatitis is a major threat to you in this country for two reasons: First, there is no sewage system. Second, Iraqis like to stand on Western style toilet bowls and engage in a game of target practice, trying to get their turd in the toilet. Unfortunately, they often miss and an American ends up sitting on it. I can't emphasize enough: wash your hands and keep your areas clean!" Buff did not need to explain the threat of hepatitis any further. We understood loud and clear.

Following Buff's class we attended a course on Arab culture. "Mr. Mohammed" (how the instructor referred to himself) presented a compelling lecture on the importance of understanding Arab culture and language in his region of the world. Mohammed, an American citizen originally from Jordan, gave us the standard story on Arab culture but provided an illuminating example to the class that I doubt any of us will forget. He asked everyone in the class to touch their right earlobe. One of the U.S. Army soldiers popped out of his seat, took his right hand, and reached up to touch his right earlobe. Everyone in the classroom looked at each other and tried to figure out the purpose of the exercise.

Mohammed went on to explain to the class and the soldier, "So, I asked you to touch your earlobes and you all quickly took your right hand and reached up and grabbed your right earlobe using the quickest, most direct method possible. This is how I would expect an American to respond to this request." He paused for a moment before continuing, "However, an Arab would do this slightly differently."

The classroom was on edge to hear how touching one's right earlobe could possibly be different for Arabs. Mohammed slowly reached behind his head with his left hand, strained to reach the right side of his head, and touched his right earlobe. "This is how an Arab would touch his earlobe." He further explained, "How I grabbed my earlobe summarizes the fundamental difference between Arab people and Western people. Western people will do what is the most efficient and the most direct when asked to do something; however, Arab people will put in the extra effort to please someone and make them feel important. The Arab will do this, even if they must go out of their way and the extra effort is wasteful or inefficient."

Everyone was perplexed. Mohammed continued, "This is a cultural difference that Westerners find hard to understand. Nevertheless, if you give up your desire to be efficient and direct and focus more on being accommodating and supportive, you will have the Arab people on your side and they will respect you as a brother versus detesting you as an occupier."

As Mohammed finished his class the crowd generously applauded his efforts. His lecture had illuminated the intricacies of Arab culture in a way that nobody had been able to do up until that point. I am still amazed there is another way one can touch his or her earlobe in this world.

After attending numerous seminars on everything from communications to Arab culture, I had much to think over. But I think the best advice came from Major Bullock, the final speaker of the course and a former MiTT member himself. He summarized the psychology of the MiTT experience: "When you guys first start advising you will have a very high give-a-fuck factor. Just like me you will be super motivated and excited about transforming the Iraqi army into a twenty-first-century fighting force." Everyone in the class nodded in acknowledgment, and the major continued. "However, once you are exposed to the Iraqis' complete lack of desire to get anything done, their intense corruption, and their cultural norms of laziness and lack of initiative, your give-a-fuck factor drops precipitously. Eventually, it drops so low, as mine has, that you resort to a give-a-fuck factor of zero, and reach the not-giving-a-fuck stage. In the not-giving-a-fuck stage you learn to accept Iraqi standards and let them do things their way as long as it has a chance of working." He paused. "You let them do it their way, even if their method is nowhere near the most efficient or intelligent way to accomplish the mission. The reason you let them do it their way? Because you ain't changing Iraqi culture anytime soon." By the end of the major's discussion, the entire class was chuckling. The thing that made the major compelling was the fact he was brutally honest and didn't sugarcoat his experience. I appreciated his honesty.

Camp Fallujah

After training we left Camp Taji and arrived at Camp Fallujah. I was glad we were back in Marine country and had left the grips of the U.S. Army's culture of bureaucracy and back rubs for everyone. The main event in Fallujah was to attend the IED training site.

When it comes to training, the Marine Corps has mastered the process. The IED training site at Camp Fallujah was a perfect excellent example of doing things right. The training site covered three acres on the outskirts of camp and was set up to represent as many real-life IED situations as possible in a small space. The one aspect of the training site that stood out was its realism. The EOD (explosive ordnance disposal) Marine in charge of the training brought actual IED material he had found in live scenarios and placed it on the training site in the exact scenario in which he had found it.

Staff Sergeant Wilkenson, our motivated instructor and an outstanding Marine, led our team through the course. Wilkenson was a poster boy Marine—a chiseled jaw, strong build, and the ability to slay dragons—but what really stood out about him was his positive attitude. He had been the victim of IED attacks many times, and a majority of his EOD teammates had been killed during his deployment. And yet he was upbeat and ready to train.

At the beginning of the IED course Wilkenson announced, "Marines, I want you to get prepared for the most fucked up Easter egg hunt in the world." This was a great analogy. Even so, we walked through the course in the 130-degree heat without a complaint. Everyone on the team was so concerned with finding the IEDs and learning the enemy's tactics that we forgot about the heat.

Throughout the course an eerie theme played out multiple times. First, the springbutts (Marine Corps term for someone who is always answering the instructor's questions) on the team, Captain McShane and Staff Sergeant Donaldson, would inevitably stop and gaze at what looked like an IED in the side of the road a hundred meters ahead of us. Wilkenson would sarcastically reply, "Wow, great eyes gentlemen. Now, how about you look below your feet . . . the insurgents left a surprise for you." As we would look to the earth, Wilkenson would explain how the IED up ahead was a decoy to get unsuspecting victims to stop in their tracks right on top of a live IED. Sure enough, we would be standing on a couple of double-stacked propane tanks filled with five hundred pounds of PE-4 high-explosive material that had been buried beneath our feet (PE-4 is a cheap Russian knock-off of what American service members know as C-4). Fortunately, we were in training.

After reaching our certain death at least five times over the next five hundred meters of the IED course, we were able to recognize an IED before it "exploded." Donaldson picked up the radio-controlled IED ignition device off the ground to see how the device functioned.

Wilkenson lunged at Donaldson and yelled, "Boom! Congratulations, you all became chop suey and made the same mistake my EOD robot made the other week. He is now chilling in the scrap yard with R2-D2 and C-3PO." Donaldson protested. "What are you talking about?" he said. "We found the IED. How did we die?" Wilkenson retorted, "Well, you're right, you guys did find the IED; however, that didn't blow you up. Look under the ignition device you just picked up." We all peered underneath the ignition device, which was a Sanyo cordless telephone base station. Sure enough the base station had been rigged with some electric tape and a short piece of copper wire that led to a 155-mm artillery shell buried beneath the base station. The artillery shell was waiting to blow up whoever got curious and decided to pick up the ignition device. Whoops.

At the conclusion of the course Wilkenson told us his favorite IED story. Some time ago he had taken a cell phone from a discovered IED site that was attached to the ignition device on an IED. By some wicked twist of fate, when his EOD team was traveling back to base, it started ringing. Wondering what the hell was going on, he answered the phone call. It was the insurgents. Wilkenson said that he and the insurgents cursed each other out and told each other to rot in hell, Wilkenson in broken Arabic and the insurgents in broken English. I am sure Wilkenson wished he could have somehow traveled through the phone, showed up on the other end, and opened a Costco-sized can of whup-ass on the insurgents.

Lieutenant Adams summed up the team's collective thoughts at the conclusion of the course: "Damn, this is gonna suck." We left the training site with little confidence and a high awareness of our mortality. Tomorrow we would arrive in Haditha. Let the adventure begin.

Chapter 4

Meeting the Iraqi Army

August 2006

Flying a few hundred meters above the ground aboard a CH-53 Super Stallion helicopter, I could see the villages' lights flickering off the Euphrates River, spinning off beautiful blue and purple colors. An eerie darkness engulfed each settlement, as if these villages were little islands in the middle of the Pacific Ocean.

Swack! Maj. Travis Gaines hollered, "Whoa, shit! What's going on?" I snapped out of my dreamy gaze on the landscape, wondering what had happened. Were we crashing? Had the pilot fallen asleep and run into something? We were still a good 150 meters in the air. The commotion felt as though we were landing the bird, but this was impossible at this height.

In Iraq, I discovered, anything is possible. It turned out we were landing, and we were 150 meters off the ground. The commotion was the helicopter landing on top of the Haditha Dam. Surprised that we seemed to be landing in midair at 0330 in the morning, each of us clutched our three hundred pounds of gear and waddled like penguins out the back of the bird. Members of the outgoing MiTT rushed to our aid with energy and excitement. Each of them grabbed at our gear like hungry hyenas, helping in every way they could.

But I was suspicious. Our hosts' generosity was in doubt. My suspicions were born out by SSgt. John Wear, who said, "Gentlemen, you don't know how excited we are to see you. We cannot wait for you to take over for us so we can get the hell out of here. Oorah!"

Once the chaos of the CH-53 engines and rotors subsided, I took a deep breath. I had arrived. From this day forward we would be making history. Here I was standing atop the famous Haditha Dam, the second largest electricity production plant in all of Iraq. To my north was beautiful Lake Qadisiyah and to the south were the magnificent Euphrates River and the civilizations that make up the Triad: South Dam Village, Barwana, Haditha, Haqliniya, Bani Dahir, and Abu Hyatt.

Once the trucks were loaded we made our way to the Iraqi camp. I fell asleep in the truck and awoke to see an armed Marine opening a steel gate. With a sarcastic tone in his voice he said, "You must be the new guys . . . that sucks. Enjoy the Iraqi side of the camp." As we entered the camp I realized we were leaving the relative safety of six hundred U.S. Marines and were now entering the Wild West. Here our neighbors would be a small group of U.S. Army Special Forces and three hundred IA soldiers.

We entered the MiTT camp, which was a small, square area about the size of a baseball diamond (see photo 2). Bulletproof Hesco barriers barricaded the camp on all sides (Hesco barriers are seven-foot-tall and six-foot-wide containers wrapped in a wire mesh that is filled with dirt and sand). Upon our arrival the boss said, "It's 0445 now. Drop your gear in your rooms and be ready for action tomorrow morning by 0830." He paused before continuing. "Tomorrow we will observe the Iraqi mission planning briefs and conduct a liaison meeting with the 3rd Battalion, 3rd Marines (3/3) battalion commander in the dam. Go to your rooms and have a nice night."

I approached my room. The dual-occupancy rooms on the camp were modified shipping containers about eight feet wide, twenty-five feet long, and eight feet tall. Each of the living spaces was outfitted with electricity and the all-important air-conditioner. I wasn't sure what to think about the accommodations. It wasn't luxury, but it was a place to sleep.

Camp Ali

I sprang up the next morning at 0800. I use the term "sprang" loosely; my mind was ready to spring, but my body was moving at an anemic pace owing to a lack of sleep. I poked my head outside and realized I had opened an oven door. I slammed the door closed, chugged a bottle of water, and took my last gulp of air-conditioned air before cracking the oven again. Now I was ready to go. Our team gathered inside the camp and took in the moment. This was our first chance to explore the area.

The MiTT camp is a Marine's paradise. Small and austere? Maybe. Filled with makeshift capabilities and livable? Heck, yeah. The camp was lacking some essentials, but thankfully, we had access to the resources of our next-door neighbors on camp, the Special Force's ODA (Operational Detachment Alpha) team. The ODA had everything the MiTT camp didn't have, including showers and a makeshift weight room. Within the MiTT camp we had a washer, a dryer that sometimes worked, and a rack on which to hang clothes. We also had a basic kitchen with a George Foreman grill, a microwave, and a deep-fat fryer. Seriously, what else could a Marine ask for?

After some exploration of the MiTT camp, it was time to move to the Iraqi Command Operations Center (COC) and watch the Iraqi mission planning briefs. Along the way Staff Sergeant Wear gave us a tour of the Iraqi camp.

Camp Ali is small, rugged, and relaxes across a flat piece of desert earth. The total area of the camp is perhaps three hundred meters across west to east and eight hundred meters from north to south. Scattered along the grounds are various guard towers, and there are berms (large mounds of dirt) across the southern and western boundaries to keep out the boogieman. The camp snuggles up to the west bank of the Euphrates about half a mile south of Haditha Dam.

It is apparent you are within Camp Ali the minute you pass through the main gate. The number of Marines, contractors, dam employees, and random coalition forces immediately goes from a ton down to one—the armed Marine at the gate leading to the Iraqi camp. This devil dog's mission is to operate and secure the gates to Camp Ali while standing in full combat gear in 130-degree heat. His life sucks.

When you exit the Marine side of camp and enter through the main gate to Camp Ali, to your immediate right you see the Special Forces camp. In many ways their camp reminded me of a grungy trailer park. Despite its rugged look this small area of earth is where the Special Forces make plans to take over small nations, find Osama bin Laden, and plan for nightly ninja raids. Or at least that was their reputation. Their real mission was the same as ours: advise and support the Iraqi battalion during combat operations. Neighboring the Special Forces camp is the MiTT camp and another hundred meters beyond the MiTT camp are fifty swahuts.

The swahuts house the Iraqi soldiers, known to U.S. military personnel as *jundi*, the Arabic term for "soldier." Swahuts are unlike any housing I have ever seen. They are simple dwellings—a square slab of concrete about twenty feet wide, thin plywood walls, and a tin roof. Scatter six to eight bunk beds throughout a small room, set up a satellite receiver to get the latest Arab news and Egyptian comedies, add fifteen to twenty *jundi*, and hang posters of Ali (a Shia Muslim hero) on the walls—now you have an idea of where the *jundi* live. It's not the Ritz-Carlton, but it's not bad considering the poverty with which most Iraqis are accustomed.

The *jundi* kept their motor transportation lot a hundred meters east of the swahuts. In many ways the lot reminded me of a Third World village. It consisted of twenty to thirty vehicles, three of which worked. In place of Oldsmobile, Cadillac, and Chevy cars, the lot had Iraqi-operated American Humvees, Leyland transport trucks (flimsy flatbed pickups), Krazes (a large and powerful Russian troop transport vehicle akin to the U.S. military's seven-ton), Wazes (Russian jeep that never works), and small Toyota pickups. In the southern end of the motor transportation area sat the "random crap" area of the camp, which consisted of rusted concertina razor wire, barbed wire, metal rods and poles, old unfilled Hesco barriers, tires, and about everything else one would find in a junkyard. Finally, and most loved by the Iraqis, was the austere soccer field, complete with no grass, thick sticker bushes, and goals made of two-by-four boards nailed together.

Fifty meters south of the swahuts were the *jundi*'s prized possessions: the shower area and Iraqi chow hall. Considering the circumstances and the civilian living conditions in the Triad area, the *jundi* had a nice shower area. It consisted of a white trailer about twenty-five feet long that was propped off the ground on a few cinder blocks.

Inside the Iraqi shower trailer were four operational showers and an amazing stench that could only be created in a confined facility that provided services to over two hundred Iraqi men on any given day. Unfortunately the only alternative for cleanliness-conscious *jundi* was to swim in the Euphrates, which contains E. coli and other wicked parasites. According to the *jundi* swimming in the Euphrates is *kullish mu zien*, (very bad).

Next to the shower facility was the holiest building on Camp Ali—the chow hall. Not unlike American service members, *jundi* love to eat. Like all the buildings in the camp, the chow hall was encased in an array of Hesco barriers to keep mortar fragments out of the food. Inside the chow hall was a small assembly line where the soldiers lined up to a large bin of rice, a large bin of beans, a stack of khubbis (homemade bread), and a small container of chicken. Aligned throughout the interior were white plastic tables and chairs of the sort one could purchase at a summer sale at Wal-Mart. It's not luxury dining, but the poor decor was complemented with engaging conversation and Iraqis wrestling each other for the last Pepsi (see photo 3).

Due west of the chow hall was the Iraqi COC, the brain of the Iraqi battalion and home for the senior Iraqi officers. It was strategically located only a hundred meters away in case the *jundi* got hungry. It was also where our first meeting with the Iraqis was to take place.

We approached the Iraqi COC. The three-man security detachment guarding the entrance to the facility awoke from their slumber, jumped from their lawn chairs, and greeted us with "Salam" (Hello). Caught off guard we replied, "Salam" and quickly entered the large swahut.

Our team had entered the Iraqi conference room a few minutes late. The meeting, which was already underway, immediately ceased. Every Iraqi in the room hopped from their seat and formed a line, waiting to greet each member of our team. It was overwhelming to say the least.

The Iraqis attacked. They swarmed around me and the rest of the team, hugging, kissing, shaking hands, and speaking Arabic. Lieutenant Le Gette, who was being mobbed by Iraqis, glanced at me. "Dude," he said, "what happened to the meeting?" Squished between a group of Iraqis, I gasped for air and replied, "I'm not sure, man, but these guys sure are friendly. Sheesh!"

Our spectacular meet-and-greet subsided quickly. Nobody on our team, aside from me, had more than a basic grasp of Arabic, the Iraqis couldn't speak English, and the two "terps" (short for interpreters) in the room could only do so much to keep communications flowing. Conversations that consist of Shlonek? (How are you?) and Anii zien, wa inta? (I am good, and you?) can only go so far. It was time to start the brief.

Captain Muhanned, the IA battalion S-3 (operations section) officer, led the mission with an outstanding orientation brief. Following his opening remarks, Muhanned called the various sections to the front of the group to describe how their section's planning efforts would affect the upcoming operation. The S-1 (administration section) talked about personnel and administration, the S-2 (intelligence section) gave the intelligence brief, the S-3 spoke to operations, the S-4 (logistics section) described logistics, and, finally, the S-6 (communications section) described the communications plan. After hearing the various S-shops give their respective briefs, it was time for a question-and-answer session and for another lesson in Iraqi culture.

Lt. Col. Owen Lovejoy, the outgoing MiTT leader, started the session. He pointed out various flaws in the operation plan and asked the *jundi* how they would address the issues. Silence. In the Iraqis' mind without their commander Colonel Abass present at the table (he was at a meeting in Al Asad), there was no point even talking about possible changes to the plan. Lieutenant Colonel Ali, the Iraqi's second in command, kept swatting questions back at Lieutenant Colonel Lovejoy as if they were pesky mosquitoes. Each time his response and rhetoric were the same: "How can I change this plan if the commander is not here to make the decision? As a commander, how would you feel if I were making decisions behind your back? Would you still be the commander?"

The Iraqis' behavior struck me as odd. In the Marines battle decisions can be made at the lowest levels of command. Subordinate Marines are expected to make decisions when their leaders are not present. In the IA the exact opposite occurs: the commander makes all decisions, even the trivial ones. If the commander does not make all decisions, his authority is undermined. I realized that changing this environment was going to be a serious challenge.

Words of Wisdom from the Marine Colonel

The sandstorm was so thick I could not see more than three feet in front of me. I was driving the Iraqis' Chevy Luv, a two-door pickup with slabs of metal bolted to the sides acting as armor. We were cruising on the top level of the dam to make our meeting with Lt. Col. Norman Cooling, the 3rd Battalion, 3rd Marines (3/3) commander. The small pickup swayed and dipped at the whims of the storm's power. At one point, when the winds were particularly fierce, we stopped the vehicle, blocked off all air-conditioning vents, and experienced the insides of a tornado. Within twenty minutes the storm passed, the tornado miraculously transformed into a cloudless, sunny day. The sandstorm had melted into the desert floor.

We faced another sandstorm in our meeting with Lieutenant Colonel Cooling. 3/3 was the unit that would save our asses if the Iraqi army ever decided to mutiny and take the entire MiTT hostage. It made sense for our team to have a good relationship with Cooling. Our meeting took place in the commander's boardroom, located on the seventh floor of the dam. The room resembled a corporate boardroom setting, save for the fact that it was 100 degrees in the room and we sat in plastic chairs. All the same we were honored and wanted to hear what the lieutenant colonel had to say.

The first words from his mouth stung our adviser team. He lectured, "Here is the bottom line gentlemen: these MiTTs are supposed to be the best of the best, the most capable Marines our Corps has to offer. If the

MiTT mission is to succeed in Iraq, that is exactly what we need to be doing." He paused, sat up in his chair, and continued. "Here is the reality. MiTTs are usually staffed with leftovers . . . no offense." We got the drift. His experience with MiTTs in the past apparently had not been that great and he intended to set things straight this time around.

The stressed-out warrior went on. "You want to know what I expect from the MiTT if we are going to get along out here? Solid leadership." We all gulped, knowing our MiTT leader was nowhere near the hottest on the planet. "You know," he continued, "here is my experience with Marines dying. For every ten Marines that die out here, two are because of dumb leadership decisions, six of them are because of individual Marine complacency, and maybe two of them are from actual enemy skill and craft. When you break that down, eight out of ten Marine casualties could be saved through solid leadership—first, by making good decisions and second, by ensuring Marines do not get complacent."

Cooling followed up with an example that still haunted him: "Five months ago a seven-ton full of Marines was told to go check out a *wadi* (dried river bed) for IED wires. When they got to the *wadi*, it was heavily pouring rain and the *wadi* was full of water. The staff sergeant on the scene made the decision to try and cross it. Suffice to say, it was a bad decision; twelve men drowned and one survived—the staff sergeant who made the retarded decision." He grimaced. "My guess is that poor staff sergeant isn't sleeping well nowadays."

Cooling abruptly moved to the next thing on his mind. "Oh, and here is another thing, you now have a microscope up your ass, congratulations." We were perplexed by his statement. "Well, gents," he explained, "if you think back about seven months ago you will remember the infamous 'Haditha Massacre' where Marines from 3/1 [3rd Battalion, 1st Marines] were accused of killing a bunch of civilians in Haditha. The press went wild with the story, which inflamed world and American opinions. Following the incident, the generals out here decided to jam a microscope up all regimental commanders' asses in Iraq, and they subsequently grabbed the microscopes from their asses and proceeded to jam them up the battalion commanders' asses—mine included. Now, following suit, I am now taking it out of my ass and jamming it up yours."

It didn't take long to realize Cooling was completely serious. "The situation is so ridiculous," he continued, "that anytime Marines engage the enemy in my area I have to do an investigation on the incident and verify it was legitimate. I fully understand this may lead to you and your Iraqis hesitating in the heat of battle—I'm sorry. You can thank the media for that one; they have no understanding of the situation on the ground or a grasp of the Iraqi people." We read between the lines; we were out here to be bullet sponges, and if we retaliated against the insurgents, we were going to be investigated under the assumption we had used force unnecessarily. The media blowback from the so-called Haditha Massacre was going to have a direct effect on our ability to operate.

Lieutenant Colonel Cooling moved away from addressing the negative realities of the war and focused on motivating our team. He lectured, stealing a page from President George W. Bush: "There are two truths to the situation out there. First, if we aren't fighting these terrorists here, we will be fighting them in America. And second, the only way out of this place is to train the Iraqi army and the Iraqi police so we can leave to fight who we really need to fight—Iran, Syria, and North Korea."

After that sad attempt at motivation, he told us more about the area. "Here's a wake-up call. Your training in America is shitty and doesn't prepare you for what you face out here. And another thing. You are going to have the urge to act like your Special Forces neighbors, who run around like cowboys on convoys, going way too fast and rarely doing the proper precombat inspections and precombat checks. Don't do that shit. You are Marines, not U.S. Army Rambo wannabes." The lieutenant colonel did not actually think our training was shitty or that we would try to emulate the Special Forces; he just wanted to stress to us his key point: complacency kills.

In conclusion Cooling said, "Gentlemen, we are ahead of these guys with the Chameleons coming into theater. This is going to stop the radio-controlled IEDs for the time being. I figure we have a one-to two-month edge on these guys. But standby, I will bet my paycheck they will figure out a work-around soon enough. Good luck, and get those Iraqis to work." We all left the meeting motivated but feeling as though we indeed had a microscope jammed up our asses.

Finalizing the Mission Plans

The mythical Colonel Abass, whom we had heard so much about from the outgoing advisers, soon returned to Camp Ali. The guy was a sight to see. He tipped the scale at 270 pounds and packed his weight in a frame that stood about five feet seven inches tall. Abass's trademark was his handlebar mustache. When he opened his mouth, it looked as if he had a small squirrel sleeping on his upper lip.

What was most amazing about Colonel Abass was his intellect and wit. He redefined what it means to be "street smart." At the time I met him, Abass had twenty-four years of service in the old IA, a fundamental understanding of the political situation in Iraq, and a deceptive ability to influence Americans. The only reason he was not at the Ministry of Defense (MOD) or in a higher position of power is that he was a Sunni, a former regime supporter, and could not speak a lick of English.

With Abass back at camp we redid the mission-planning brief. This time around a different feel was in the air. When Abass entered the COC conference room, everyone snapped out of their seats and jumped to attention. He spoke to the crowd, welcomed our new MiTT, thanked God for our safe arrival, and told Captain Muhanned to begin the brief. The brief was similar to Lieutenant Colonel Lovejoy's brief, except with more formalities and more questions from Abass to his staff. Abass brought up many of the same points Lovejoy had, which was a testament to his ability to notice the same issues and concerns as our top military leaders.

Once the brief was over I had a vague idea of what we were getting ourselves into and a decent level of confidence in the *jundi* to accomplish the mission. I wouldn't say the *jundi* are Marines, or that they could execute half of what they had planned, but I was pleasantly surprised at their ability to give a thorough brief.

But I knew the operation would be intense. Our MiTT was going to be thrown into the steaming cauldron on our first mission. The Iraqi battalion's mission was to conduct a seventy-two-hour operation to search and clear every home in Bani Dahir and Kaffijiya.

At the time of this writing Bani Dahir is the most violent area in the Haditha Triad and is the buffer zone between Haditha and Haqliniya, the two largest towns in the area. The insurgents attack every patrol that goes through the area. Staff Sergeant Wear, the outbound MiTT's intelligence adviser, claimed he would give us his next paycheck if we were not attacked during our mission. On the upside, though, the town has about two hundred homes, so we knew the search would take less than a day.

Kaffijiya is almost the opposite of Bani Dahir. Currently it is one of the least violent areas in the Triad, and many of the residents provide timely intelligence to the Marines and IA. In addition Kaffijiya has about a hundred homes, so we knew that searching this area would take only half a day to complete.

The day ended with an Iraqi confirmation brief at 2100, an odd hour for a meeting. It soon became apparent why Iraqis have meetings either early in the morning or late at night, and why they sleep during the day. Originally I thought it was because they were lazy, but I now realize it is because they are smart: it is far too hot to do anything during the day.

The evening meeting was exhilarating. Lieutenant Adams and I learned we would be the first guys on our team to get a piece of the action. Adams was assigned to 1st Iraqi Company with 1st Lt. Jesse Cope (the outgoing adviser), and I would be embedded with 4th Iraqi Company and Capt. Rodd Chin (also an outgoing adviser). The rest of our MiTT would be stationed with the mobile Iraqi COC on the outskirts of Bani Dahir. From there they would listen in on the action and direct support and logistics to the fight, if needed.

During the mission 4th Iraqi Company would be the cordon element during the Bani Dahir search and 1st Iraqi Company would be the search element. During the Kaffijiyah cordon and search, the roles would be reversed. We would be living, fighting, and bleeding with the Iraqi army. Excitement was on the horizon.

Part 2

LEARNING IRAQI ARMY SYSTEMS

AND CULTURE

Chapter 5

The First Fight with the Iraqi Army

August 2006

ieutenant Adams and I were set for our mission to clear Bani Dahir and Kaffijiyah. The intelligence brief claimed we should brace for gunfights. Don't gunfights only happen in the movies? I wondered. In any other scenario I would have been nervous, but I would be accompanied by flesh-and-blood Iraqi soldiers who had lived amid war and chaos their entire lives. These guys were willing to send every 7.62-mm round from their AK-47s into the hearts of the enemy. What could be more comforting than knowing I would be surrounded by thirty of these guys at any moment?

Bani Dahir

Captain Chin, thirty-five motivated Iraqis, and I set up perimeter security around the town of Bani Dahir. I spent the day moving from one Iraqi defensive position to the next, witnessing the glaring differences in how the Marines did things and how the Iraqis did things. The first position we visited consisted of five Iraqi soldiers, some breakfast chow, a full set of tea cups with a tea pot, and an Iraqi Humvee with a PKC 7.62-mm machine gun pointing down the southern road leading into town. The Iraqis' priorities in their defensive blocking position were not what I expected.

When it comes to prioritizing efforts during defensive operations, the Marines follow a commonsense acronym: **SAFE**. It stands for security, avenues of approach, fields of fire, and entrenchment:

- **Security:** Check surrounding buildings, check for IEDs underneath the Humvee, look for nearby booby traps, and so forth.

- **Avenues of approach:** Make sure the machine gun is pointing in the direction from which the enemy will be approaching.

- **Fields of fire:** Everyone needs to have a general idea of where to point their weapons to ensure the entire area is covered.

- **Entrenchment:** In our scenario entrenchment meant setting out road blocks or posting signs a couple hundred meters in front of the defensive positions.

The Iraqis also follow a commonsense acronym when it comes to prioritizing efforts during defensive operations: **REST**. It stands for relax, eat, sleep, and tea:

- **Relax:** Make sure everyone has a comfortable position in the Humvee or finds a nice shady spot under a building because of the extreme heat.

- **Eat:** Always bring homemade chow from the camp—fresh *khubbis*, oranges, and perhaps some rice and beans.

- **Sleep:** As long as someone in the turret is partially awake, everyone else can sleep.

- **Tea:** When everyone needs a pick-me-up, break out the tea set, complete with sugar bowl, teakettle, and teacups, and have a tea party in the middle of a combat operation.

From an Iraqi perspective, SAFE is for dimwits and REST is the way to go. Security? Why check for IEDs and booby traps in the middle of the street? Any IEDs or booby traps insurgents had placed would have ignited when we initially drove on the position. Avenues of approach? Why waste energy pointing the machine gun in the direction of the enemy's likely approach when it means you have to stand in 130-degree heat? Fields of fire? What a complete waste of time. AK-47s make a loud cracking sound when fired so you know exactly where the insurgents are the minute they start shooting. Entrenchment? Okay, so the Marines want us to put signs two hundred meters ahead of our position? That makes a ton of sense; now if someone is approaching us, we'll give away our position so we can't surprise them. Great idea, Marines (see photo 4). I'm afraid Iraqis and Americans will never see eye to eye on this.

I continued walking to the different positions, bounding from one place of cover to another, doing what I had been taught in all my training. I looked at every weird spot on the ground and rushed past danger areas. On the other hand my comrade, Captain Chin, strolled along calmly. "Sir," I asked him, "aren't you worried about the snipers from across the Euphrates shooting at you?" Chin casually said, "Gray, don't follow my example and make your own decisions, but heed my advice. At the pace you're going you'll last a few hours out here. You're wearing eighty pounds of shit and it's 130 degrees outside. I know it seems counterintuitive to be complacent at times, but it would be a shame if I had to write your wife a letter because you died of heatstroke." I thought Captain Chin was speaking the truth. I'd die if I kept this up. I had a much higher chance of kicking the bucket from heatstroke than from an insurgent sniper on the other side of the river with a broken AK-47, no aim, and a reliance on Allah to put the bullet in my head.

For the rest of the day I operated with less tension, but only to a level where I still felt comfortable—I was not taking any stupid risks. I was not a salty combat vet yet. I wanted to ease my way into this. After a few rounds of checking out Iraqi blocking positions and realizing they were up to Iraqi standard, I decided it was time to go chill with the Iraqi medics.

The medics were the smartest Iraqis with us. They had established a foothold on a great shade spot under a former bank building that had been crushed by a 500-pound bomb a few years earlier by coalition forces. The building was in total shambles, but the warped roof structure provided amazing shade (see photo 5). I figured I could kill two birds with one stone: I could learn a little Arabic and I could cool off a bit.

"As salama aleikum" (Peace be upon you), I muttered to the two Iraqi medics. "Wa aleikum salam" (And upon you peace), they eagerly replied, smiling from ear to ear. After a five-minute exchange of pleasantries in Arabic, the two Iraqis showed me to a piece of choice rubble that made an excellent seat. I was not at a Starbucks, but the discussion I was having was fascinating. Luckily, one of the medics, Hussein, was a former English teacher in Baghdad. With my developing Arabic skills and his rudimentary ability to say some English words, we pieced together a great conversation.

Hussein was a private in the Iraqi army. He had a well-groomed mustache, embracing smile, and soft features—a sure sign his life had not been rough. He was thirty-eight and looked his age, which is saying something for an Iraqi. I have met a few Iraqi soldiers in their thirties and forties and all look as though they were only a few steps away from a six-foot hole in the ground. Hussein was different. He was a modern man, well educated, and had led a simple middle-class life. He had a wife and two young boys of whom he was very proud. I could not figure why this guy was a *jundi*.

Things changed for Hussein when OIF (Operation Iraqi Freedom) commenced in 2003. After the initial invasion and chaotic aftermath, he was left with limited options. He could move to southern Iraq and make $50 a month continuing his craft as a teacher—a fifteen-year career—but he would not have enough income to support his family. Hussein's second choice was to join the new Iraqi army. In the IA he would start off making about $350 a month and would be able to give his family a much better life. The choice was easy. Providing for one's family is the foundation of an Iraqi man's pride and honor. Nothing takes precedence over this sacred duty, even if it means leaving for the chaos of Al Anbar Province, risking one's life on a daily basis, and returning home to face constant death threats.

My conversations with Hussein and Muhammad, the other Iraqi medic, eventually led to the topic of conversation that is universal to all military males regardless of culture or creed: beautiful women. Hussein and Muhammad were interested in hearing about women from California. They wanted to know what made them special. A litany of questions came flying at me: "Why are all of the beautiful women in California? What is the magic that moves them to this area?" Clearly these men had watched too many old episodes of *Baywatch*. I debated whether I should make up an interesting story as to why all the hot women resided in California. I decided to be honest and explained to them that this was a stereotype from television and that beautiful women live throughout America.

Trying to temper their fantasy, I told Hussein and Muhammad that many Mexican women were moving into the area. I found it hard to translate "Mexican" into Arabic, but it did not matter. Hussein and Muhammad blurted out in almost perfect unison, "Mexicii? Me love Mexicii ma'am!" (Mexican? Me love Mexican women!) Apparently Mexican women hit a hot spot with these Iraqi men. It turns out Mexican women look very similar to Lebanese woman and are thus more in line with the ideal of Arab beauty. I was still confused. I could not think of a classic American television show that would have exposed Iraqi men to Mexican women. I asked my friends where they had seen Mexican women. "Television," they responded in English. "On the Mexican television." A light flashed in my head. How many times had I spun through the channels in the United

States and stopped on Telemundo to look at the gorgeous and scantily clad Mexican women dancing around on some game show. The Iraqis had done the same thing.

After conversing with the medics I made my way to Gunnery Sergeant Horvath's and Captain Chin's position in an abandoned school. I took a seat in the corner of a room where they were resting.

Boom! I felt the earth shake beneath me. My heart sank. "Oh shit, Gunny. What the fuck was that?" Unfazed, Horvath responded, "Not sure, Sir, by the sound I'd guess an IED across the river in Barwana." My heart was racing. The combat vets continued to snooze and talk about the peculiarities of the *jundi* while I wondered when I was going to die.

In the midst of our conversation the sound of Arabic came over one of the Motorola radios. We went to check it out. Civilians were gathering near our position, requesting entrance into the town. At first there were only two civilians, moaning that they needed to get to their homes. The crowd swelled to thirty and we had the Iraqi squad leader dispatch a *jundi* to calm the scene.

In our training we were taught to approach Iraqi civilians in a peaceful manner and only elevate the level of force according to the situation. If the civilians are peaceful, we were told, approach them peacefully; if the civilians are firing guns at you, approach them with your machine gun on full automatic. The Iraqis had a different perspective. The dispatched *jundi* moved forward with his RPK machine gun pointing directly at the crowd. He requested the leader of the jumble come to him and discuss the situation. Talk about negotiating from a position of power.

Watching the event unfold I thought that this scene would end up on the cover of the *New York Times*. This *jundi* was going to have a negligent discharge, shoot someone in the crowd, and all hell was going to break loose. I was overreacting. It all ended peacefully and cordially; the *jundi* just do things differently.

After the incident with the crowd I was ready for the day to end. Adams came to my rescue. At around 1600 I got a call over the radio that the *jundi* conducting the search of the homes were done. Adams radioed, "Hey, we are all clear here. We have a shitload of confiscated AK-47s as well, over." I replied, "Roger, out."

The reason Adams and the *jundi* had piles of weapons became obvious later. Colonel Abass had ordered his troops to take all weapons from the town, unknown to us. The official national rule is that the townspeople in

Iraq are allowed one 30-round magazine and one AK-47 per household. Colonel Abass disregarded this rule and gave the order to confiscate all the weapons. His logic was sound: in a town of insurgents, why would he leave every person an AK-47? The Iraqi people's excuse is that they use their AK-47 for protection. Complete baloney. A single AK-47 won't protect anyone from an insurgent. If the townspeople need protection they can tell the Iraqi army or U.S. Marines and they will soon have three hundred automatic weapons to protect them. Colonel Abass's decision made a lot of sense.

We cleared all of Bani Dahir without a single violent incident. Not even a single shot was fired. Not a single weapons cache was found, and there was barely a soul in the street. I imagined we would chalk this up as a victory. But the operation was too easy. Something was obvious to me: All the insurgents in the village knew we were coming and had managed to leave town. I hoped that when we cordoned and searched Kaffijiyah word would not travel and we would surprise any unsuspecting insurgents. Perhaps we would get lucky.

Kaffijiyah

Gunnery Sergeant Horvath, Captain Chin, and I split up and went with three Iraqi squads into Kaffijiyah, a small village nestled alongside the Euphrates. The Iraqi squad I was with would clear the north side of town, Horvath's would clear the center, and Chin's would clear the southern portion. As in the Bani Dahir operation, Colonel Abass ordered us to take all weapons from the residents of Kaffijiyah. The local civilians were not happy. I tried to explain Abass's order to the townspeople, and the common response was that the Iraqi soldiers were corrupt and want to sell their weapons in Baghdad when they go on leave. I tried to convince them otherwise, but to no avail. According to the residents of Kaffijiyah, the *jundi* are Ali Babbas, a colloquial term for "thieves." Iraqis tend to believe that any Iraqi who is not in their family cannot be trusted.

The biggest issue with the operation was the tactical incompetence of Captain Najib, the 4th Iraqi Company commander, who was everything Iraqis look for in an officer. He had a sense of entitlement and confidence, his manners were precise and his professionalism was keen, and he was feared by his men. The general Marine opinion of Captain Najib, however, was that he was an idiot in an Iraqi uniform.

The original plan for the operation was to have three squads move in line from west to east. This way we would ensure the town was cleared systematically. According to the plan every few hundred meters the Iraqi squad leaders would check back with Najib and make sure everyone was in line. The intent of keeping the squads roughly in line was so one squad didn't get too far out in front of the others. If this were to occur, the danger of Iraqi friendly fire would increase dramatically.

Halfway through the town it was clear the squads were out of whack. Our squad was at least five hundred meters behind the center squad, and the southern squad was probably three hundred meters in front of the center squad. If we were attacked from any direction, we were in for disaster. Realizing the tactical dilemma we faced, I left my squad to find Najib and help him rectify the problem. He was nowhere to be found. I talked to *jundi* in the center squad and they directed me forward. Sure enough, five hundred meters in front of the center squad was Najib with a few soldiers scouting the area. Horvath and I approached Najib, who was sitting in the direct firing line of his center squad, oblivious to where his troops were in the town. Horvath picked up his pace and mumbled under his breath to me, "This fucker is going to have my boot in his ass."

Horvath caught up to Najib and addressed him in broken Arabic. As Horvath berated Najib, Najib seemed to lose his ability to understand Horvath's broken Arabic and English. Iraqis sometimes have bad cases of "selective hearing." Horvath gave up and stomped off. I figured I would take my shot with Najib. I tried the friendlier, helpful approach, thinking I could appeal to the Arab in Najib. "Najib, why are you in front of all the troops? If there is a firefight you will be shot. Do you even know that the squads are all misaligned?" Najib responded confidently, "I need to see the battlefield up ahead. My men will not shoot me, they know where I am. Plus, there are no insurgents in this area anyway." From Najib's tone I knew he had resorted to a "fuck the Americans" attitude and I would have no luck in changing his mind. We were destined to clear Kaffijiyah in the least tactically sensible way.

Najib's poor tactical decisions throughout the day were dragging down our morale. Something good had to be coming our way, and indeed the good news came. We ran into a police colonel who worked in the area and could provide us with much-needed human intelligence. Najib called back to Colonel Abass to report the news.

Without giving details Najib told us we would be in the police colonel's home for a while until he had updates from Colonel Abass. We apprehensively agreed and posted security on the police colonel's home. Remarkably it turned out that Abass and this man had a long history in the old Iraqi army.

Five minutes later an entourage of Iraqi Humvees came flying through the town. In true Iraqi fashion, Abass has decided to bring his entire personal security detachment to this man's house in the middle of our searching operation. He wanted to have tea, talk about the local area, and get an assessment of the situation in Kaffijiyah.

Colonel Abass and the police colonel conversed in Arabic for fifteen minutes before I lost interest and noticed a cute Iraqi boy, no older than five. He sprinted to me and spoke in perfect English, "Give me." I responded in English, "You sure are direct, aren't you?" He snapped, "Mister, give me." I ruminated. On the one hand, I did have some toys, but this kid was rude. On the other hand, if we could get in with this kid's police colonel father, we would have access to a lot of intelligence. I made my decision and threw the kid one of the toys I had in my drop pouch.

The little boy dived on the toy, ran into his house, and came dashing at light speed toward me to shout again, "Give me!" I played the kid's little game for a few more rounds, not able to resist the idea I could win his heart and mind. I snapped back to reality and realized I was being used. This kid had ratholed a pile of the things I had given him and was coming back for more. As long as the gravy train was in town, he was going to get more than his fair share.

I focused my attention back on Colonel Abass, who had finished speaking with his old friend. The police colonel's parting words were that the insurgents in the Triad were in their last throes of survival and were depending on thievery and burglary to support their attacks on the Iraqi army and Marines. According to him they would be out of the area within months because the people were fed up. I knew one thing. I wasn't holding my breath for this guy's prediction to come true. *Insha'allah* (God willing) this guy is right!

Despite all the minor setbacks with Najib, the day clearing homes in Kaffijiyah was successful. No insurgents attacked, we received some solid intelligence from the local residents, and we found no caches or evidence of insurgents working in the area. It was time to get some chow. We helped Najib round up his men and headed to the battalion mobile command post (CP), which overlooked Kaffijiyah from a hill eight hundred meters away. Captain Chin and I started our walk to the CP when the Iraqi ambulance came screaming in our direction. I thought to myself, what is wrong now?

The ambulance stopped right alongside us as the dust cloud following engulfed us, proving that being invisible is possible in Iraq. It was my medic buddies Hussein and Muhammad. Excited, they yelled at us to hop in the back. We obliged after a short calculation: we could either hitch a ride in the back of an Iraqi ambulance with no armor and no turret gunner and be driven by a couple of crazy Iraqis or we could walk a mile wearing over eighty pounds of gear, suffering in 125-degree heat. Sometimes comfort-based decisions are the way to go. We hopped in the back of the medical vehicle and grabbed onto whatever we could find as Hussein put the pedal to the metal.

Making Friends with Najib

After returning from the mission in one piece, I was ready to hit the rack. Sadly, Colonel Abass made a request to speak with the advisers who were embedded with Najib. He had correctly sensed problems during the Kaffijiyah mission between the embedded advisers and Najib and wanted to smooth over the situation. Abass had unique insights to share. He gave me, Horvath, and Chin a lesson on how to deal with Arab men. His lecture was directed mostly at Horvath, but we all gained insight from his wisdom.

"Gunny Horvath," he began, "you are as stubborn as Captain Najib. I respect this quality in men and I believe it contributes to your success and pride as a military man, however—" Colonel Abass interrupted himself. "Captain Najib will be punished for not cooperating with you today on the battlefield. I am sorry for his actions. However, I want to lend you some advice. In our culture, you must give a little if you want to get anything. If two stubborn people meet, it always creates problems. For example, Arab people are similar to a taut string. At one end you have the reasonable people; on the other end you have the maniacs. They are both connected by this taut line. If the maniacs want something, the reasonable people must soften and give him some line and vice versa. Unfortunately this line is not strong. If one group pulls against the other, the line breaks and everything is broken."

Abass continued his lecture. "Here's a more personal example. The U.S. Army Special Forces team that previously worked here were bossy. They were smart men, had excellent tactics, and trained my scouts well. But they were stern, demanding, and stubborn. On one mission they asked me if they could take my scouts. I agreed with them that the mission was valuable, however, I would have none of it." Abass got louder. "Why should I allow them to order my scouts around without consulting my advice and without respecting my stature as commander? We were not friends. I was merely their pawn. The Special Forces team was terrible with relations and I made them pay!"

At this point Colonel Abass was excited, but he began to calm down. "The next Special Forces team to come in was different," he said. "Their tactics were terrible and their advice incompetent. However, they were my friends, drank tea with me, and consulted me on the best employment of my scouts. I would try to please them and I allowed them to employ my scouts in any matter they chose, even if I felt it was unwise. This is something Iraqis do. We take the extra step to please a friend. It is important to compromise and keep the string I spoke of from breaking." Abass was wise. We decided to build our personal friendship and military relationship with Captain Najib and the other *jundi*.

Chapter 6

Vacationing with the Iraqi Army

August 2006

Improvised explosive devices, better known as IEDs, are the biggest threat in Iraq. The number of devices and tactics insurgents use to build and employ IEDs could fill a book. Breaking it down "Barney-style" (Marine term for synthesizing things so even the dumb purple dinosaur can understand it), these devices can be separated into three categories: pressure-plate IEDs (PPIEDs), command-wire IEDs (CWIEDs), and radio-controlled IEDs (RCIEDs) (see photo 6).

PPIEDs are any IED initiated by the victim. The classic example is the homemade land mine. Imagine you are walking through a rice paddy in Vietnam and step on a metal or plastic object stuffed with C-4 explosives by the local villager. The next thing you know your leg is flying through the sky and you are collapsing to the ground. This is a type of PPIED. A more complicated example of the type found in Iraq might be a couple strips of thin metal separated by Styrofoam wafers on each end. These metal strips connect to four 155-mm artillery shells buried on the side of the road. The idea is to have a vehicle roll over the metal strips. The pressure from the weight of the tires then causes the metal strips to touch, completing the electric circuit and setting off the artillery shells. This makes a bad day for the Marines or Iraqi army.

Insurgents love PPIEDs because they are "fire and forget"—drop it, leave, and hope Allah will find the right victim. Tactically, though, insurgents have two drawbacks they must consider: accidentally killing the local populace and emplacement. The PPIED is not discriminating. Because whoever happens to drive over the top of a triggering device ignites a PPIED, an insurgent may end up blowing up his uncle, his sister, or his neighbor who is cruising down the street. Insurgents place these IEDs on military-only roads or place them on the civilian roads after curfew hours, when no civilian traffic should be traveling.

But this placement presents a conundrum to the insurgent: How can he emplace the IED on a military-only road if he will be searched if he is seen on this road? Also, if he instead decides to place the IED after curfew hours on a civilian road, he will be searched because he is driving after curfew. All of this makes emplacement appear impossible. It is not, as evidenced by the countless dead Marines and *jundi* who have died from PPIEDs.

The simplest of IEDs are the CWIEDs. If you think back to the Wile E. Coyote cartoons, you already know about CWIEDs. Remember how Wile E. Coyote would set up a bunch of TNT on the road and trace his wire back to a hidden spot where it would be connected to a large ignition switch that said "ACME" on it? When the roadrunner, his target, was in his kill zone, Wile E. Coyote would push down on the igniter box. Unfortunately for the coyote, something would invariably be screwed up with his CWIED; he would get fried and the roadrunner would run off.

Insurgents do the exact same thing as Wile E. Coyote, but their CWIEDs work. First, they place a large amount of explosives: 155-mm artillery shells, four-hundred-pound propane tanks filled with PE-4, satchel charges, metal barrels stuffed with rusty nails and shrapnel, and so on. Second, they trace a copper wire back to their hidden ignition point. This hidden area could be an old sheepherder's tent, a civilian's house, or a stack of rocks. The third step in the CWIED phase is to wait for an unlucky convoy to enter the kill zone and then count, wahid, ithnien, thlathe (one, two, three)—boom!

Owing to their simplicity and ultralow technology (which limits our ability to defeat them with expensive technology), command wires are an insurgent favorite. The added bonus of CWIEDs for insurgents is that they eliminate the issue of accidentally blowing up their neighbors. Yet there are drawbacks to CWIEDs. Insurgents have to sit and wait for a target, which takes time and manpower, not to mention that sitting in the searing heat for hours on end is no fun. Also, CWIEDs are difficult to hide—concealing two thousand meters of copper wire is not easy!

The final category of IED is the RCIED, also an insurgent favorite, consisting of explosives connected to a modified electronic receiving device. Examples of RCIEDs receiving devices include Sanyo base stations, cell phones, and Motorola radios. These devices can be programmed to detonate explosives at the insurgent's desired time. The RCIED is the lazy man's IED. Imagine an insurgent sitting on his patio smoking his hookah pipe. When he sees a convoy passing a few miles away, he dials a special code on his cell phone and detonates the IED, goes back into his house, collects a five hundred dollar check from Al Qaeda, and takes a nap as if nothing ever happened. The chances of the Marines finding this guy? Zero.

What the insurgents can achieve with IEDs is amazing. Roughly 20 percent of every American's tax bill goes to the defense budget. And yet a bunch of relatively uneducated sheepherders with twenty bucks can kick our asses all over Iraq. Luckily a new electronic countermeasure device called the Chameleon is now employed on every Humvee in Al Anbar. At one hundred thousand dollars per Chameleon, these devices are worth every penny. The Chameleon blocks every radio-controlled device. What this means in Al Anbar is that the RCIED threat is gone. The insurgents are left with the PPIED or the CWIED, both of which are difficult to emplace and are easily seen. Because of the Chameleon the challenge of emplacing IEDs has become more difficult for the insurgents.

The Leave Run Process

After checking that our Chameleons were fully functional, we left for our first IED-dodging convoy to Al Asad Airbase, the "Club Med" of Al Anbar Province, located thirty-five miles south of Haditha Dam. The mission was to conduct a leave run ("leave" is the military term for vacation). I am still trying to figure out the peculiarities of how the leave run process works. Apparently everyone in the IA works twenty days and then takes ten days of leave to see their families. This is the standard set by the Iraqi Ministry of Defense. The Iraqi army makes the French work schedule look like a Chinese sweatshop.

Every ten days a leave run was required. All *jundi* going on leave from 2nd Brigade, 7th Division Iraqi army, which included our battalion in the Haditha Triad as well as battalions in Hit (an insurgent hotbed forty miles southeast of Haditha) and Rawah (a small town located thirty miles west of the Triad), converged at the 2nd Iraqi Brigade headquarters camp on Al Asad Airbase. From there the *jundi* were jammed onto civilian buses, integrated into a U.S. military convoy, and moved southeast from Al Asad, where the convoy picked up other IA soldiers going on leave from various divisions in Al Anbar.

The buses moved through some of the more treacherous areas in Al Anbar Province. Their first "scenic" city along the drive was Ramadi, which was followed by another "tourist attraction," Fallujah. If the buses survived they skirted south of Baghdad and moved south toward Najaf, the final destination. Najaf is a large city in southern Iraq and is midpoint between Baghdad and Basrah. It is a reasonable destination for our brigade, as more than 90 percent of the soldiers in 2nd Brigade are Shia Muslims from the southern areas of Iraq.

Under the current method of operations this generous leave schedule means every ten days the MiTTs are risking their lives so the *jundi* can see their families every twenty days. Remarkably, Iraqis were angry at their twenty-days-on, ten-days-off schedule and threatened to quit if they did not get their leave. This was ridiculous to us, considering all MiTT members were on tours ranging from seven to fifteen months.

The leave process did not lend itself to minimizing risk for MiTT members or the IA. Leave operations were especially convoluted for our battalion, which was spread between five locations in the Triad. A MiTT joke was that the primary objective of the MiTT is not to train, support, and advise the IA on how to conduct counterinsurgency operations so we can leave Iraq but to gather *jundi* throughout the Triad so they can go home to see their families every twenty days.

The easiest way to understand the leave process is to think of it as a school bus. The school bus gets the kids from school and drops them off at their bus stops. Similarly, the first stage of a leave convoy involved convoying to Al Asad to pick up Iraqi soldiers coming back from leave. We typically went one day prior to the *jundi* arriving and spent the night in Al Asad so we could take care of any business we needed to conduct there. The following day the *jundi* arrived, at about 0400 to 0500. After the Iraqis inventoried who was returning from leave, the convoy headed north, back toward Camp Ali (see map 2).

Our first two stops on the route back to Camp Ali were Baghdadi, home of 3rd Iraqi Company, and Haqliniyah, 1st Iraqi Company's base. In the respective locations we dropped off the *jundi* coming off leave and picked up *jundi* who were ready to go on leave. Essentially we were making a one-for-one *jundi* swap.

Once we reached Camp Ali we offloaded everyone except for the *jundi* who were from 4th Iraqi Company, which was located on the Marine FOB (forward operating base, pronounced "faub") in central Haditha. The

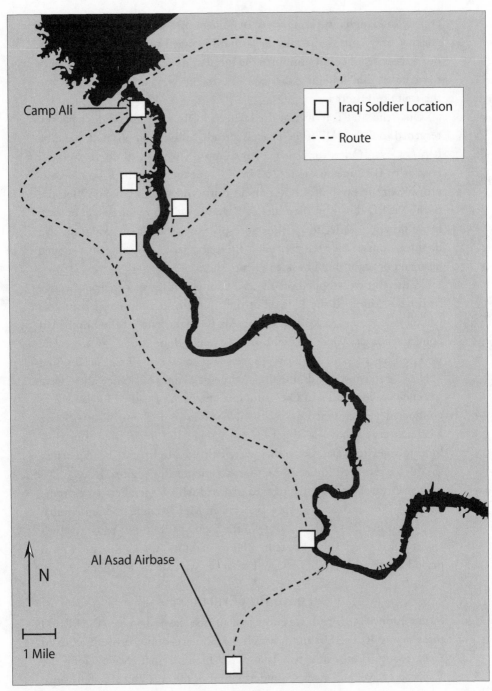

Map 2. Iraqi Army convoy operations during a leave period.

convoy to Haditha was dangerous. By reforming a smaller convoy at Camp Ali that only consisted of the *jundi* that belonged to 4th Iraqi Company, our adviser team could minimize the number of vehicles and personnel in the convoy, thus lessening the exposure to the inevitable IED attacks on the route to Haditha.

Once the MiTT arrived at the Haditha FOB, we swapped the *jundi* and returned to Camp Ali. If the process already sounds complicated, stand by, it is not over. Once we returned to Camp Ali we had to do yet another convoy to Barwana, home to 2nd Iraqi Company. Barwana is on the eastern side of the Euphrates River about thirty miles from the dam. Because of the PPIED threat on the route to Barwana (which required a convoy to move slowly in order to spot pressure-plate switches), a convoy took two to three hours. Once we arrived at the Barwana FOB we again swapped *jundi* and brought them back to Camp Ali.

In the end we dropped off all *jundi* coming off leave at their respective firm bases (dropped the kids off at their bus stops) and managed to collect all *jundi* going on leave at Camp Ali. Keeping track of the number of convoys thus far? We're on eight, and we're not done yet.

The final stage in the leave process was to screen all the *jundi* going on leave for contraband and theft while at Camp Ali. Once they were screened we loaded them like cattle into the back of flatbed Leylands and conducted yet another convoy to Al Asad to drop them off at brigade headquarters so they could get on buses there and begin their fourteen-hour journey to Najaf. Once they were delivered to brigade headquarters, the MiTT returned to Camp Ali that same night (see photo 7).

Leave runs were exhausting and exposed MiTT members to extreme danger. In the end, on a single leave run, an MiTT conducted ten combat convoys, drove 250 miles on some of the highest IED threat routes in Iraq, and traveled over twelve hours in a Humvee in less than a thirty-six hour period. I hoped the IA appreciated what we were doing for them.

Leave Run Execution

Route Bronze is the path we chose for our first leave run, given the PPIED threat along Route Uranium, which is a military-only road leading to Al Asad. Route Bronze is a two-lane paved highway that weaves along the Euphrates River and gives a wonderful tour of the area. But Route Bronze was also infested with CWIEDs. Grim reminders of IED death and destruction were evident everywhere along the road. There were massive

IED craters spattered along the road, making it look like a piece of asphalt-colored Swiss cheese. Combat engineers filled and marked the holes as fast as possible, but they could not repair the damage as fast as the insurgents could plant IEDs (see photo 8).

Aside from the massive IED potholes along the road, the route was well maintained and at times scenic. Part of the route moves on the outskirts of the major towns and villages. To the east are various villages in the region, which snuggle up next to the Euphrates River. The view to the west is treacherous desert. All we saw there was the occasional blank stare from a random sheepherder who was providing reconnaissance for the insurgents. I never saw any grass to the west of Route Bronze: why did sheepherders graze their flocks there?

Along Route Bronze we were kings. The Iraqis led the convoy and their lead turret gunner waved a large orange flag as a reminder to the locals to move it or lose it. Locals knew the drill: if they did not move, a hail of 7.62-mm metal slugs from *jundi* AK-47s and RPK machine guns would come flying toward their craniums.

Crowds parted like the Red Sea when our convoy moved through. The locals veered into the desert a hundred meters off the road, got out of their cars, and faced away from the road. Some adhered to the rules better than others. Thankfully for the civilians, Iraqi turret gunners knew how to distinguish between a credible threat and a lazy Iraqi who wasn't following the rules. It was unfortunate to disrupt civilians' lives in this way, but the threat of vehicle-borne IEDs was constant in the Triad.

The atmosphere changed as we moved farther south. Here civilians standing outside their cars gave us looks that said, "I am going to cut your heart out with a spoon." Things changed when we get near Baghdadi, a small town about five miles north of Al Asad. As I write this Baghdadi is under the control of Colonel Shaban, the Iraqi police commander in the area who quelled the insurgent threat with little help from the Americans.

It was relatively peaceful in Baghdadi. Rolling through the town, my biggest threat was not IEDs but ensuring I did not run over a kid while driving the Humvee. They lined the streets, begging and yelling, "Mister, mister, give me! We love America, give me, mister." Some kids gave us a thumbs-up, while others waved both hands above their heads. Parents waved and gave us bright smiles. Captain Chin, our turret gunner, sometimes tossed a bag of candy and toys to the kids. The instant the candy hit the ground, I witnessed true war. The kids turned into animals. The boys punched the girls to the ground and then proceeded to beat one another. They resembled a pride of starving lions after a large kill, each lion vying for his fair share, snapping and biting at the members of his own pride. These people are poor.

Past Baghdadi was a long stretch of road that rested between a cliff and the Euphrates River. The arrangement made for both an excellent location for attacks and a great scenic route. As we rolled down this section of road, Captain Chin and the old MiTT crew in the Humvee with us enjoyed scaring us. During one drive down this road Capt. Peter Morales started counting loudly, "Three, two, one—bang! This is where we got hit a few weeks back." Here I was, trying to drive my first combat convoy, scared to death, and I had these jokers trying to rev me up. Concealing my nerves, I responded, "Sir, are you trying to scare me? It ain't working." I heard a chuckle from my response and we continued along the route.

We finally reached the turning point where Route Bronze turns into Al Asad Road—the equivalent of getting an invincibility star on the Super Mario Brothers Nintendo game. We sped up and tried to cover as much ground as possible, completely forgetting about the enemy. Everyone on the old MiTT claimed this final three-mile stretch of road leading into Al Asad Airbase had never seen an IED and never would. I took their word for it and slammed on the gas in an attempt to catch up with the Iraqi Humvee ahead of me.

Once on Al Asad we had sugar-plum visions of what looked like a kingdom of POGs ("people other than grunts," a derogatory term for nonactive combat participants), civilian contractors, and desk jockeys. Al Asad Airbase is another fortress we erected in Iraq. We drove around the base to see the magnificent structures. The disgruntled old MiTT members talked about how amazing life was in Al Asad.

The old MiTT crew was jealous for good reason. Al Asad comes complete with four different KBR chow halls (each the size of a football field), huge gymnasium structures complete with swimming pools and basketball courts, a Moral Wellness and Recreation Center that could fit an entire Marine battalion inside, and a shopping section with a Subway, Burger King, Pizza Hut, and an AT&T phone center. Were we really in Iraq?

I was excited about luxury living again. My excitement ended abruptly, however. As we toured the base, we moved farther from the amenities and closer to the outer regions of the base. We were going to the Iraqi brigade camp. A motivated Marine, decked out in combat gear, asked for rosters, verified our convoy clearance, and greeted us upon our entrance into the U.S.-controlled fortress. Everything was methodical and organized. The situation at the Iraqi camp was completely the opposite.

Approaching the Iraqi entrance into the brigade camp there were two *jundi*, one asleep, and the other trying to stay in the small portion of shade that the guard shack provided. The guard's weapons were in the guard shack, sitting on the ground, filthy. The guards were very friendly. Passing through the gate, the *jundi* awoke, jumped up, and with a wide grin gleefully yelled to the convoy, "As salama aleikum" (Peace be upon you). Welcome to the Second Brigade Iraqi camp, I thought to myself. God save us.

We twisted along the one-lane paved road that snaked through the brigade camp until we reached the MiTT camp. We pulled our Humvees into their camp, which was a bunch of swahuts and other small facilities surrounded by a fence of Hesco barriers. Our accommodations were rugged. The brigade MiTT stuffed sixteen of us into a swahut. After we settled in, our next stop was a KBR chow hall, a treat we had not had in almost two weeks.

Entering a KBR chow hall was equivalent to entering heaven. There were lines of tables, many overweight civilian contractors and service members, and large flat screen televisions playing Fox News and SportsCenter at all times. On the perimeter of the enormous indoor spaces were various buffet-style choices. You had the option of the fast food lines, where you could order any fast food imaginable, or you could hit the main course line, where you could always get a healthy dose of steak, lobster, shrimp, chicken, or lamb. If you were not satisfied with a plate full of fast food and a gourmet steak, you had the option of indulging in the sandwich bar, where double or quadruple meat is standard.

If you were still hungry you could move over to the Mexican buffet to get enchiladas, tacos, quesadillas, or beans. If you wanted some greens to go with all your other chow, no problem. There were two identical fruit and salad bar stations in the facility.

At this stage you might have four or five plates of food on your tray. But then there was the comprehensive ice cream bar featuring a variety of flavors of ice cream, yogurt, or sherbet. If you weren't satisfied with the ice cream sprinkled with fudge shavings, sprinkles, and strawberry syrup, you could head over to the pie and fine desserts bar, where you could get four varieties of cheesecake, walnut pie, pumpkin pie, chocolate cake, and "you name it they probably have it" pie. KBR chow was outstanding in my opinion. Regulars at the facility complained, but KBR put to shame some of the best restaurants I have been to in the States. Thank you, American taxpayer!

After recouping, in one meal at the KBR chow hall, the seven pounds I had lost in the previous two weeks, I waddled back to our swahut on the brigade camp. At 2100 we were told that the buses returning the *jundi* from Najaf were coming in at 0400 the next day. It was time to hit the rack.

Staring at the tin roof ceiling of the swahut, Lieutenant Adams and I came up with estimates for our chances of death in Iraq. It was a sick exercise, but talking about our mortality was more therapeutic than internalizing the worry and stress associated with these thoughts. Based on our calculations, we had about 270 potential meetings with the grim reaper. We had 180 convoy legs to do for leave runs, an estimated forty combat missions similar to Kaffijiyah and Bani Dahir, and perhaps thirty random chances associated with miscellaneous events. I did not include potential small-arms attacks on foot patrols or mortar attacks. For argument's sake we agreed that the total number of chances at death was five hundred.

Heck, I had lived in West Philly for two and a half years and on Chicago's South Side for two years. If I had a random chance of being killed each day I'd lived in those areas, that would mean I'd survived 1,642 (365 days x 4.5 years) shots at death, or three times the risk of my tour in Iraq.

The Clown Show Returns

An important lesson about Iraqi culture is that time lines are meaningless. The returning *jundi* arrived at the brigade Iraqi camp at about 1100, seven hours later than scheduled. The inbound *jundi* arrival scene was another lesson in Iraqi culture: Iraqis are, by American standards, lazy.

Being Americans, we had everything squared away and prepared for efficiency and time management. All the Humvees and Leylands were in convoy formation prepared to move out. The way our MiTT envisioned it, the Iraqis would come off of leave, we would conduct a quick accountability of everyone, we would load the convoy, and would rush out the gate to make up for our seven-hour time deficit. Our plan did not work (see photo 9).

Iraqis are intense friends and comrades. This became evident when the arriving Iraqi soldiers exited the buses after vacation. They started hugging and kissing one another as if they were at a family reunion. Everyone was overjoyed to see their comrades. This was a good thing, but keep in mind it had only been twenty days since these guys had seen each other.

We sat in the scorching 125-degree heat in full battle-rattle for forty minutes. Waiting patiently for the Iraqis to finish greeting one another so we could actually be doing something, the boss' patience wore thin. "Gray, tell them to get off their asses," he said, "and get their counts so we can get the hell out of here." I responded, "Sir, I spoke to Captain Chin, and he said we have to wait this one out and let the dust settle." Exhausted, he replied, "Roger, well kick them in the asses to get them rolling—this is ridiculous!"

I went up to Abdulrachman, the Iraqi administrative chief, and asked if he could start taking a roll call so we could load the Leylands and return the *jundi* to their respective bases in the Triad. He responded in his standard asinine fashion, "We are working on it." I pondered different methods of engagement with Abdulrachman, since the one I was using was not working. Chin suggested talking to one of the Iraqi officers to force Abdulrachman to do his duty. Chin's advice worked like a charm. Iraqis tend not to take orders or suggestions from an American unless you are in their inner circle—a position I had yet to attain in my short time with many of the *jundi*. However, Iraqis will listen to the Iraqi officers, who wield the power to take their pay or leave away from them as a form of punishment. With a credible threat behind him, Captain Natham spoke to Abdulrachman and the roll call was finally completed. The Iraqis loaded into the Leylands and we were ready to go dodge IEDs on Route Bronze.

On the return convoy our MiTT took over leadership on the operation, with the outgoing MiTT members there for guidance. I moved from Humvee driver to vehicle commander for the rearmost Humvee. As we moved north on Route Bronze, I noticed a consistent screeching on my radio. I tried to respond to the incoming radio traffic but was unable to do so. "Don't worry about it, it's the Chameleon—they fuck up comm [communications] all the time," blurted Captain Chin, who saw I was struggling. Apparently the boss and Captain McShane had not received the same memo. The entire time on the radio, when I could actually hear them, it was a bitchfest: "Gray, get your comm unfucked! Gray, why aren't you responding to my radio check?" Chin comforted me, saying, "Gray, don't sweat it. It takes about two months for everyone on the team to understand that comm is going to suck, especially in the rear of the convoy. Until your team realizes and accepts this fact, there will be constant bitching at each other. From the sounds of your major and captain, you guys may need the entire deployment." I chuckled and said, "I sure hope not." Knowing I was not screwing things up gave me confidence. For the remainder of the trip I concentrated my efforts on IED awareness and gave up trying to communicate on the radio.

Our first stop was the Baghdadi MHC, a residential compound protected by Colonel Shabam's police foot soldiers and home to the Baghdadi FOB. Unfortunately we had to stay at the MHC longer than anticipated. Shabam wanted to hobnob with our boss. As we waited hordes of Iraqi kids bum-rushed our positions. A wave of small humans ran in our direction and fear took over. Even though the kids were four hundred meters off when they saw us approach, their collective voices yelling, "Mister, Mister, give me, give me, give me" could be heard for miles. Where was Santa Claus when you needed him?

Iraqi people in general, and Iraqi children in particular, believe Americans have infinite wealth and infinite possessions. If we did not give them everything we owned, we were considered stingy. The kids wanted everything from your pen or your last water bottle in the Humvee to your M-4 assault rifle or the Humvee itself. (Yes, one of the younger boys asked me for my Humvee and told me to get a new one.)

Doc McGinnis and I had a crowd of ten kids surrounding us, picking on our gear as though we were zoo specimens, yelling at us to give them everything we owned. The next thing I knew the *jundi* came to our rescue. They swooped in. Samir yelled, "Get the fuck out of here, before I kick your little asses!" The kids scattered like flies.

Samir explained to me in broken English spliced with Arabic, "Seyidi [Sir], you need to let these kids know minu il masuul [who is boss] or you will have them on you all day. Bil [In] Basra, I would beat these kids if they begged for things. They have fathers and mothers whom to ask for things. They beg minek, besebeb inta Americii [from you because you are American]." Samir was right.

Samir, Barak, Karim, Hydr, and Muhanned lectured Doc and me on the realities of Iraqi children and the mistaken view we had regarding their innocence. The *jundi* tempered my vision that Iraqi children are innocent blank sheets ready to become freedom-loving democrats. I realized I was dealing with ten-year-old kids with doctoral degrees from the school of hard knocks. My focus was so much on winning hearts and minds that I forgot these kids only cared about survival. They were begging us for things because they thought they could swindle us into giving them something. Afterward they would go to their friends and brag about how they outsmarted an American. It was all bullshit. Naïve generosity is a sure way to appear as a fool in Iraq.

The boss returned. We mounted the Humvees and continued north to Haqliniyah along Route Bronze. We completed our bus stop at Haqliniya and rushed to Camp Ali. We still had to swap out *jundi* in Haditha and Barwana before we could do the return trip to Al Asad so the *jundi* could catch the bus to Najaf.

Once we completed a hasty security check of all the *jundi* going on leave at Camp Ali, we stuffed the Leylands and raced to Al Asad before dusk settled on the area (see photo 10). We made it to Al Asad in record time, offloaded the Iraqi soldiers due for Najaf, and quickly turned around for Camp Ali. Remarkably, we made it home by 2300 with all limbs intact. Il hamdu Allah (Thanks be to God). The team was exhausted and emotions were getting squirrelly.

Mission Recap

Our first leave mission really opened our eyes to the realities of working with the Iraqi army and the monumental challenges we faced. No amount of firsthand stories or Iraqi culture briefs can prepare anybody for the levels of ineptitude, laziness, and lack of motivation rampant in the Iraqi army. The frustration within our team was mounting. I was more worried about seeing a friendly fire incident within our team than I was about an insurgent ambush.

Despite my disappointments with certain adviser team members, following the stress, chaos, and hysteria of the leave convoy I had a chance to sit down with one of the great warriors in the Iraqi army, Captain Hasen. As an eleven-year veteran of the old regime army, Hasen was a proud Iraqi, faithful Shia Muslim, and dedicated family man. He was built like a small bull, with a broad chest and shoulders, a Santa Claus stomach, and a friendly smile. Hasen is also one of the few *jundi* who speaks outstanding English, something many of us on the MiTT appreciated.

Hasen lectured me on Iraq's past. "Lieutenant Gray, I sat for three years in my home during the American invasion. I was ashamed we had lost to American forces. Do you know how humiliating this was for those of us in the old Iraqi army? It took me three years to overcome my disappointment." He continued in a solemn voice. "I had eleven years in the former Iraqi army, I had a bright future ahead of me, and in one instant the Americans destroyed my future by telling me I was banished from the Iraqi army. When they asked me to come back to the army, I wasn't sure I had the will to restart from the ground up. Eleven years of my life—wasted."

Captain Hasen elaborated on his past positions with pride. During his service as an SPG-9 antiaircraft gun company commander, his unit destroyed American planes and tanks during the initial phases of OIF and the first Gulf War. I listened to Hasen's stories of leadership and success on the battlefield, knowing his successes were our American losses. Hasen understood I had respect for him as a fellow warrior. It was fortunate our interests were aligned this time around.

Captain Hasen is a great man. I am certain he has his Iraqi quirks and oddities that seem selfish and ridiculous through an American lens, but there is something genuine about him. With men like him, perhaps there is hope for Iraqis to create a prosperous Iraq.

After speaking with Hasen I returned to my hooch. I quickly realized it was the first anniversary of my wedding and I had no way to contact my wife. The Iridium phones were out of batteries that day. Of course, my wife had come to expect this from the Marine Corps. The day after we got married we didn't go on a honeymoon; instead, we moved all my stuff down to Dam Neck, Virginia, so I could attend Ground Officer's Intelligence School. It wasn't exactly a romantic escapade. Sadly, our first anniversary wasn't romantic, either. C'est la vie.

Chapter 7

Jamal in the Swahuts

August 2006

The *jundi* loved my "top-secret weapon." I want to reveal it here so that future ambassadors to the Arab world can take advantage of my technique. In reality my top-secret weapon was neither secret nor a weapon. It was a family photo album I stuffed in my cargo pocket.

During predeployment I put in a lot of time learning about Arab culture. One thing I took away from my studies was that family is central in Arab life. In the Arab mind anyone who keeps God and his family as the highest priority in his life cannot be a bad man. I knew the Arabs perceived Americans as Godless heathens, more concerned with material wealth than family. To combat this stereotype I created a family photo album that I could show the Iraqis.

In my top-secret weapon I included photos of me working with the sheep on our ranch, my family baling hay on the farm, and photos of us hanging out at our cabin in the mountains. I was quick to throw out pictures of me raising pigs, hugging our dogs, and my wedding at a fabulous mansion (rented for the occasion) in Pennsylvania. Those, I knew, would not go over well in Iraqi culture.

This worked much better than I expected. It allowed me to cut through all the perceptions Iraqis had of Americans, and I was one step closer to being inside the Iraqi army. The *jundi* loved seeing pictures of my family and of me doing things similar to things they did. Coupling my top-secret weapon with my growing ability to speak Arabic, I felt I was forming quality relationships with the *jundi*.

One night, armed with my album, I made my nightly visit to the *jundi* hooches (living area) to learn some language and learn about Iraq. I sat down with an Iraqi named Sermen. He was Sunni, his mother was Shia, and his grandmother was Catholic—go figure.

Sermen had an almost frightening amount of knowledge of the insurgency. He claimed he got his information from his friends who were insurgents, but I was not convinced. According to Sermen the going rate for firing an RPG at Americans was five hundred dollars, the going rate for emplacing IEDs was three hundred dollars, and for actually killing an American you received a thousand bucks. Sermen described a sniper in Baghdad who had killed over a hundred troops from the coalition forces. Apparently this insurgent had a garage full of BMWs and stacks of cash. It sounded like being an insurgent made economic sense.

The *jundi* in our battalion made roughly $350 a month. The highest paid Iraqi in our battalion was Colonel Abass, who cleared about $900 a month. Put simply, being a *jundi* was bad business. The alternative to serving in the Iraqi army was to commit one insurgent attack per month (make five hundred dollars for an IED) and watch television for the other twenty-nine days of the month.

After chatting with Sermen I passed by the scout's swahut on my way back to the MiTT camp. Kareem greeted me. "Lieutenant," he said, "take a seat, stay a while, drink some tea, let's talk about your family." One of the Iraqis, Ali, asked for my name in broken English. I replied in Arabic with a wide smile, "Ismee Mulazim Gray, sadeeki" (My name is Lieutenant Gray, my friend). The Iraqis repeated together, "Mulazim Gay?" I looked at them and said, "La [no], Mulazim Guurray." The Iraqis tried again. "Mulazim Gaaay?"

I knew that I could not have the Iraqis calling me "Lieutenant Gay" or it would be a never-ending joke with the Marines for the remainder of my deployment. I needed to rectify the situation. I struggled with the Iraqis to help them pronounce my name correctly. Luckily, Ali came up with a better solution. "Let's give him an Arabic name," he said. The swahut erupted with applause. The scouts thought this was the greatest idea since the Arabic numeral system. Everyone started shouting suggestions. Ali said, "Mohammed or Khalis?" Another fired, "No, I like Jaffer, or Ali." Kareem butted in. "No way. Let's call him Riath or Rasheed." Finally, Hyder, the most respected scout, proclaimed, "Inta warda, inta tkoon Jamal, Mulazim Jamal!" (You are a flower, you will be Jamal, Lieutenant Jamal!) Before I could even respond and tell the Iraqis that I thought being called a "flower" in a room full of twenty Iraqi soldiers was awkward, it had already caught on. The swahut shouted in unison, "Mulazim Jamal, Mulazim Jamal, Mulazim Jamal." Oh well, I thought, Mulazim Jamal it is.

The History of Iraq . . .
and Everyone's Desire to Take Their Oil

It seemed that every day I went to the Iraqi swahut area I learned something about Iraqis. One day the terps gave me lessons on the history of Iraq and how Iraqis perceive altruistic people. I cracked the door on the terp swahut and was promptly greeted by Martin. "Is that Mulazim Jamal at the door?" he asked. Somehow word had already traveled throughout the camp that the Iraqis had named me Jamal.

Martin invited me in and gave me his "history of Iraq that Americans need to understand" lecture. With a title like that, I was all ears. Martin mentioned how Americans, Brits, Turks, and the Persians have all come into his country with the thought they would pacify the people. Their basic strategies have been similar: kill everyone who resists in the beginning, see where the dust settles, and then rely on selected Iraqi leaders to show initiative and tie the society together in a peaceful society where people let bygones be bygones and everyone respects the rule of law. But, he said, that does not apply to Iraq. In two thousand years of documented history, there had been a few constants: tribal infighting, sectarian violence, and war with outsiders.

Martin continued. "Jamal, two people have controlled Iraq in our history. One was our good friend Saddam Hussein, and the other was a man named Al Hajaj, who ruled Iraq over a thousand years ago. They controlled Iraq because they had key characteristics that Americans and outsiders need to understand. Saddam and Al Hajaj were brutal tyrants who ruled with fists of steel and hammers of iron to crush all those who wanted to oppose them."

I looked at Martin. "And this is a good thing?" I asked. He laughed and said, "Yes, that is the key point to understand here. Let me give you an example. Currently the Marines try to get information from the locals about IEDs. As you know, placing an IED takes a long time to dig, set the wiring, and so forth. Thus if an IED is in the middle of a neighborhood, everyone knows about it. Yet when Marines go in to ask, 'Who did it?' after having their Humvee blown in half, they get blank stares."

Martin paused before continuing. "You want to know how this situation would be solved using proven Iraqi methods? First, the Iraqi army would tell the people that unless the people who did the terrorist act were turned in during the next twenty-four hours, a single residence would be demolished. If after that first day nobody had spoken, the army would demolish an entire street of homes. Within hours of this engagement, I can promise you that you will have names, addresses, and the family members of the insurgents. The Iraqi army will then take this information and execute the insurgents. This is how Saddam did things, and this is how things work in Iraq. Period."

I sat speechless for a moment and told him I would have to think about my response and get back to him. Martin smiled. "Think long and hard," he said, "and when you figure it out, become the president of Iraq."

If Martin is correct, it will be difficult to accomplish our strategic mission in Iraq of creating a peaceful, stable, and democratic-based government that serves the people, especially if we let them decide how to do things. Paradoxically, if we let Iraqis do things the way they want to do them, it means Iraq will end up as a tyrannical military dictatorship again. This would bring us full circle. And if we confine the Iraqis to using our methods, they will end up in the same situation our troops find themselves in: asking the locals where the IED makers are and getting blank stares.

As Martin and I chatted, Moody woke up. Moody inquired, "What are we talking about today?" I smirked and said, "The history of Iraq." Moody laughed. "You mean the history of America trying to take our oil and claim they are helping us become democratic?" I said, "Yep, exactly. You think I came to this place for my own health?" Moody replied, "You Americans are way too naïve. I truly believe your president might be stupid enough to think he can get Iraqis to trust him." Confused, I asked Moody what he meant, and he explained altruism to me. "Jamal, to Iraqis, the concept that somebody would actually want to help another person without some material benefit is ridiculous. Attempts at altruism are a strong signal for one thing—the person you're dealing with is an Ali Babba!"

Moody's description helped clarify why Iraqis have such a deep suspicion of America's proclaimed desires to help the Iraqi people. He outlined it best when he said, "Americans may think Iraqis are towel-head idiots who are still living in the ice age, but we are not naïve; we know we sit on more oil than all of Saudi Arabia." He continued. "How can any Iraqi believe Americans have come to our country just so they can improve the lives of Iraqis? Your country has spent billions of dollars and countless lives fighting here—all of that for nothing? You must think we are crazy. Plus, why hasn't America gone to the countries in Africa who are ten times as poor and actually need your help? Do you see what I am saying?"

Moody and his fellow terps agreed. I tried to convince them that American policy in Iraq was genuine. The terps simply laughed and said, "Jamal, you are crazy." Maybe they were right.

Babysitting Iraqis

Being the only one to learn Arabic on the team became a curse. The boss designated me "leader of all Iraqi babysitting operations." Not a great job, but somebody had to do it, and I was the most qualified. I figured it would give me more time to learn Iraqi Arabic and Iraqi culture.

When I pulled my first duty as an Iraqi babysitter, I was fortunate enough to be babysitting the leadership of the newly restarted Haditha Police Department—Colonel Farooq and his three captains, Arkon, Yunis, and Harat. Colonel Farooq was in and out, speaking with sheiks in Haditha, but Arkon, Yunis, and Harat were with me all day.

After ten minutes of small talk, Arkon realized there was no need to feed me the standard lines he gives Americans. He loosened up. "Jamal, let me show you what the insurgents have done to my family." He pulled out his cell phone and showed me the pictures and video eulogies of fifteen close family members who have been killed in the past few months by insurgents in the Triad. He growled, "I want to kill every one of these bastards!" Yunis and Harat nodded in agreement. Yunis spoke next. "We are in this business not because we want to help the Americans," he said, "but because we want to get revenge."

I thought to myself, I have a hard time when one of my family members dies. I can't imagine how I would feel if fifteen of my close family members died within a few months. Imagine if three of your brothers were shot in the head, your mother was shot in the stomach, two sisters were stabbed to death, five cousins were killed, an uncle was decapitated, and three aunts were murdered. Hell, I wanted to get revenge for these guys and I did not even know them.

In true Iraqi fashion our conversation went from hysterically emotional to completely normal within one minute. I asked my new friends, "Can I get you guys anything? A drink? Some food?" Yunis responded with a smile then said, "Hey Jamal, you guys have sexy magazines, right?" I paused for a moment, trying to remember if nudie mags were taboo or going to offend Islam and cause Iraqis to commit jihad on me. Finally, my common sense hit me: every man loves to look at beautiful naked women.

I rushed to get my guests some chick magazines to ease their minds. I returned, and when I barged into the room, Harat was on his prayer rug facing Mecca. He mumbled under his breath, "Allah Akbhar, Allah Akbhar. La illah il Allah." (God is great, God is great. There is no God but Allah.) I gave him a puzzled look and muttered, "This is really weird." I stood speechless with a *Penthouse* magazine, a *Buttman* magazine, and a *Club* magazine in my hand as the Iraqis conducted their prayers. Allah is definitely sending me to hell for this one.

Yunis blurted, "Jamal, throw me those magazines, man. What are you waiting for?" After finishing his prayer session, Harat snapped to his feet and ripped the magazines from Yunis. "Hey, share those," he said. I chuckled to myself. This was definitely not in the cultural classes I got in the States.

Not surprisingly, Iraqi men are addicted to hot women. Yunis flipped through the various photographs, saying, "Man, I would drop my wife this instant and move to America if I could get one of these women." I responded in jest, "Dude, you know not all women are like that in America, right? Only in South Florida do they all come like that." Somehow my Arabic did not convey my intended humor; Yunis, Atron, and Harat all want to move to Florida now.

Iraqi Shenanigans

Everyday with the *jundi* was an adventure. Lieutenant Le Gette, the adviser team's artillery officer, and I walked to the motor transportation area of the camp to inquire about the Iraqis' pressure washer that was rumored to be destroyed. We approached the motor transport area, stumbling over random Humvee parts, tools, lubricants, and inoperable tactical vehicles along the way. We approached Amir and Hussein, who were washing one of their Humvees with the pressure washer, and I explained the situation. "Have you guys had any problems with your pressure washer? We were told it was busted." Both men gave us a blank stare. What a stupid question; we were sitting there watching them use the pressure washer, which was obviously functional. The Iraqis laughed. "Jamal, as you can see, the pressure washer is fine. Who told you it was broken?"

Le Gette and I immediately knew what had happened. Captain Hasen, a decent guy most of the time, had tried to pull a fast one on us. Hasen had a functional pressure washer; however, what he really wanted was a fleet of pressure washers. His method to attain this was to tell the MiTT his old pressure washer was broken. He assumed he could simply sit back and wait until we bought him a new one. That might have worked in the past, but this time we actually followed up on his claim. Le Gette and I had learned our lesson: Iraqis will milk a sugar daddy as long as you let them.

"Gray," Le Gette said, "I'm going to tell Adams that the *jundi* don't need a pressure washer." I replied, "Roger, dude, I'm going to go see what Qatan is up to. Major Gaines, Staff Sergeant Haislip, and I are supposed to meet him. He's taking us fishing."

I rolled over to Qatan's swahut to meet Gaines and Haislip. Qatan answered. "You guys ready to go fishing?" he asked. I translated for Gaines and Haislip. Gaines responded, "Na'am [Yes], Let's catch some fish." I looked at Gaines and said, "Sir, I have no clue what we are about to get ourselves into." He smirked and replied, "Well, I guess we'll find out." Qatan grabbed his fishing nets and the remainder of his gear and signaled for us to follow him to where the eastern edge of Camp Ali snuggled up next to the Euphrates River.

We approached the wire fencing that surrounded the boundary of Camp Ali. A man-sized path had been cut through it. Haislip looked at Gaines and me. "Isn't that the wire that is supposed to deter insurgents from sneaking on Camp Ali and killing us in our sleep?" he asked. Before I could respond, Qatan, who had already walked through the hole in the fence, hollered, "Come on, you guys are slow!"

We passed through the cleared section of the protective wire and moved to the shores of the Euphrates. Ten feet off the shore was a blanket of thick reeds, six to seven feet above the water's edge. We quickly realized Qatan's concept of fishing was different from our own. We thought fishing involved fishing poles, hooks, and worms. We were not thinking like Iraqi fishermen; they use nets.

I asked Qatan, "How are you going to get past the reeds?" Qatan replied, "You see that long board that leads to the reeds? Crawl along that board to the reed line. There you will see a flat piece of tin from a swahut roof. Stand on that—it's our boat." I looked at Qatan. "Our boat?" I asked. "It's a piece of tin resting on some crushed reeds." Qatan said, "Yes, Jamal, exactly." He hopped on the five-inch-wide board, ran across it, and effortlessly moved to the reeds, where he stationed himself on the makeshift boat he had positioned in the reed line. I looked at Major Gaines. "Shit Sir, that looks pretty easy." I followed. But my adventure to the reeds was not as graceful as Qatan's; I ended up swimming. After doggy paddling my way to the reed line, I crawled my way onto the flat piece of tin.

Haislip, being the only sane one of the bunch, decided to stay on shore and take pictures of the scene. Once Gaines, Qatan, and I were stationed on the boat, Qatan threw his net into the river. We had a stunning view of the Euphrates. I felt like Huckleberry Finn. This was the ultimate adventure (see photo 11).

When we returned to the MiTT camp, Doc quickly scolded us. "You guys were in the Euphrates?" he said. "You know that thing is crawling with E. coli and parasites, right?" We had no response. Doc was right—as usual. Then the boss followed up with his concerns. "You guys could have been taken prisoner by the insurgents," he said. Unlike Doc, the boss was undeniably wrong. It would take a brass-balled insurgent to try to swim up the Euphrates and somehow take us prisoner. Plus, seven months without a little fun would lead to insanity. All business and no play is a recipe for a mental breakdown.

The Other Secret Weapon

Later that evening I stopped by the Iraqi S-1 (administration section) shop in the Iraqi COC. My stop at the S-1 earned me some wasta, an extremely important concept in Iraqi culture. Wasta is a mysterious combination of your pull, connections, subject-matter knowledge, and charisma, all of which allows you to get favors and respect from others.

After meeting with the various Iraqis working in the S-1, they pointed me to their copier and asked if I could fix it. Captain Chin, the Marine previously in my position, was unable to get them a new one or fix this old one. Thankfully, in a lifetime before the Marines, I had worked with computers and office equipment for a living.

I confidently opened the case of the copier and was greeted with copious amounts of dust and debris. I am no rocket scientist, but a layer of superfine sand dust is not good for a copier. Sure enough, after cleaning the machine, it worked like new. The Iraqis were amazed. I was a hero. I had saved them hours of having to handwrite copies of everything.

Fixing their copier was not a long-term solution, however. I had given the man a fish, but I had not taught him how to catch them. I gathered the group of S-1 personnel around me and explained the importance of weekly and daily maintenance on electronics and office equipment.

I explained that maintenance would extend the life of their equipment anywhere from three to five years. They all nodded in agreement and asked me the most effective way to clean the copier, what places needed the most attention, and how to open the various panels. Sadly, I knew they were simply asking me what I wanted to be asked. Captain Chin had warned me of this. If his experiences held true, the copier would be broken again in a matter of weeks and the *jundi* would be begging me to buy them a new one.

Chapter 8

Simple Things Made Difficult

August–September 2006

When the Iraqi battalion received its annual dump of new supplies from the Iraqi brigade, I decided to act as interpreter and help Lt. Rob Adams, who usually dealt with supply issues but was having a tough time communicating with the Iraqis. "As salamu aleikum," I said to the crowd of Iraqis preparing to offload the supplies. I was greeted as though I were an Arab rock star. "Jamal, Jamal, you speak Arabic? You are a good man. Come on over, sit down, we want to talk to you." How do these guys know me? I wondered. I mustered together some Arabic words and all of a sudden I was Lawrence of Arabia with the *jundi*.

Supplying Iraqis

Amazingly, the Ministry of Defense had sent supplies for three hundred soldiers, more than enough to cover our needs at the battalion. Of course the supply count was based on necessary items such as camouflage blouses, camouflage pants, and boots. To say the MOD had actually sent full supplies for each of the three hundred soldiers would not be true. For example, we had fourteen sweatshirts, forty pairs of tennis shoes, and sixty-five pairs of gloves. Don't ask me how those numbers worked out.

Captain Hasen explained why he was disappointed the MOD did not take all of the odd lot supplies. "Jamal, let me explain to you something about Iraqis. If you give one guy something and don't give another guy the same thing, the bitching and complaining will be so persistent, you will wish that we all had nothing. Trust me, you will see."

Adams suggested a great idea to Hasen. "Why don't you use the extra items as rewards? The Iraqi officers can give these to soldiers who do exceptional things in the battalion." Hasen quickly responded, teaching us another lesson in survivor culture. "Listen, if I give one soldier an award, all of the soldiers will immediately berate me for playing favorites and giving special treatment to a single soldier. Plus, the soldier who receives the award will be scolded for being an ass kisser. In the end, it ends up being a worse deal for both me and the soldier receiving the award. This is crazy, but true." Adams and I nodded in agreement. In our short time interacting with Iraqis, we knew Hasen was correct. Sadly, what Americans deem to be great ideas seldom work within the Iraqi culture.

Astonishingly, the handling of the new supply dump went extremely well, thanks to Captain Nihad, the S-4 logistics officer. Nihad was the closest thing to a Marine officer in our battalion. He worked extremely hard, he took pride in his work and duties, and his troops faithfully executed his well-conceived plans and orders.

For all the praise I could give Nihad, there was one aspect of leadership that even he failed to perform: leadership by example. Marine officers learn in their first days at Officer Candidates School (OCS) the concept of ductus exemplo, or leadership by example. The idea is simple and time tested: an officer, or any sort of good leader for that matter, does what his subordinates do, regardless of how dreadful the task may be. This in turn gains the subordinate's respect and encourages them to accomplish the mission. The ductus exemplo concept is foreign to Iraqis. Leadership in their minds is not an opportunity to show the troops any task is possible but an opportunity to force someone under their command to do all the unwanted tasks.

The day the supplies arrived provided a perfect example of the Iraqi leadership trait I call lazimus maximus. Adams and I, feeling sorry for the *jundi* who were hauling the boxes of supplies in the burning heat, decided to help them finish their job. Nihad immediately scolded us, saying, "Jamal and Adams, what are you doing? Come over here with me in the shade, have a drink, and let the soldiers do that work. Work is not for you!" Samir and Ali, the *jundi* we were helping, said, "Shukran" (Thanks) and told us to go with Nihad. It was obvious they appreciated our help and respected us for putting in the effort. We wanted to continue helping the soldiers, but our basic knowledge of Arab culture gave us the good sense to go with what Captain Nihad wanted. Telling him he was wrong in front of his troops would have led to bigger issues. Later, in a more private arena, we explained to him the concept of ductus exemplo. I doubt he listened, but perhaps over time he learned.

The Iraqis finally squared away their new supplies into the supply area. Overall, it was an impressive effort by Iraqi standards. Nobody shot themselves in the foot, nobody slept on the job, and the actual mission was accomplished. After the event Samir and some other *jundi* demanded Adams and I come to lunch with them. There was no getting out of this one. Beans, rice, chicken, and khubbis are good for perhaps the first twenty times, however, by this point it was getting old. Nevertheless, in an effort to continue to build relationships with the *jundi*, we ate with our friends (see photo 12).

Counting Iraqis

Here is a paradox. Modern mathematics is based on the number system developed by the Arabs, yet somehow many Arabs do not understand simple arithmetic. My guess is there is some other element involved. In the case of the Iraqi S-1 shop, this other element is lying. Abdulrachman, an Iraqi soldier who still held grudges against the Americans for whipping his unit in Nasiriyah during the march up to Baghdad, gave me a lesson in Iraqi math, which uses the Arabic numeral system but has an uncanny ability to defy logic.

For a few weeks Abdulrachman had been telling me they had 134 *jundi* on leave. During my first couple of weeks here I went with this number, because I assumed a level of professionalism within the S-1. I am a gullible American.

I interrogated the S-1 on their leave counts. "Abdulrachman, I was in the swahuts this morning watching the morning formation and there were only 64 soldiers from H&S battalion present, yet you say there are 84 present?" He responded as though it was obvious. "Jamal, of course, there are only 64, it is just a mistake in the report." I had him by the balls. "So Abdulrachman, if you agree with me there are only 64 soldiers on hand, that must mean there are 20 soldiers who took two consecutive ten-day periods of leave, correct? You really have 154 currently on leave, not the 134 you keep telling me?"

Abdulrachman acknowledged the mistake. "Jamal," he said, "I am sorry, you are correct, I will fix it now. Sorry for all the confusion, you can trust me in the future. I am a very good S-1." I played the part of the ignorant

American and smiled in response. He took the bait and assumed I did not figure out his hidden agenda, which was to fake the accountability numbers so certain Iraqi soldiers could take extended twenty-day leave sessions. It seemed Iraqis were often trying to cheat the system, a trait heavily reinforced under Saddam Hussein's regime.

I finally understood why the generals told us that accountability, leave, and pay issues are the Achilles heel of the Iraqi army (logistics are the Iraqi army's kryptonite). Accurate accounting of Iraqis is an impossible business when the incentives for numbers to be accurate are not there. I remember a *Washington Post* article in late 2004 in which the Iraqi government claimed it could do a nationwide census in a day. The idea was to shut down the country and send out 150,000 schoolteachers to get an accurate number of the country's population. My question was this: if Iraqis cannot account for a battalion's worth of soldiers who they can physically line up and count, how can they expect to count the unorganized masses throughout Iraq? When you add the multiple layers of incentives for the census data to be tilted one way or the other by various religious, tribal, and ethnic groups, it only adds to the potential confusion. My guess is that any census data compiled in the post-Saddam era has a 20 to 30 percent error rate—at a minimum.

Feeding Iraqis

When it comes to chow distribution, the U.S. military is hands down the most effective military organization on the planet. One day on a leave run, Adams and I, with the help of Amir and his Leyland flatbed pickup, went to pick up food items at Al Asad's food distribution center. We followed a U.S. Army sergeant around the chow supply area and loaded up on various goods. We were sweating our asses off in the 130-degree heat. Thankfully we soon came to the meat freezer. When the sergeant opened the door on the freezer, a crisp blast of air engulfed us.

Amir seized the opportunity to cool off. He dropped out of the driver's side of the Leyland and moved around the Leyland's engine compartment to help us load supplies. At the first hint of cool air, he sprinted for the freezer. Amir dove into the meat freezer at full speed and bellowed at the top of his lungs in his best English, "Welcome to Amreeyca! I love Cali-forniya!" He fell to the freezer floor and rolled on the ground. He continued his rant, shouting, "I love Cali-forniya, I hate Iraq, please take me Amreeyca!" We all laughed hysterically. Although we could not believe what we were seeing, we definitely understood the logic behind it. It was hot as hell, the freezer felt damn good, and food was plentiful.

After loading all the frozen meats we could carry, we closed the large freezer doors. We had one problem, though. Amir would not leave. He was clinging to the floor like a leech. We eventually had to peel him off the ground. We next moved to the dry goods food area and filled the Leyland to the brim with food. Now the MiTT could survive happily for at least a few weeks without resupply and we could help the Iraqis if their situation became even more dire than it already was.

The U.S. military chow supply is abundant and organized, but the Iraqi chow supply system is criminal. We returned to the brigade camp on Al Asad to wait for the Iraqi chow to arrive. As usual the Iraqi food contractors had collected their paycheck without providing a service. No food arrived. Once again the Iraqis would have to rely on the U.S. taxpayer to provide their food. We were at a point that our battalion might starve. Just the week before, during an inventory of Iraqi chow, the counts were sparse: ten bags of potatoes—all of which were rotten, a box of tea, a few cans of peas, a small container of tomato paste, and seven twenty kilogram rice sacks. Ahmed Rial, the food contractor on our camp, gave me his assessment of the situation. "Jamal, we have enough chow for roughly three days, but they will be fed like prisoners." I could not have agreed more with Rial's assessment.

The Iraqi food situation was dire, and it opened my eyes to happenings around the camp. One day I saw the Iraqis throwing small wires with fish hooks attached across the electric lines running through the camp. They were using these wires to get the power to cook in their swahuts. Why are they cooking in their swahuts? I wondered. I noticed that when I was in the *jundi* swahuts learning about Muslim prayer practices, they were eating fresh-caught fish from the Euphrates. It appeared that the entire camp of Iraqis was sustaining themselves by fishing. At this stage we were effectively an agrarian army. I understand that a soldier's life is sometimes rough, but any professional army should not have to spend 50 percent of its time engaging in hunting and gathering activities while the contractor is collecting fat checks and not providing anything.

I asked a few soldiers and officers around camp what the deal was with the food contract. The problem was multifaceted, they told me. The first issue had to do with security, which may have explained 10 to 20 percent of the shortfall. On occasion the Iraqi supply convoys and food contractors were pirated and everyone was murdered on their way west through Al Anbar Province. The second, and more important issue, revolved around a kink in Iraqi culture that developed over time due to a history of chronic supply shortages: Iraqi people hoard things. In the context of the Iraqi army this occurred when the chow was dropped at the higher-level head-quarters, which was then given the responsibility to pass it down to sub-ordinate units. The higher-level units often decided to keep the chow and never sent it to the lower units. They hoarded it for a "rainy day."

Looking back on my experience at Camp Taji, which is a high-level training headquarters for the Iraqi army, I realized that I had witnessed chow hoarding firsthand. While at Taji we ate lamb chops, chicken breast, and steak; yet the Camp Taji *jundi* were on the same chow contract our battalion was using. The *jundi's* theory is that soldiers at Camp Taji horde all the chow supplies and send table scraps to the brigades, who then sub-sequently horde the table scraps and pass their gas to the battalions. It is not surprising that all our *jundi* leave their AK-47s in their swahut and hang a "Gone Fishing" sign on their front doors.

We May Die from Starvation

Word came one morning from brigade that the emergency supply that had been en route from Baghdad would not be arriving. The Iraqi con-tractor, the Jabber Company, had been ambushed by Al Qaeda elements near Ramadi. Every one of the workers had been murdered and all the supplies, including the eighteen-wheeler that was hauling the chow, had been stolen.

What did this mean for the *jundi* and the MiTT? In a nutshell, more fishing in the Euphrates and more wasting of U.S. taxpayer money so the *jundi* can eat. We needed to purchase the chow using the MiTT's four-thousand-dollar-a-month slush fund, which pays for things the Iraqi army needs. Food obviously qualifies as a need.

My motivation level wasn't exactly "sky high" after hearing this news. I had originally bought into President Bush's rhetoric that if we trained Iraqi security forces to take on the security of their own country, it might allow democratic institutions to flourish throughout Iraq. What I realized was that I would not be risking my life for Iraqi's future but for hungry Iraqis and an inept and corrupt logistics system that has no chance of being reformed any time soon.

We decided to execute Operation Hungry Tiger. The operation's name was a parody on the fact that we were heading into town with the sole purpose of buying chow for the Iraqis so they would not go hungry. We commenced the operation at 0600 and convoyed to Barwana. The Iraqis cruised on the way to Barwana; we arrived at 0730 (record time) without incident, il hamdu Allah (thanks be to God). After generating a basic mission plan to secure the market area, buy the necessary chow, and securely egress, we left the northeast Barwana FOB wire and headed through the rustic town of Barwana.

Before we left the gate a short, overweight Marine tottered to an Iraqi Leyland driver and yelled at him in English, "Switch positions in the convoy!" Perplexed, I looked at Adams and asked, "Who the hell is that?" Adams responded in a disgusted tone, "Dude, it's the boss. He's yelling at the *jundi* to get in position. What an idiot." I replied, "Are you serious? When is he going to figure out we are advising the Iraqi army and not commanding the Iraqi army?"

The market in Barwana was notorious for small-arms attacks. Situated along the eastern bank of the Euphrates, the Barwana market allowed terrorists on the western side of the river to easily shoot across the river and escape without incident.

The lead Iraqi Humvee barged into the Barwana market. Crack! AK-47 fire came screaming through the air, trying to punish the front of the lead Iraqi armored Humvee with little success. I immediately ducked into the armor of the turret and started scanning for the enemy. Luckily, the small-arms fire was aimed squarely at the lead Humvee, which had already entered the market and was far from our Humvee.

Private Ali, the lead Iraqi gunner, who was in the hail of gunfire, ducked into the body of the Humvee, cautiously reached his arm up, and pulled the trigger on his PKC, letting a burst of thirty rounds fly in a skyward direction. These unaimed rounds were not going to hit any insurgents, but they did scare them enough to force them to evacuate the area before anyone else could return fire.

Once the scene calmed down, Adams said, "Dude, this is retarded. We're risking our lives to buy chow for the Iraqi army? I ain't walking out in that shit!" I responded, "Seriously man, let's make sure everything is calm before you guys do anything. I don't want to tell your wife you died in a heroic battle for Iraqi chow." The *jundi* sent out a small team of men to search in the immediate vicinity to ensure there were no ambushes waiting in the wings as our convoy pushed completely into the market area.

"Gray, what's it looking like up there in the turret?" Adams inquired. "Well, to be honest," I said, "I can't see shit to the west, because there is a big-ass palm grove forest; I can't see shit to the east, because there is a big-ass hill in front of my face; and I can't see shit to the south, because an Iraqi Humvee is in my way." Adams interrupted me. "Gray, where can you see?" I replied, "Well, to the north things look clear. You can get out and buy some chow, I think." I paused for a moment and then further antagonized Adams with false motivation. "Oohrah, Devil Dog. Go get some action!" Adams, not amused, responded, "Jamal—fuck you."

Once security was set Adams, the funds handler (Corporal Jellison), and Moody (terp) exited the vehicles to negotiate prices and quantities with the locals. As Adams and his posse worked with the locals, I took a moment to enjoy the scene. I had to pinch myself. The Barwana market was so foreign to my American eyes that I needed to check that I wasn't dreaming that I was in the Indiana Jones movie *Raiders of the Lost Ark*. The marketplace itself was small, perhaps a football field in length, but it was vibrant with life. Each shop was a stall the size of a small garage space, typically fitted with a tin awning and a couple of wrinkly faced merchants sitting in chairs enjoying the desert heat. Freshly slaughtered lamb carcasses hung from meat hooks outside stores, shoe stores had their shoes nicely assorted in lines, jewelry shops had all their goods on display, and the farmers had their produce products nestled in the shade. My guess is that when the Ottomans came to these same Arab lands many centuries ago, they saw the exact same thing.

"Gray, we bought the entire thing!" Adams exclaimed proudly as he approached the Humvee. I was not involved in the conversation, but from the looks of it, Adams had managed to buy the entire marketplace. Every shop had a Leyland backed up to it and four *jundi* loading sacks of rice, bags of potatoes, and various other food sacks. Bravo! (See photo 13.)

After emptying the Barwana market we marched the convoy back to the Barwana FOB. As we were moving out of the market a young boy waved and offered us some Pepsi. His father sat back and watched approvingly as his son handed us four sodas, expecting nothing in return. Adams graciously gave him a five-dollar bill. I waved at the kid from my turret and said, "Shukran jazeelan" (Thank you very much). He returned my wave and smiled. I think we may have won one heart and mind today. Of course, we also may have been bamboozled into paying five dollars for four Pepsis; we will never know for sure.

Chapter 9

Iraqi Payday Operations

September 2006

At their core Iraqi soldiers are not much different from U.S. Marines. If you do not feed or do not pay a Marine, do not expect him to accomplish anything. This same holds for the *jundi*. Fortunately for Marines, getting chow and pay are rarely problems in a world of computers, laws, and honest people. The situation in Iraq is a lot different.

The Iraqi pay system is broken but improving. As the Marine in charge of overseeing Iraqi pay operations, I wished I'd had the power to fix the whole system. But this wasn't possible. I couldn't create a banking system in Iraq, eradicate extortion and violent robbery, and eliminate corruption in Iraqi society. All I really could do was be the focal point for the *jundi* for all their complaints regarding pay. I also could see to it that their pay processes at the battalion level were fair and just and that I reported all discrepancies to the next higher level unit. What happened beyond battalion level I had no control over.

Payday was approaching and it was obvious. Nearly every *jundi* in the battalion had confronted me with pay issues. The pay system was counterproductive to the Iraqi army's future. The more the *jundi* relied on Marines for solving their problems, the longer Marines had to stay in Iraq. I had told the *jundi* multiple times that they needed to consolidate all their pay issues and give them to the Iraqi battalion S-1. The battalion S-1 would then send the pay discrepancy report to the Iraqi brigade, which would send it to the Iraqi division, which would eventually send it to the MOD, where all pay issues would be resolved.

Every time I told Iraqis to talk to their Iraqi leadership to solve their problems, they looked at me weirdly. And I got the same general response: "Jamal, Iraqi officers are Ali Babba. Colonel Abass is Ali Babba, General Bassam [Iraqi brigade commander] is Ali Babba, MOD is full of Ali Babba, and everyone else in Iraqi is Ali Babbas. Are you kidding me? You are the only person we can trust!"

I understood the Iraqi perspective. They had lived in a harsh environment with limited resources, had been inculcated by tribal culture, and were used to operating within Saddam Hussein's corrupt regime. It was no wonder they only trusted people with whom they had a personal relationship.

Payday

Iraqi payday began. A reckless convoy of unfamiliar Iraqis came crashing through Camp Ali. This "convoy of chaos" was the *jundi* from the Iraqi brigade based in Al Asad. When the dust finally settled, Colonel Abass and the other Iraqi officers greeted the brigade officers as though they had not seen them in many years (it had been less than a week). I waited thirty minutes as the Iraqis hugged, kissed, and reminisced about days of old.

"Tseen, Jamal is the new MiTT pay officer. He is over there." Colonel Abass directed Captain Tseen, the Iraqi pay officer, in my direction. Tseen, obese and just a few pounds from claiming the title of "fattest Iraqi officer" from Abass, waddled his way to me with open arms and a wide smile. He bear-hugged me, kissed me on both cheeks, and shook my hand. "Jamal, I heard you are a very good man, how are you? How is your family?" I responded with a firm handshake and a firm bear hug. "Tseen," I said, "I am quite well. I hear you are the best pay officer in Iraq? I am happy to hear you arrived safely."

Captain Tseen ordered a few of the *jundi* on guard to grab his gear from the Iraqi Humvee. It took me a minute to realize that the large hay bales the *jundi* were struggling to take from the Humvee were not Tseen's luggage, they were 350,243,100 dinar (roughly $250,000). Inflation had not only broken the Iraqi economy but also the backs of these poor *jundi* carrying the cash. The next step was to count the money. We entered Colonel Abass's hooch to secure the money in his safe, the only secure environment on Camp Ali. I say "secure" in the sense the safe was fireproof and under lock and key; however, the fact that Colonel Abass had access to this safe was not reassuring.

Tseen grabbed the 100,000-dinar wads of cash from his assistant's hands and counted them. "100,000 dinar, 200,000 dinar, 300,000 dinar." I verified with the MOD roster that the amount of money arriving to our camp was the amount we should be receiving. Amazingly, we had exactly 350,243,100 dinar. We locked the safe. Tseen said, "Jamal, it is now time for tea. Come with me." I obliged and we went to drink tea with a group of Iraqi officers in the battalion swahut.

Our first pay operation was to pay the Headquarters and Service Company (H&S Company) Iraqi soldiers who resided at Camp Ali. We set up shop in Captain Hasen's swahut, which was in the center of the *jundi* swahut area. To the untrained eye it seemed as though the *jundi* payday scene was absolute chaos. The *jundi* were simultaneously excited and stressed. They yelled and fought with each other to get a favorable position in the line. They relied on the paychecks to survive and to feed their families. No paycheck meant an Iraqi could not take care of his family, a dishonorable position in the Arab world.

There were seven individuals involved in the management of the pay process. Sergeant Major Kasem, the senior enlisted Iraqi in H&S Company, stood at the door to the swahut and asked for three identification (ID) cards at a time; he acted like the bouncer outside a club. He continually yelled at the pay line, which consisted of anywhere from fifty to a hundred Iraqis, all of whom were trying to push their way to the front of the line.

Inside the swahut Tseen and I set up a long table with six chairs behind it. The Iraqis receiving pay started at chair one and moved down the line. The first and second chairs were for me and a terp, usually Imus, Mark, or Moody—the most honest terps. While I rarely used a terp, during pay operations I relied on them heavily to give me the honest scoop. Pay operations were notorious for various kinds of shady business, which my basic Arabic skills might not have caught (for example, officers paying favorite soldiers more money, stealing soldiers' pay, forging signatures on the pay charts, and so forth). Sadly, I had no real function at the table except to monitor the process and assure the *jundi* that the Iraqi officers would not engage in nefarious activity. No matter how much Iraqis publicly claimed that Americans are dishonest, stingy, and generally rotten people, in private situations, they relied on us heavily to provide oversight.

The third chair was for Naji, an S-1 warrant officer with over twenty years in the old Iraqi army who is respected throughout the battalion. Naji's duty was to verify IDs, verify names, and keep a written record of payment for the battalion's pay records. Iraqis love to keep paper records of everything. Their record-keeping ability is old fashioned and inefficient but functional. Next to Naji sat Tseen. Tseen read names and pay amounts from the official pay rosters from MOD. When the pay recipient verified that his name was correct, he signed on the official MOD pay rosters. Tseen also acted as an impact zone for *jundi* complaints, bearing the full brunt of every emotional *jundi* who found out he had a pay issue—a sight women and children should never have to witness.

Once Tseen had read the payee's name and pay amount from the roster, the payee moved down the line to the money counter. Typically Captain Hasen acted as the money counter. He grabbed a lump of cash and started flipping through it so fast he could have used it as a small fan. He had to be fast since each *jundi* received about 500,000 dinar. Once the money had been counted, he handed it over to the soldier receiving it, who then stepped out of the line and counted it to verify Captain Hasen's work. If he had problems with the amount, he told Hasen, who would either recount the money if he thought the *jundi* was lying or grab a few bills from his cash stacks and hand it to the *jundi* who was shorted.

The sixth seat in the process was reserved for the pay overseer. In our battalion this was Lieutenant Colonel Ali, the executive officer (XO) of the battalion and the only officer trusted by the *jundi*. His primary duty was very similar to mine: ensure the pay process is orderly, fair, and honest. His additional duty was to clarify and mediate any issues with pay punishments, a highly contested and passionate affair. Fortunately, my role in the pay punishments was passive. I had to understand the process and ensure it was not leading to further corruption or creating impediments to the Iraqi army's future success. Ali actually dealt with the emotional or distressed Iraqis who wanted to argue their case.

Pay punishments are the only method of reprimanding Iraqi soldiers, aside from restricting leave. Because restricting leave usually guarantees a soldier will never return to active duty, restricting pay is the preferred punishment. Pay punishments are necessary because the Iraqi army doesn't have a functioning or enforceable Uniform Code of Military Justice or similar government construct that allows for a more fair and orderly method of punishing poor soldier behavior.

In the old Iraqi army there were many more ways to impose good order and discipline among the troops: beatings, threatening families, sending soldiers to jail, and so forth. In the new Iraqi army the easiest way to enforce standards is for the battalion commanders to be the judge, jury, and executioner for Iraqi soldier misbehavior. Unfortunately this system is prone to nepotism and corruption, but most of the time it accomplishes its objective of motivating Iraqi soldiers to do the right thing.

Payday Problems

The pay process for H&S Company went relatively smoothly for an Iraqi operation. The same held true for the pay operations we carried out in Barwana, Haqliniyah, and Baghdadi. But the hinges came off the doors when we paid the *jundi* in Haditha. There we were down to the last group of soldiers to be paid, none of whom had received pay for the past few months because of the bureaucracy and corruption at the MOD. The first *jundi* approached Tseen, smiled with a mouthful of five teeth, and said, "Sir, have you worked my pay problem out with MOD yet? It has been five months since I have been paid." Tseen responded, "I am sorry, I am still trying to figure it out. God willing, we get it next payday."

This was obviously not the answer the *jundi* wanted to hear. The *jundi* and his comrades approached the table and verbally attacked Tseen. The situation appeared beyond control. I was getting worried, but my terp said, "Jamal, Arab people are very emotional. I will let you know if something needs to be done." I sat back in my chair and watched the bedlam as the group continued to confront Tseen, calling him names, calling him a liar, and accusing him of theft. I was amazed at the disrespect the *jundi* were showing to a senior officer. It is expected that emotions will sometimes run high, but if the *jundi* had done this in the U.S. military it would have resulted in a court-martial. In the old Iraqi army, it would have ended in a beating.

In my short experience with Iraqis it seemed they chilled out after venting for a few minutes. In this case, however, they didn't. They did not calm down; they got more furious as Tseen exited his seat and sprinted to Captain Najib's office to get away from them. Tseen's exit meant the fury and anger of the *jundi* would be directed to the next best candidate—me.

"Jamal, you must help us, Tseen is Ali Babba!" the group exclaimed. I was facing a dilemma. I could agree with their sentiments and reinforce their distrust and disrespect for Tseen or I could tell them their pay system was valid, that Tseen was working hard, and that their system simply needed time to work (a blatant lie). I took a compromise position and used a trick I learned from some of our predeployment culture training—blame problems on a higher unit or organization. I told the disgruntled *jundi*, "Listen, I will help you as best I can. I think Tseen is an honest man and is trying his best, but he has to deal with all of the corruption at the MOD."

I had detonated a "bitching bomb." The *jundi* went on a tirade of complaints, hoping I could fix all the problems in Iraq. "Jamal, we have no pay, no new clothes, no new uniforms, no food, we get shot at every day. How can we continue this way of life?" Qasem, the driver of the Iraqi Humvee I had ridden in during the Kaffijiyah and Bani Dahir operations, approached me and said, "Jamal, look at my socks." Qasem pulled off a boot and showed me his decrepit sock. I said, "Good God! We just received a new supply of socks, shoes, boots, and uniforms at the battalion. They still have not sent any of this gear to the fighters in 4th Iraqi Company?"

I knew I could not help these men with their pay problems, since those issues were fixed at the highest and most corrupt levels of the MOD; however, I could possibly get these guys supplies by asking Lieutenant Adams to put his boot in the ass of Nihad, the battalion supply officer. Before I gave the *jundi* an honest assessment, I remembered Mohammed's key point during his Arab culture brief at Camp Taji: when dealing with an Arab do not be direct in your responses and criticisms; instead, go out of your way to be helpful and accommodating, even if what you are saying is not the complete truth.

I rejected the American culture tendency to be candid and instead gave the *jundi* my culturally aware response. "Friends, I will try my best to work with the brigade to ensure Tseen is rectifying your pay problems. I think there is hope. I will also ask the battalion where your supplies are located. Please be patient." I paused before continuing. "Bil mustekbel rah yakoon maku mushkila. Insha'allah." (In the future, there will be no problems. God willing.) The soldiers appreciated my sincerity. "Jamal, my brother, thank you for caring about us, God willing you can help us, may God be with you." The Iraqis each gave me a hug and their best wishes. Mohammed's cultural insights had served me well.

On our way out of the Haditha FOB, Imus mumbled under his breath to me, "Money is the root of all evil. People who want everything are no good. I am sorry you have to deal with those Iraqis." Imus, in his ideal world where every Iraqi loves one another and praises God, was angry at the *jundi* for telling me their problems. A very proud Iraqi, Imus was trying to convey to me that greed, poverty, and begging were not the norm with his people. His people were not these problem-ridden Iraqi soldiers; his people were part of the historic Arab kingdoms, which oversaw a glorious Islamic society along the Tigris and Euphrates rivers. To ease his fears I said, "Imus, dude, it's all good, man. Every society has a group in need. I won't hold it against you."

On the convoy home, as I was searching for IEDs, I thought about the supply issues within the Iraqi army and how we could fix them. How could it be that battalion headquarters had recently received a shipment of new supplies and yet the actual fighters at the company level had nothing? How could we help these Iraqi soldiers?

My thoughts on helping the Iraqis solve their supply problems had changed by the end of our thirty-minute convoy. At the end of our trip the *jundi* started throwing boxes of their meals, ready-to-eat (MREs) onto the side of the road. I could not believe it. How could they bitch to me about not having supplies then throw boxes of chow off their Humvee because it did not appeal to their taste buds? We had just risked our lives in the Barwana markets buying these guys food and now they were throwing away their backup chow? This episode only reinforced what I had seen earlier when we were unloading all the new Iraqi supplies. The Iraqis showed me their bin of used equipment. The bin was filled with used flak jackets, boots, and uniforms from soldiers who had quit or been fired. If these guys were so desperate, why didn't they use some of this stuff? It was not in poor shape. What's wrong with these people? I thought.

I think the answer lies in the Iraqi perception that American taxpayers have an infinite supply of money. Guess what, Mr. *Jundi*? The Marines recycle gear all the time and never throw out boxes of MREs needlessly. At times the Iraqis annoyed me with their sob stories, especially when their whining was followed by a bout of wastefulness and an attitude that Americans "will just buy us new things, as they always do." But then again—MREs do suck!

Chapter 10

Insights on Iraqi Culture

September 2006

Every day I was in Iraq I learned more about Iraqi culture. The most shocking lesson came from Colonel Abass, who gave Lieutenant Colonel Cooling (the 3/3 commander), a few U.S. Army Special Forces soldiers, Staff Sergeant Haislip, and I a lesson on Arab marital relations at a lunch gathering.

A Dinner Date with Colonel Abass

After the standard thirty minutes of chit-chat over lunch, Cooling said to Abass, "Seyidi [Sir], what do you think about the insurgents in this area?" Abass responded through Martin, the terp, "My honest opinion is they are all faggots and homosexuals and do not follow the Koran. They probably don't even beat their wives." We all chuckled at the statement, but we could not believe what we were hearing.

Cooling asked Abass the same question we all wanted to ask: "So you said the insurgents do not beat their wives—is not beating your wife considered a bad thing?" Abass got out of his seat with a wide grin on his face and spoke, "In Iraq, it is mandatory you beat your wife!" We all looked at each other, puzzled but curious to see where this conversation was going. He continued, "To not beat your wife is considered unmanly. Men who do not beat their women allow their women to take advantage of them through their powers of seduction. I think Western pressure to stop wife beating will only lead to a systematic weakness in Iraqi men."

Cooling asked, "Now, Seyidi, what if your wife is not causing any problems? Would you still beat her?" Abass replied, "Gentlemen, that is a good question. Let me explain. It is important to beat your wife to remind her you are in control. For example, I have two wives. One of my wives is a disaster and I beat her all the time; however, one of my wives is absolutely perfectly behaved, yet despite her good behavior, I still must beat her."

We all listened intently, trying to decipher the absurdity of this statement. Abass continued, "It is not like I just start beating my good wife for any reason—that is senseless. I make sure she knows why I am beating her." He paused to collect his thoughts. "One trick I have used in the past has worked quite well. Let me tell you the story. I had just returned from the doctor's office and the doctor told me that I had very high cholesterol and that I must cease my intake of sodium. I told my wife this bit of news and she responded by ensuring that all of my food was prepared without any salt. Everything was fine for a few weeks. Even so, one evening I knew I needed to beat my wife."

I halted the conversation. "Seyidi, you felt a need to beat your wife?" Abass replied, "Yes, of course—but let me continue with the story. So my wife brought me a bowl of soup without any salt, just like she was supposed to do. When she looked away, I sprinkled salt on my soup. I ate the soup and after a few bites, I started yelling at her for trying to kill me. She was a bit surprised there was salt in the soup, but assumed she had made the mistake. I proceeded to beat her as punishment and she accepted the beating."

We sat around the table and watched the Iraqi officers in attendance nod in agreement with Abass's story. This story made perfect sense to them. In contrast none of us could believe what we were hearing. Colonel Abass, aware of our concern, announced, "I understand this must sound cruel to you, but it is just how we operate in Iraq. It is part of our culture and is accepted as the proper way of doing business."

Cooling followed up with a question. "Seyidi, I understand this is your culture and I want to understand it; however, what if some man pulled these same tricks on your sister or mother? Wouldn't that offend you?" Abass chuckled and rolled his eyes at the lieutenant colonel. "Let me tell you a story about my sister," he said. "She came to me one day trying to address the issue of her husband beating her. She thought that I would be able to stop it and help her situation. She asked me to talk to her husband so he would stop beating her." He paused. "You know what I asked her?" We all had blank stares on our faces. Abass continued, "I asked her why she was getting beaten. She told me she had been complaining a lot because of disagreements she had with her husband and she was refusing to do some of the things he was telling her to do." Captain Pitts, the Special Forces team leader, inquired, "Did you kick the husband's ass?" Abass, taken aback, responded, "No, of course not. Instead, I beat my sister on the spot and then told her husband that I was sorry she was being disrespectful to him and that if there were any problems he could contact me."

Colonel Abass's solution was a double whammy for his sister. We were all in disbelief at what we had heard. And yet the Iraqis were all nodding in agreement. In this part of the world, I figured, that's just how things work. It is a man's world over here. Or in Colonel Abass's words, "The only time a woman is allowed on top in Iraq is in the bedroom."

After hearing Abass's thoughts on the theory of wife beating, we moved on to another topic of interest: Iraqi infantry tactics. "Seyidi," I asked, "I have another question for you. Can you explain why Iraqi soldiers shoot all of the ammunition in their magazines in the general direction of insurgents when we take fire? It seems like a waste." All the Americans in the room waited for the explanation to one of the biggest puzzles in Iraq.

Colonel Abass responded, "Jamal, I know this behavior perplexes Marines. They say my soldiers are undisciplined or cowards. Here is the difference, though. Marines have all kinds of fancy scopes on their weapons, more accurate weapons, and much more marksmanship training. Of course they are going to sit back and take well-aimed shots." Abass paused before continuing. "Here is some advice for the Marines. As opposed to telling me my soldiers are cowards and undisciplined with their fire, Marines should be giving me money to ensure my *jundi* keep fighting the way they do."

We all wondered what the colonel meant by this. Abass explained, "You remember a few days ago when the Marines shot an insurgent a couple of times, but he didn't die? The Marines ended up evacuating the insurgent to Al Asad for medical care. This is a waste. If my *jundi* were out there, I can assure you the insurgent would have had thirty or forty bullet holes in his body and wouldn't have lived."

Abass paused for emphasis then continued. "Listen to how much I would have saved your government. First, you had to bring a helicopter to pick this guy up; this costs manpower, gas money, and precious pilot time. Second, you had to bring a QRF [quick reaction force] to the situation so you could have some Marines tend to the casualty; this is wasting your Marines' energy and lowering their defenses at the base because you had to take the QRF from the base defenses. If we add up all the expenses and the time taken to take care of this insurgent, it is quite expensive. Is this additional cost worth having disciplined fires?"

Colonel Abass switched his focus from the group to Cooling. "Lieutenant Colonel Cooling, next time you send your Marines on patrol, let me be certain my *jundi* are out there with them and I will tell my men to make sure they kill anybody they shoot. We will then split the cost savings. Deal?" Everyone in the room erupted in laughter. This guy broke things down so simply and peppered them with so much common sense, it was hard to argue with his logic.

After a few hours of great conversation and insight from Colonel Abass, we headed back to the MiTT camp. Regardless of what happens on this deployment, I thought, I will never forget Colonel Abass. This guy could talk about beating women with a straight face and convince a room of Marines why undisciplined firepower makes sense. It was nothing short of amazing.

Man-Love Thursdays

Homosexual intimacy has always wigged me out at some level. To me it's a lot like trying to play football with a baseball bat. People are free to engage in the practice, but they are never going to convince me it makes any sense. This same philosophy applies to some of the unique practices Arab men engage in with one another. I really don't care if Iraqi men enjoy holding hands, rubbing each other's bellies, kissing each other's cheeks, or having sex with each other—I just don't want to be involved.

For whatever reason, one day the Iraqis wanted to get especially friendly. Love was in the air, I guess. I am well aware that in Arab culture men have much tighter relationships, they touch each other more, and their bonds run much deeper than in Western cultures. I am willing to learn new cultures, but I could not adjust to this aspect of Iraqi culture. Abit, the Iraqi S-6 communications chief, ran up to me with open arms, hugged me, kissed me multiple times on the cheek, told me he loved me, and then grabbed my hand in the same manner my wife and I would use on a romantic walk through the park. It caught me off guard.

Abit and I walked to the MiTT camp holding hands. The entire time we walked, he relaxed his head on my shoulder and caressed my forearm as if I were his lover. The last time I'd felt this awkward was when I crapped my pants in the fifth grade. Nevertheless I resisted every temptation to tear my hand away from him for fear I would offend him in some way. Eventually, we parted ways and I hustled back to the MiTT camp to clear my mind.

The man love did not end with Abit. Later a pair of 2/3's Marines from the S-6 (communications section) came to Camp Ali to install the SIPRNET (Internet that is classified Secret) in the Iraqi COC so the MiTT would have better connectivity. Both these Marines were around five feet four inches, eighteen years old, and had no facial hair. They looked like prepubescent boys.

I was on my way to the Iraqi COC in the Chevy Luv (similar to a Toyota Tacoma) when I saw a huge crowd of *jundi* around the two S-6 Marines. I rushed to the scene to see what was going on. I asked the Iraqis for a situation report, saying, "Shaku maku?" (What's happening?) Ayad and Juwad explained the situation in a mix of Arabic and English that only I could understand. "Jamal, those two Marines are wasiim [pretty] and nreed fikki fikki wiyahum bil swahuts. Nreed nshoofhum minu il masool [we want to have sex with them in the swahuts. We want to show them who is boss]." Floored by the comment, I said, "You guys are sick. I don't want any of you ever touching these Marines—nasty bastards." The Iraqis all laughed. Juwad retorted, "Jamal, you know we are all going to masturbate to the thought of these two guys from now on, right? Just give us one of them for some fun! A few minutes is all we need." Sadly, I knew Juwad was serious. I smirked and shook my head in disgust.

The two Marines, who had no clue what was happening, asked me, "Sir, what was that all about? What did you tell them, what is going on?" I did not want to break the news to them that they were objects of desire to the *jundi*; nonetheless, I responded, "Gents, the Iraqis think you're cute and want to take you behind a swahut. The sick thing is they are only half joking. I am going to get you guys the hell out of here before this gets out of hand."

The two Marines' eyes widened. They did not have to say a word; their body language was more than enough to communicate what they were thinking: The *jundi* are warped! We left the area.

After I dropped off the potential rape victims in the Chevy Luv, I returned to address the *jundi*. Fifty *jundi* started yelling, "Jamal, come over and talk. Jamal we love you." Within thirty seconds forty curious Iraqis had surrounded me. I rushed to lock the doors on the Chevy. Ayad, a goofy-looking Arab and the comedian of the crowd, addressed me: "Jamal, you like boobs and asses, don't you?" I replied, "Of course." Ayad continued. "Well you know why you need to try gay sex?" I asked mockingly, "Why, Ayad?" He responded, "The ass is much tighter, feels better, and you don't have to deal with an emotional woman afterward."

I addressed the crowd from my uneasy, outnumbered position. "Dude, Ayad, I realize you are too ugly to get women and must resort to men. If you need me to help you get some Iraqi women, let me know and I'll make a few phone calls." The crowd erupted in laughter. Ayad slapped me a high five and gave me a huge hug through the truck window. "Jamal," he said, "you are an Iraqi. We love you." I smiled and dissed Ayad one last time to the amusement of the crowd. "Ahebbek Ayad," I said, "bess ma tshoof ila Marinesee. Inta Faregh!" (I love you Ayad, but don't look at my Marines. You are gay!)

Corruption as a Way of Life

Corruption is a means to an end. I used to think it was a dishonest way of carrying out business; however, I am slowly coming to grips with the fact that corruption is as much a part of Iraqi culture as is greeting friends and guests with *as salamu aleikum*. Moody, our top terp, and Ahmed, my stellar S-1 clerk, who spoke very good English, gave me a crash course in the economics and social dynamics of the corrupt Iraqi pay system. What he taught me can go a long way in Iraq toward helping Americans at all levels—from my level to the strategic level—understand how business gets done.

Our discussion began quite innocently. "Ahmed," I said, "I am trying to understand why there are so many discrepancies in what Captain Tseen is telling me regarding the pay status and what he is sending to the Ministry of Defense." Moody looked at Ahmed, giving him the nod that he would explain to the uninformed American how things really worked in Iraq. Moody said, "Jamal, the first thing you have to understand, is that Captain Tseen is looking after his *jundi* and does want them to get paid. You also have to understand that Tseen is a highly connected individual in the MOD. This is a huge asset." I reluctantly said, "Okay." Moody continued, "Jamal, let me ask you something. Do you know why our battalion is paid at the highest rates in the brigade and do you also know why all *jundi* in the 1st Division Iraqi Army are paid at higher rates than everyone in our 7th Division?" I shook my head and said, "No, why?" He replied, "We are paid at the highest rates in the brigade because Tseen knows the most

people at MOD from our brigade and is able to cut the most deals. First
Division is paid at a higher rate than everyone in our division because their
pay officers know even more people than Captain Tseen does at the MOD.
Americans like to call this corruption. We call this 'getting things done.'"

I inquired further. "Moody, I understand that it's all about who you
know in this country, not what you know. My only concern is if Tseen
is skimming money off the soldiers and lining his own pockets under my
watch." Moody and Ahmed responded as if the answer were completely obvious. "Yes, of course he does. All pay officers skim pay. Why do you think
being the pay officer is such a highly regarded position in the Iraqi Army?"
I immediately replied, "He is stealing money from the *jundi*? How is that
possible? I keep track of everything he does here at the battalion level. Plus,
the higher level MiTTs do the same thing all the way up the chain until it
reaches MOD." Moody jumped in. "Jamal, Jamal, before you go any further,
let me tell you about my trip to the MOD with Tseen last year."

Moody shared his experiences of corruption, money, and power at the
MOD. It played like a Shakespearian drama. He explained to me that the
MiTTs do a wonderful job of ensuring there is very limited corruption
regarding the pay process. Without them, he said, there would be massive
levels of fraud and abuse within the Iraqi pay system. However, because of
the American military presence within military units, all the checks and
balances worked efficiently and correctly.

Unfortunately, the true corruption happens at levels beyond the U.S.
military's purview, namely, in the MOD. At the MOD two corrupt officers
will forge documents or submit false rosters and split the winnings. Their
oversight is minimal and everyone expects them to be corrupt. After all,
that is one of the benefits of being in the pay officer position.

Moody gave me examples of pay officers engaged in corruption. A
favorite technique of pay officers was to create false rosters of soldiers. The
rosters included the names of anywhere from fifty to three hundred soldiers who had recently quit the Iraqi army. But because of the slow process
of updating rosters and the bureaucracy at the MOD, these pay officers
were able to collect the pay for these "ghost" *jundi*.

The final punch line from Moody and Ahmed was that corruption had
happened, and was going to happen, whenever money was involved. In
Iraq, they said, corruption is a form of payment to individuals who are able
to make it to positions of power or to those who have spent time creating networks of friends. The basic logic is as follows: if I spend an entire

lifetime building relationships and forming bonds that allow me to reach a position of power, I should be able to extract economic benefits from my position in the form of corruption. Otherwise, what would be the incentive to rise to a position of power?

The more I think about the corruption problem in Iraq, the less I feel the solution is to crack down on these practices. Iraqi corruption is as respected and commonplace as hard work is to the Japanese. Can we tell people in Japan that hard work is bad and that they should simply quit and become lazier? Likewise, I am not sure that telling Iraqis they need to stop being corrupt is the best way to approach Iraq's corruption problem. If we want to fix this issue, first we need to understand the role it plays in the culture.

Tribalism in Iraq

Tribalism. For most Americans the word conjures up the image of a group of Indians sitting in teepees smoking peace pipes. My experiences in Iraq dispelled this idea. I slowly came to understand that a different sort of tribalism pervades Iraqi society. Tribalism has been in this area of the world since the dawn of humankind—before the Crusades, before Islam, and before Christianity. It has been part of the Arab culture for thousands of years. I will save some time by compacting thousands of briefs and papers on Iraqi tribalism into two statements. First, tribalism exists because it helps facilitate survival in austere environments. Second, the method of survival in a tribal context is to ensure members of the tribe focus on community survival versus individual survival.

While no exact parallel exists, the closest Western organization that works on the same fundamental principles is the gang. Gangs are tight-knit groups that bond people together for purposes of survival. Put simply, a solo gangster with an Uzi cannot maintain drug-trafficking turf in Los Angeles because he is an easy kill; however, thirty gangsters with Uzis are much more difficult to defeat. Similarly, in the desert there may be only one watering hole for fifty miles. A few Arabs alone cannot expect to defend this key turf, but a larger group can maintain their resources and livelihood.

Gangs also tend to deemphasize individual efforts and focus more on the efforts of the group. For example, the members do not say, "I am Mike the Maniac and I am also a Crip." To the contrary, they will say, "I am a Crip." This focus of attention on the Crips, or the community and not the individual, ensures unity of effort in defending the gang turf. Anyone who shows signs of defecting from the gang is killed or banished from the gang for fear they may ruin gang integrity and thus the strength of the gang. The exact same mindset of gangs applies to Iraqi tribalism and to Arab culture as a whole.

Moody was always a great source for interesting insights into how tribalism works in Iraq. It was perplexing that he, as the most highly educated and civilized of our terps, also had the greatest tribal pride and adherence to tribal culture. This was just another example of how pervasive tribal identity is in Iraq, even within the well-educated and highly civilized population of Iraq. Tonight's discussion revolved around the tribal concept of "blood money."

Moody told me about a typical homicide situation in Iraq. Let's say Ahmed, who is part of the Dulaym tribe, kills Hyder, who is part of the Janabi tribe. Based on tribal custom, if someone from another tribe kills someone in your tribe, you must get revenge for this action or all honor in your tribe is vanquished. To lose the honor of the tribe is to lose all credibility in bargaining, to lose all your friends' respect, and to become an outcast in society. Because honor is so important, there is a logical reason why revenge is a good idea in tribal society.

Revenge, in the context of a homicide, means killing someone in the other tribe—quid pro quo. Obviously, the logical progression of this system would imply that all tribes would eventually kill each other off. Fortunately, it does not work like this.

There is another way to get revenge and restore honor that does not involve killing a member of the other tribe. This alternative comes in the form of cold, hard cash. This cash, or "blood money," can serve as retribution for one member of a tribe killing a member of another tribe. Fortunately, when blood money is involved there is no actual blood shed after the original homicide occurs. The exact blood money amount to be exchanged is determined between the sheikhs of the two respective tribes and is negotiated in a systematic and civilized manner. The system is very similar to the way the Vikings and Anglo-Saxon clans did things over a thousand years ago in northern Europe.

So while on the face of it the tribal system of revenge may seem primitive, it actually is quite civilized and relies on money as the diplomat. The U.S. military has even embraced the blood money concept. Many times the U.S. military will pay off sheikhs or families for accidental deaths. The idea of paying off Iraqi families for their pain and anguish may seem very crass to Americans, but the payment suffices as blood money and serves to prevent any retaliatory attacks from the tribe affected.

While money solves nearly all tribal conflicts, it is not foolproof. Moody told me about a famous sheikh who lived about sixteen hundred years ago in Iraq. "Jamal, this sheikh was the only sheikhh in history who would not accept blood money—and it led to disaster. As the story goes, a member of an opposing tribe killed the sheikh's brother. As is customary, the opposing sheikh came to negotiate with the affected sheikhh for the blood money amount he would need in order to restore his honor. The affected sheikhh's response was 'I do not want your money—I want my brother!'" I stopped Moody. "Wait, why didn't he accept the money? Doesn't that mean there will be a war?" Moody replied, "Yep, the sheikh called for war. Eventually, one revenge killing led to another. The downward cycle of death decimated both tribes in the end. Here is the moral of the story Jamal: accept blood money payments." I concurred with Moody's assessment. Moody responded in jest, "Jamal, you want to know what is even more remarkable about this story? This is the only time in the history of Iraq it was not about the money."

Moody expanded his discussion of Iraqi tribalism. "Jamal, do you know who understood the tribes better than anyone? Saddam Hussein. He was a master." Moody followed his praise for Saddam with an example. "Not long ago, two tribes were in a bitter feud because the tribal sheikhs could not agree on the appropriate blood money amount one tribe owed to the other," he said. "After two days of fighting, there were thirty-eight dead on one side, and forty-five dead on the other, with no resolution in sight. This situation looked like it would end in the destruction of the two tribes."

Moody paused to catch his breath. "The next day, when the two tribes were standing toe to toe with guns, mortars, artillery, and RPGs ready to destroy each other, Saddam Hussein came to the rescue." I replied, "Did he fly to the scene in his Superman costume?" Moody laughed. "No, Jamal, there were no Superman costumes involved, but he did send an MOD official from Baghdad to help mediate the issues within the tribes. He asked each sheikhh how much blood money would be required to compensate for the mounting losses on their side. Once the two amounts were negotiated, the official paid the sheikhhs on the spot and told them it was courtesy of Saddam Hussein. The groups quit fighting and went back to a peaceful existence and a high appreciation for Saddam." I said, "So Saddam became the peacemaker and hero at the same time?" Moody sneered. "Exactly. And now you Americans want to kill the guy who finally got the tribes to agree on something—you're crazy!"

Our tribal discussion continued. All these new ideas infiltrating my mind were creating new questions I needed Moody to answer. I gave him the best "what-if" scenario I could muster. "Moody, what would happen if some poor man in a tribe accidentally rams his car into someone in another tribe. He will obviously not have the cash to cover the blood money and this simple event could effectively lead to tribal warfare. How do the tribes control these situations?"

"The tribes have a solution to this situation and many like it," Moody replied. "Effectively, all the tribes in Iraq collect a tax from their members. Personally, I pay around a thousand dinar a month, which is roughly one American dollar. This money goes into what I'll call a blood money fund. When the poor tribal members run into problems with rival tribes and cannot afford to pay the blood money on behalf of the tribe, the fund is used to ensure the money is paid and no further violence takes place. It's like an insurance policy."

I had more questions for Moody. "This sounds like a welfare policy. Do you have any freeloaders who look at the blood money fund and say, 'this is a great opportunity to kill someone from the other tribe that I really hate with the added benefit that I won't even have to pay for it?'" Moody answered, "The tribes have this one figured out as well. Before the tribe will use the blood money pot to pay off a member's blood money debt, the sheikhs make certain you are a good member of the tribe and investigate the circumstances of the death. If the tribal sheikhh senses a member was freeloading on the system he would simply hand them over to the other tribe who would subsequently kill the individual responsible for their member's death." I said, "Wow. Sounds like you have it figured out."

Just Beat It

My discussion with Moody on tribalism somehow shifted to the topic of beatings. After learning about tribalism's peculiarities, I was not sure Moody could shock me any further. I was wrong. Moody began his lecture on beating people. "Jamal, there is a beating chain of command in Iraqi society. The oldest males sit at the top of the chain of command and the youngest sit at the bottom." Puzzled, I asked, "A beating chain of command?" Moody said, "Yes, a beating chain of command. Here is how it works. Say you are around the dinner table and the youngest son calls the oldest son a 'weakling.' The eldest son, the middle son, and the father, whose honor and respect have been violated, are obligated to beat the offender. And the instigator is obligated to let the beatings happen without a struggle." I asked, "The older brother, middle brother, and father are obligated to beat the youngest brother? Are you kidding?" Moody responded, "Yes, obligated. One time I had to beat my brother for three hours in the shower until my father said I had gone too far. My heart was broken for beating him, but we both knew it was necessary."

I had to ask Moody another question. "Wait a second. Why exactly was it necessary for you to beat your brother for three hours? That seems excessive." Moody explained his logic. "Jamal, this is very difficult for Americans to understand, but I will explain it to you anyway. Let's say I did not beat my brother. Let's also assume the word gets out to the rest of the community that my youngest brother disrespected me and was not punished. This would effectively show the community that the males of my household can't even take care of our own internal affairs." He paused before continuing his lecture. "Not only does my youngest brother lose his honor in the community, but I lose my honor, my father loses his honor, my grandfather loses his honor, and the entire lineage of males related to my brother lose their honor. Because of this, the family must be sure the youngest brother is beaten. Likewise, the youngest brother will be more than willing to take his beatings, because he understands the consequences of his actions."

I thought about Moody's beating story. I think I understand the logic. Effectively, if individuals know they will get harsh punishments for doing something wrong, this acts as a strong deterrence. The logic of this system helps explains why Arab nations are more apt to do public beheadings, public beatings, and public limb amputation. The government wants the community to know that if they do not respect society, they will be punished severely.

Iraqi culture is fascinating and very different from our own.

Chapter 11

Death Operations

September 2006

W e got a call one afternoon from the brigade MiTT. The news was terrible: a *jundi* from the Iraqi brigade had been melted by a mortar shell that landed on the Barwana FOB. When an Iraqi soldier becomes an "angel" (what the U.S. military calls a dead *jundi*) a lot of work is involved. One of our jobs as a MiTT is to coordinate for transportation of the deceased angel from the location of his death to Baghdad. We are also in charge of ensuring there is a MiTT member and an Iraqi soldier with the body at all times until it reaches Baghdad. Once the body reaches Baghdad, the family takes custody and the situation is no longer in the U.S. military's hands.

After some discussion, Major Pyle determined that SSgt. Daniel Valle, or "V" as he was called, would be the Marine escort. With V as the designated hitter for the escort mission, it was time to conscript a *jundi* to be the Iraqi escort. I was sent to ask the Iraqis who they wanted to send. I sprinted to the Iraqi swahut area and rounded up any *jundi* who had a relationship with the angel or knew his family. Luckily, I was able to find Hussein Ali, who was a distant relative. I waited for Hussein to get his gear together and we hurried to the MiTT camp. The helo was leaving in fifteen minutes and we still needed to drive to the helipad, which was located on top of the dam. If we were going to make it, we would need a miracle.

Hussein and I rushed back to the camp. I had both his duffle bags of clothes and Hussein had his body armor and Kevlar in one arm and his AK-47 swinging in the other. We reached the MiTT camp completely exhausted. Lieutenant Adams gave us the latest news. "Gents, it looks like air is red [pilots cannot fly], so this dead body escort mission will be rolled to the next day."

Once my heart rate had settled, I asked an obvious question. "Where is the angel's body?" Major Gaines replied, "Hrmm, Jamal, that's a good question." He turned toward Adams and yelled, "Figure out where the hell that body is." Throughout the evening Adams called the 2/3 Marines living in the dam and asked everyone he knew if they had seen an angel come in recently. Nobody knew anything about it. The situation appeared hopeless until a Humvee came flying into our camp.

A young Marine lance corporal jumped out of the driver's seat and said, "Lieutenant Adams, Sir, we were told to bring this to you." We opened the back hatch of the Humvee. Body bags full of the angel's main corpse, smaller pieces of the angel's body, and blood-soaked combat gear were strewn about. Adams was pissed. "Devil Dog, who the hell told you to drop this body at the MiTT camp? We do not have a large refrigeration capability and we aren't escorting the body until tomorrow!" The stunned lance corporal replied, "Uh, Sir, I have no idea. I'm just doing what I'm told. My boss is the 2/3 S-4 logistics officer." Adams sneered and said, "Roger, thanks. I'll talk to your boss this evening. Bring this back to the dam and tell them they need to refrigerate the body."

As the lance corporal left our camp, the team burst into laughter. Nuts, in his trademark sarcastic tone, said, "So let me get this straight. When I get blown up by an IED, 2/3 is going to throw me in the back of a Humvee. I will then sit there for a day or two until they figure out what to do with me, and at some point they will send me to my family half rotten. Friggin' awesome."

It was 1415. I called the air officer before we departed for the top of the dam. The helo would be inbound at about 1530, plenty of time to reach the helipad. The air officer told me, "Roger, Lieutenant Gray, bird is inbound at 1530." With the air officer's confirmation we loaded up the Waz, a Russian made pile-of-crap jeep, and pulled out of the MiTT camp.

Captain McShane came sprinting to us. "I just got a call from the air officer," he said, "and he tells me the bird will be here in ten minutes. You'd better hurry!" I gasped. "What the heck? Are you serious?" I turned to V. "V, it takes fifteen minutes to get to the dam. You think we can get there in ten?" V replied using one of the few Arabic phrases he knew: "Insha'allah."

I put the Waz into high gear and slammed the gas. We somehow made it to the top of the dam in time. I asked the air-control Marine on duty, "Is the bird still inbound?" He responded, "Roger, Sir, should be inbound in five minutes." I further asked, "Where is the angel's body?" He responded, "Uh, I'm not sure. The S-4 said you guys would have it with you." My jaw hit the deck. I could not believe this was happening again.

I rushed into a nearby office on top of the dam to borrow a phone. I called the Marine S-4 shop and asked them to explain what was going on. The S-4 Marine on duty explained the situation. "Sir, we are tracking on the body and there was a miscommunication between us. However, that said, we don't have anyone able to bring the body to the top deck right now, you will have to get it out of the freezer on the seventh deck if you want it there in fifteen minutes." I hung up and sprinted to the Waz.

I said to the air-control Marine, "Hey, can you have the bird wait twenty minutes while we go get the body?" He replied, "Sir, I can give you fifteen, at most." Irked, I said, "Shit, well, we'll take what we can get." We remounted the Waz and raced to the seventh deck of the dam to retrieve the body. Unfortunately, to reach another level of the dam you have to drive nearly a mile along the dam where there is access to drive to the lower levels. The dam levels are similar to terraced agricultural fields, with minimal crossing points with which to move from one level to the other.

With the Waz in high gear we went flying through one of the Azerbaijani security checkpoints. Amazingly, they did not open fire on us and understood we were experiencing an emergency. We made it to the seventh level in record time, eight minutes and forty-five seconds.

Our next mission was to find the freezers. V, being the designated chow Marine for the MiTT, knew of only one set of freezers on the seventh deck—the chow freezers. "Dude," I asked him, "you think they would be sick enough to store the body with all the meat, milk, and other perishables?" I was hoping to get a negative response. "Sir," V said, "to be honest, those freezers are the only freezers on this level, they must have done that." I screeched on the brakes as we approached the row of four large shipping container sized walk-in freezers.

V searched the first two freezers and I searched the second two. We both came out empty-handed. I asked V, "Shoot man, where the hell could they have stored that body?" At that moment, a Marine corporal wandered over to us, wondering why a Marine first lieutenant and a staff sergeant were rummaging through 2/3's chow supply with sweat pouring down their faces. V took the lead. "Devil Dog, we are looking for a dead body. Seen one?" I thought for sure the Marine interrogating us was going to tell us to visit a psychiatrist, but he responded, "Actually, I heard the S-4 moved a body down here last night. Let me check real quick in the meat locker."

The Marine plowed to the rear of the meat locker, smashing boxes out of his way. Sure enough, in the corner of the meat locker sat a bloody body bag and some bloody combat gear buried next to a stack of hamburger patties. V and I immediately needed to figure out the best way to get the angel's body into the Waz. I established a plan. "V, you go to the Waz and figure out how we are gonna stuff this guy in the back. Corporal, you stay here with me and help me put all the pieces together so we can easily carry this body to the Waz."

The corporal and I slowly moved the various parts within the body bag—arms, feet, and others—into the form of a human and propped it onto a stretcher. Once we loaded the body bag, we stacked the angel's bloody flak and Kevlar on top of the stretcher and gingerly evacuated him from the freezer and into the Waz. V had a clearing in the middle of the Waz and had dropped the tailgate. "Shit, Sir, he ain't gonna fit," V proclaimed. I responded, "V, we don't have much choice, hang on to this guy with your life. I'll try and keep the ride smooth."

The scene that followed was straight out of the movie *Weekend at Bernie's*, in which a couple of young executives have to manipulate their boss's corpse through precarious situations without being discovered. I put the pedal to the metal in the Waz, and V held the body with outstretched arms. We made it to the intersection in the dam where we could move to the top deck. It was going to be a steep drive uphill. To V's horror I floored the Waz. "Sir," he shouted, "I think I'm going to drop him. My forearm is 'bout to burst!" I encouraged V, saying, "Just a few more seconds till we get to the tenth deck. Hold on buddy!"

"V, we made it," I said. "Il hamdu Allah." V and I were now on the tenth deck and needed to race to the helipad before the bird left. We screamed along the top of the dam and arrived a few minutes later to the helipad. Hussein came running to us, "Shaku maku? Aku mushkila?" (What's up? Are there any problems?) I replied, "La. Maku mushkila. Kullshi kullish zien wa sahel." (No. No problems. Everything is very good and was easy.) Hussein looked at us with suspicion. V and I were dripping in sweat and obviously stressed. Even so, Hussein shrugged his shoulders, grabbed his gear, and sprinted to the bird, while V and I loaded the corpse.

I wished V and Hussein safe travels and bid them farewell. As I exited the rear of the helicopter, Hussein looked at his dead cousin. He was disgusted, shaking his head in sorrow. "Jamal," he said, "last month my only brother was killed in a suicide car bomb attack in Al Qaim. I cannot deal with more death in my country." I tried to console him. "Hussein, Allah wiyak wa ahelek. Rah ykoon maku mushkila bil mustekbel." (Hussein, God is with you and your family. There will be no problems in the future.) I paused, shook his hand with a firm grip, and said, "Insha'allah."

I felt extremely sorry for Hussein. The state of life in Iraq is treacherous. It is almost standard operating procedure that Iraqis bury a loved one every month in this country. Meanwhile, in America we are worried about unemployment rising from 4.5 percent to 5.5 percent. Who cares? Imagine if the tables were turned and we had to worry if we had four and a half days or five and a half days to live. The Iraqi people are faced with challenges that dwarf the typical American sob story.

Chapter 12

The Iraqi Officer and Enlisted Relationship

October–November 2006

Outlaws

On the return trip from Haqliniyah, Maj. Travis Gaines and I stopped a bit short of Camp Ali along South Dam Road. Gaines turned to me and said, "Jamal, do you know why the Iraqis decided to stop"—he raised his voice—"in the middle of the road?" I replied, "Sir, I have no clue."

Thirty seconds after we had stopped, Sermen, an Iraqi soldier, came jogging past our Humvee and approached the rear Iraqi Humvee. At the same time Ayad sprinted past the side of our Humvee and headed to the Iraqi Humvee in the front of the convoy. Gaines said over the radio, "Does anyone have a clue why the hell Sermen is coming to the rear of the convoy and Ayad is moving to the front of the convoy while we're still outside the wire?" The radio was silent. Nobody on the MiTT knew what was happening.

I found out what had transpired once we arrived at the camp. According to the Iraqis there was a huge fight between Sermen and Captain Natham, the Iraqi convoy commander. Captain Natham had requested that Sermen refrain from driving like a maniac and slow his Humvee. Sermen had refused the order, told Natham to go to hell, jumped out of the Humvee, and gone to the rear of the convoy because he could not stand Natham any longer.

After hearing the story I did not know whose side to take. On the one hand Captain Natham was the convoy commander and had the authority to tell his subordinates what they could and could not do. On the other hand Sermen realized that if he drove as Natham desired, the convoy would become an easy target for insurgents. I decided I was with Sermen. Speed and unpredictability keep you alive in Iraq. Even so, because Sermen was in the military, he needed to respect his officer's commands.

This incident highlights the relationship between officers and enlisted men in the Iraqi army. In the U.S. Marines, if an enlisted Marine defies an officer or senior enlisted, he isn't allowed to carry on as if nothing happened. He is punished through the Uniform Code of Military Justice. Without respect for the chain of command, a military organization will have no ability to maintain order and discipline.

Sadly, the Iraqi army is set up so that soldiers have no service obligation and face no legal punishments. If a *jundi* decides the Iraqi army sucks and wants to quit, he can. Likewise, if he wants to tell a superior officer to rot in hell, he can. In the Iraqi army it is nearly impossible for officers to maintain military rule that is necessary to execute combat operations. A formal legal system simply does not exist. The only way for officers to punish the *jundi* is to take away pay or leave, but when they implement this punishment, the *jundi* just quit.

The Monarchy

There is another side to the Iraqi officer and enlisted relationship, of course. The Iraqi officers treat the soldiers like servants. It is very difficult for enlisted soldiers to take orders from their officers if they believe the officers do not care about them. Here is a perfect example. One day we were rolling through the Haditha market and spotted a vehicle that looked like one of the vehicles on our BOLO (be on the lookout) list. Our Humvee immediately flagged the vehicle to pull over, then we called up the rear Iraqi Humvee to go search the car.

After five minutes the Iraqi Humvee finally pulled up. We waited for another five minutes and began to wonder why nobody was searching the car. We asked our terp Mark to call them on the Iraqi radio net to find out what the situation was. Mark explained, "Gents, the Humvee alongside us is full of Iraqi officers and they are refusing to do "soldier" tasks. They see their role as commanders and thus do not have a role in actually conducting any of the work." Major Gaines and I each looked at each other, dumbfounded. Gaines replied, "Mark, are you kidding me or are you serious?" Mark replied, "I'm not joking, Gaines. The Iraqi officers just called on some enlisted soldiers from one of the front Humvees to come back and search the vehicle." Confused, I said, "Mark, the officers are twenty feet from the car. The soldiers they called on are two football fields away. I don't get it." Mark smirked and said, "I know. It's stupid. Welcome to Iraq."

I guess none of this was surprising. The concept of king and servant seems to be pervasive in Iraqi culture. The sad part is that we are supposed to change these people somehow. In the words of one of our Camp Taji instructors, "Teach the Iraqis the concept of the leader being the servant of his men. Teach the Iraqi officers that they must respect their enlisted soldiers." Are you kidding me? That's equivalent to asking us to convince the American people that they need to stop watching NFL football and start watching professional soccer. Changing a culture is not a mission, it's a pipe dream.

The Status Quo Cannot Go

Major Pyle and I spoke to Lieutenant Colonel Ali about promoting Sergeant Major Kasem to the highest position of enlisted leadership in the battalion. We suggested that he replace Sergeant Major Nayim, who maintained the current position and had failed miserably in his role. Major Pyle stated the facts. "Seyidi [Sir], Kasem is a stellar leader, has impressive initiative, and gets things done on camp. We believe Kasem should be in the highest enlisted position. He can have a positive influence on the entire battalion, show off his work ethic, and reinforce the concept that meritocracy wins over nepotism."

Lieutenant Colonel Ali was visibly confused. He gave Pyle an odd look. "Why would I promote Kasem? If we promote Kasem we have to get someone else to fill his current job and he is doing a great job where he is. If I move him to Nayim's position, he has to learn another job. It makes absolutely no sense. And if I give him a promotion, all of the *jundi* will want promotions. Finally, if Nayim gets kicked out of the top enlisted position, he will lose all respect in the battalion. I will not do this. Nayim is my friend." Major Pyle's jaw dropped to the ground—and for good reason. How can a Marine respond sensibly to something like this?

Sometimes the Iraqis just don't get it. Their deep-seated tribal influences reinforce some of their least productive traits: maintaining the status quo, nepotism, playing favorites, and fixating on pride and honor. The concept that the hardest-working, most-qualified individuals should be rewarded for their efforts is completely foreign to them.

Chapter 13

Iraqis Speak on the Nation, Region, and Military

September–October 2006

Mark," I said to our Kurdish terp, "I'd like to hear what your opinion is of the American invasion. When the plan was written up, we would free the country's people from Saddam's oppressive grip and these people would then rebuild the society and become the beacon of democracy in the Middle East. What went wrong?" Mark smiled and playfully punched me in the shoulder. "Jamal, I never thought an American could admit that something may have gone wrong in the Iraq invasion. Are you sure you are not an Iranian spy?" I said, "Mark, shut up. Get on with your story." He said, "Jamal, I think America screwed up in four categories when they came in during the original invasion."

The Nation

Mark lectured me on the situation in Iraq before the U.S. invasion. "The majority of people in Iraq were excited the Americans were coming, particularly the Kurdish, Shia, and highly educated," he said. "Despite the misinformed Western vision of a Saddam-controlled media feeding Iraqi people propaganda that vilified the United States, many Iraqis had their eyes wide open to the Kuwaiti and Saudi Arabian media outlets through illegal satellite dishes. This opened our eyes to the good things Americans could bring to Iraq. Basically, the stage was set for a successful American campaign."

Mark paused before going on. "Listen, Jamal, it was no secret Saddam was in a desperate fight for the population's support. His groveling for support actually made the Iraqis feel more and more that what America had to offer was better, even if we weren't sure what this offering would be. It got so pathetic that Saddam ordered banks to give everyone a hundred dollars if they would support him in the war against America. They would never admit it in public, but my guess is the majority of Iraqis wanted the Americans to invade."

"Mark," I asked, "if people were excited about us invading, why am I here three years later dodging IEDs?" He replied, "Well, everything went down the crapper because of four key mistakes: opening the borders, disbanding the army and police, leaving the military bases open and unguarded, and leaving the banks unsecured." In his professional manner Mark elaborated:

When the Americans opened the borders, or at least left them unsecured, it let Al Qaeda fighters, Syrians, and Iranians come into the region to create chaos. This was the first sign to the Iraqi people that there was a weakness in the American's ability to secure the situation. Then you guys had the brain-dead idea of disbanding the Iraqi army and Iraqi police. The Iraqis would have accepted this if the Americans had maintained the security these services provided, but instead you guys fired the security forces and at the same time let the thieves and bandits run rampant. This was strike two against America. Next you left the Iraqi army camps unguarded after the invasion. This allowed everyone in the country to arm and prepare for guerrilla warfare. Hell, with my own eyes I saw grandmothers carrying RPGs out of the camps so they could sell them for money. It was a free-for-all. If the United States put in a simple effort to secure these facilities the number of weapons and ammunition available to the subsequent insurgency movement would have been erased. Finally, strike four for America was leaving the banks unsecured. This was the straw that broke the camel's back, Jamal. Iraq went from a semimodern banking system to the stone age after the invasion. Thieves were robbing banks without consequence and the American soldiers simply watched it happen. All the money that was once held in the hands of decent Iraqis transferred into the paws of the nefarious Iraqis. You guys fucked us, plain and simple.

Mark's comments tore at my heart. If we had brought in a much larger invasion force and planned more appropriately for the fall of Saddam, Iraq may have actually ended up as a success story. Tragically, any good will Iraqis had toward America all but vanished.

The Region

In the two weeks after 2/3 took over the area from 3/3, they suffered twenty-two wounded and two Marines killed. Before 2/3 arrived, 3/3 had experienced numerous combat casualties. The Triad was nothing short of a bloodbath for the Marines. I decided to get the Iraqi perspective on why 3/3 and now 2/3 were getting waxed by the insurgents.

I grabbed Moody, the most experienced terp we had. Moody had been with our battalion in Haditha since it had been formed almost two years earlier, and he had seen four different Marine units rotate in and out of the Triad. "Moody," I asked, "why have the past two Marine battalions been crushed by the insurgents?" Moody responded, "Jamal, the problem with Marines is that you do not understand Iraqi people." He hesitated. "Well, actually, the only Marine I have seen that really understood Iraqi people was Lt. Col. Jeffrey Chessani, the 3/1 commander. Do you know what happened to him? The Marines fired him for the 'Haditha Massacre.'"

Moody continued his praise for Chessani. "Jamal, the guy was a genius. You know the entire time his battalion was here there were only two Marines killed? He was the only Marine commander who would come to the Iraqi camp and ask for advice on a regular basis from the *jundi* and the terps." I retorted, "Are you kidding me? He's the only Marine commander that sought out Iraqi advice on how to deal with Iraqi problems?" Moody replied, "Jamal, I am dead serious." I said, "Well, what exactly did he do that was so different than what we are doing now? We don't want to create another Haditha Massacre. That isn't an option at this point."

Moody said, "Jamal, the so-called Haditha Massacre was the best thing that ever happened to the Marines." He sat back and smiled. "Until the Marines realize that violence is how politics and policy are solved in Iraq, they will never be successful. I guarantee when the Americans leave us alone, the solutions to our country's problems will be solved by violence. That is just how it is and how it always will be. We are different."

Moody continued with his insightful lecture. "What Chessani finally realized after speaking with Iraqis, myself included, was that the people in this region need to feel pain in order to respond, because the insurgents put pain on them everyday. Unless we reciprocate we are not going to convince anybody to do anything." I fired back, "So you suggest we just go grab civilians and start torturing them or something?"

"No, the key is to implement policies that put the pressure on the tribal sheiks to act," Moody responded. "The sheiks control the populations and do what is in their best interest. The trick is to shape the decisions they must face. For example, we suggested to Chessani that he button down the cities and eliminate vehicle traffic, implement curfews, and shut down the power. The sheikhs were forced to come out of their holes and negotiate with the Marines. The Marines have the power to put the pain on the people without resorting to the violence the insurgents use. Chessani knew this and was highly successful in protecting his Marines."

Playing the devil's advocate I responded, "Well, if we implement those policies then we will continue to anger the people and they will just want to side with the insurgents." Moody burst out with laughter. "Jamal, you and I both know the Americans will never, never, never win the hearts and minds of Sunni Arabs in Al Anbar Province; however, you can win their respect for your authority, power, and money. This is how you will get them to do what you want. They are never going to like you, but they may be willing to work with you if it is in their interest."

What Moody said made so much sense. From an Iraqi perspective the facts are very clear: to beat the insurgents one needs to fight fire with fire or one will lose the fight. If the sheikhs can collect thousands of dollars from insurgent groups by promoting violence against Marines, without incurring any cost, the decision is simple: continue supporting the insurgents. Likewise, if the Marines put a little pressure on the sheikh—take his electricity, his ability to drive, his food, his water, and so forth—he now has a cost associated with accepting money from insurgent groups. You have now shaped his decision-making process in your favor.

Toto, we aren't in Kansas anymore.

The Military

I got my last dose of Iraqi perspective this evening speaking with Colonel Abass. I addressed Abass with the standard litany of greetings, pleasantries, and small talk Iraqis need before getting down to business. But then I asked, "Sir, what are your thoughts on implementing some sort of awards system to recognize the work of *jundi* who are doing excellent work?" Abass sunk into his leather chair and twisted his handlebar mustache. "Jamal, what exactly are you thinking?" I replied, "Sir, to be quite honest, I'm not sure. I know what works in the Marines, but I'm not sure how our system would translate into the Iraqi Army. One idea I had would be to give the *jundi* formal letters of appreciation signed by you. What do you think of something like that?"

Colonel Abass chuckled in a low grumble and propped himself upright. "Jamal, Jamal, Jamal, I love your enthusiasm. You are a happy fellow and I think it is wonderful. God has obviously blessed you." I quickly replied, "Sir, I know you think I'm full of shit on this one and I actually realize that I probably am. I'm really just fishing for some ideas from you. Why won't a system like this work? Didn't you have an awards system in the old Iraqi army?"

Abass proceeded to lecture me. "Jamal, in the past the Iraqi army was a job of pride and honor," he said. "Today, it is purely a way for people to make ends meet. Iraqis no longer have any pride in the country or their military anymore. God willing, we can fix this over time, but I doubt it. The only thing that will motivate my *jundi* is more money, more leave, or less work. These men are not soldiers, they are civilians."

Colonel Abass summarized his thoughts. "Jamal, did you know the brigade tried to write me a formal letter of appreciation a few weeks ago? It was a wonderful gesture, but even I have become disillusioned in this new Iraqi army. I don't command anything, the Americans do. I can't kill insurgents, because the Americans won't let me. Civilians don't even respect the power of the Iraqi army anymore. How can I have pride in it? You know what I did with the letter I received?" I replied out of courtesy, "What?" Abass said, "I wiped my ass with it and used it for toilet paper. That's how much that paper was worth to me. The same holds for a majority of the *jundi* in my battalion."

At the conclusion of the initial Iraqi invasion, we should have never dissolved Iraqi's only functional organization. It now may be irreparable.

Part 3

COMBAT OPERATIONS WITH
THE IRAQI ARMY

Chapter 14

Operation *Nimer*

September 2006

Five years ago, on September 11, 2001, terrorists blew things up in New York City and Washington, D.C. At Camp Ali terrorists decided to celebrate the five-year anniversary by sending a 107-mm rocket screaming over the MiTT camp. It landed thirty-five meters north of us. Luckily it was a dud or it could have killed our entire team in one shot. Death was a reality we faced in combat. We had been lucky thus far to have experienced relatively few casualties in the Iraqi battalion. But in September we headed into our biggest operation yet, and I was certain that at the end of the operation someone would be dead or missing a body part. Surviving the operation would be a serious relief.

We began the operations briefs. Even by Iraqi standards the preliminary Iraqi order had failed. Don't get me wrong, the content was solid. The briefer communicated his ideas and everyone understood how we would accomplish the mission. Even so, the Iraqis made a rookie mistake in formulating the plan. They assumed they could fit 222 individuals into the Haditha FOB, a space designated for a maximum of 100. The Iraqis may enjoy the idea of being stacked on top of one another, but I didn't want an Iraqi sleeping on top of me.

Captain McShane did not endorse their plan either. "What about the idea of using peoples' homes as patrol bases?" he asked. "We can switch every day or so." Although such an idea would certainly infuriate the locals, we thought it was better than stacking 222 bodies in a shoebox. But McShane's ideas did not persuade the Iraqis. Captain Hasen said, "We are

119

Iraqis; we do not want to invade another Iraqi's home. The Americans may be willing to do this, but we refuse to do this!" Hasen's critique was correct, but he did not offer any alternative solutions. McShane, visibly frustrated, fired at the Iraqis, "We must do this. You have presented no solutions—we are doing it our way now!"

McShane's plan angered every Iraqi in the room. Unfortunately Iraqis are not Marines. Marines will come to the position of attention, salute, and carry out the mission their commander gives them, even if the commander is a dope. Iraqis will do no such thing. McShane, who was used to being in command, still had not grasped the difference between commanding and advising. There are two things Americans should never do with Iraqis in public: Never tell them they are wrong and never command them to do something. Both of these infractions shred an Iraqi's pride and honor, effectively murdering him in the eyes of society. An equivalent offense in our culture would be to get on a bus, call the first black person you saw a "nigger," and tell him to sit in the back of the bus. These things do not sit well.

The Iraqis had a point. McShane's counterproposal was an untenable option. It would rightfully cause Anbar Sunnis to view Americans as occupiers and was sure to create even more insurgents in the region. In addition, setting up patrol bases in local homes would expose us to VBIED and grenade attacks. It would not work.

The upcoming operation was causing tempers and emotions to fly sky high, not only between the MiTT and the IA but also among the MiTT members. During our nightly MiTT meeting Lieutenant Adams asked Staff Sergeant Haislip to get batteries for all the Humvees. Haislip responded, "That ain't my job." Adams, a prior-enlisted Marine for twelve years, responded in the way he knows best. "Haislip, I didn't ask you if it is your job. Just fuckin' do it!" On Haislip's behalf Staff Sergeant Donaldson said, "Lieutenant Adams, aren't batteries your issue as the supply officer? Why aren't you taking care of that?" Adams was seething. He said, "Stay in your fuckin' lane, intelligence boy. How about you figure out what the hell is going on in the area of operations and let me figure out how to get the batteries?" The team was on the brink of mutiny. The boss jumped in, but his yelling only heightened the frustration. "Everyone shut up and quit fuckin' bitching! No more talking." These people cannot handle the stress of planning the mission, I thought, God help us when we move to the execution phase of the mission.

The Mission Begins

The day came to kick off Operation *Nimer* (Tiger). All the soldiers from our battalion would be in the operation, along with elements from 3rd Iraqi Battalion in Hit and 1st Iraqi Battalion in Rawah. With a mere 222 *jundi* involved, the Marines thought it would be routine. But no matter how routine an operation might be for Marines, nothing is routine for Iraqis.

As is typical in Iraqi operations, of the 222 *jundi* involved, only 80 would actually see combat; the rest would sit back in the COC at the Haditha FOB. I will never understand why Iraqi communications and coordination can be so poor when they keep a vast majority of their troops in the command center to alleviate these problems. I guess the answer is simple. The more Iraqis you have involved in planning and coordination, the more arguing and disagreement you will receive and thus the worse performance you will have.

The basic operations plan was to flood the Triad cities with Iraqi soldiers conducting heavy combat operations. The hope was that this offensive would keep the insurgents occupied just long enough so that 2nd Battalion, 3rd Marines (2/3) would be able to transition into the area to replace the outbound Marines from 3rd Battalion, 3rd Marines (3/3). Insurgents historically time their attacks when new Marine units RIP (relief in place) into the area of operations. They correctly assume that the new Marine battalion will be slow in adjusting to the environment and the stress of combat. Our goal was to keep our fresh marines, 2/3, from being blown up by IEDs, shot at by small-arms fire, or mutilated by RPG explosions.

In preparation for battle we assembled an enormous convoy with supplies, soldiers, weapons, and a bunch of bad attitudes. The first stop on the convoy would be the Haditha FOB. There we would coordinate with the 3/3 Marines on how this operation was going to work. We had a vague plan, but we needed to iron out the details. We had traveled with the *jundi* before in enormous convoys with upward of thirty vehicles, but we had never traveled through the narrow, IED-infested streets of Haditha with a convoy larger than six vehicles. This mission would require navigating ten vehicles through the city (see photo 14).

On pins and needles we zigzagged through the one-lane streets of Haditha. We hauled ass through the main marketplace, ensuring that no insurgents had any time to stage an attack or toss a grenade into one of the Leylands full of *jundi* and gear. Miraculously we arrived in one piece at the austere Haditha FOB.

Although the Haditha FOB is perhaps the size of a football field, it has living conditions that would make a caveman cringe: bullet-ridden walls, collapsed roofs from mortar damage, trash and barbed wire strewn about, shattered glass and shrapnel along the ground, and more sandbags than someone could count in a lifetime. Haditha is one of the most dangerous places in Iraq, if not the entire world.

Pulling up to the FOB with ten vehicles was not an impossible task; however, pulling up to the FOB with ten vehicles operated by Iraqi drivers was. After multiple vehicle wrecks and collisions, the chaos began to subside and we got our orders. Our convoy would be broken into two elements, one staying at the FOB and the other heading to the Water Treatment Facility (WTF), our proposed combat patrol base. The WTF element would include me, Doc McGinnis, Major Gaines, and Staff Sergeant Chesnutt from the MiTT; Martin and Moody would be our terps. We also would have six infantry Marines from 3/3 who operated exclusively in Haditha. The final piece of the pie would be a crapload of motivated *jundi* with four Leylands full of gear to accomplish their mission. "Let's move out," Major Gaines ordered. We started the convoy out the east gate toward the center of town. The motivation level was striking. Everyone was gung-ho for combat.

Swack! The convoy immediately stopped. Two of the Iraqi drivers had managed to smash their Leylands into each other—not an auspicious beginning. We continued out the east gate. As we rolled into the town Nuts shouted, "Gents, the streets are clearing up ahead and people are running the hell out of the way, I recommend you get in the truck and standby." All Marines know that you are screwed when the locals evacuate a bustling area because it is a sure sign an insurgent attack is imminent.

Before we knew it we were taking incoming sporadic machine-gun fire from insurgents flying across the intersection. The insurgents had planned an ambush, but our slow departure meant we did not advance into their ambush at the time they desired. If we had progressed at our original pace, we would have been in the teeth of the ambush. We wanted to hunt insurgents, but we needed to establish a patrol base at the WTF before dark. We would fight the insurgents in the future, but it would be on our own terms and not theirs.

We snaked the convoy around, headed away from the insurgent ambush and toward the west exit, which led us into the outskirts of town. Going out the western gate created another problem. We had never been on this route before and were entirely at the mercy of the Iraqis' navigation skills to get us back to the center of town. Relying on Iraqis for anything besides a cup of chai (tea) with heavy sugar was rarely solid advice. To make matters worse we were being led by the infamous Mulazim Jaffer, a young second lieutenant Iraqi army officer who was a few 155-mm artillery rounds short of an IED.

Moving at fifty miles per hour along a single lane dirt road, the only thing I could see was the road directly in front of me, dust clouds the size of a tornado coming off Jaffer's Humvee, and perplexed townsfolk in my peripheral vision. I yelled to Major Gaines, "Sir, you think we should try to get him to slow down before he gets in a serious wreck and this operation is over before it even begins?" With all the bustling on the road, and the radio traffic in both Arabic and English flowing through the cab of the Humvee, he could only respond, "Jamal, I can't hear you."

Jaffer somehow had managed to snake through the outskirt village and find his way back to the main road through town, Route Boardwalk. Just as I felt relief as a result of our seemingly good luck, I witnessed Jaffer's lead Humvee come screaming around a blind corner onto Route Boardwalk. As soon as his Humvee banked a left onto Boardwalk, a chubby Iraqi man driving a red motorcycle came flying along the left side of the Humvee. The next thing I saw was a vintage 200-cc motorcycle violently careen off the road and a short fat Iraqi go flying through the air spinning around in a helicopter-like fashion.

The motorcycle crashed fifty feet away along a house fence and stalled. The Iraqi man was not so lucky. While flying at twenty feet in the air, the man had blasted into the nearest telephone post at twenty-five miles an hour, bounced off the post, helicoptered a few more times in the opposite direction, and crashed to the ground. For a few seconds I could not see the man, as the dust cloud from his landing engulfed him completely.

"Holy shit, Sir, that guy has to be dead!" Major Gaines was equally shell shocked at what we had witnessed. We both took a deep breath. We were in the middle of the hottest neighborhood in Haditha, we had just killed a local, and we were traveling in a large convoy with limited firepower. What in the hell were we going to do? Gaines made a quick decision. "Jamal," he said, "pull up on the south side of the road to block traffic, the Iraqis will block north, and the rest of the convoy will have to standby. We'll give Doc five minutes to assess the situation."

"Roger, Sir, makes sense to me," I responded as I smashed the accelerator to block the road, hoping to stop any traffic from entering the scene. "Doc, get your ass out there and tell us what we need to do next," Major Gaines commanded. "Roger, Sir," Doc replied. "If this guy is dead, or not about to die, we are going to get the hell out of here. If he is about to die, we need to abort the mission and bring him back to the dam so they can perform surgery on him."

The situation was getting tense. It seemed everyone in the town had come out to see what was going on. By my count twenty-five locals were on the scene and the crowd was multiplying by the second. We were in the worst possible situation imaginable. Furious Sunni Iraqis surrounded us and were ready for vengeance.

My heart was racing for Doc. That poor bastard was out there trying to explain to the Iraqis through an interpreter that it was an accident and that the Iraqi soldiers were sorry for causing the man harm. It seemed as though he was out there for an hour, but in just a few minutes, he returned. "I don't know if that guy has Allah on his side or what," Doc said, "but he is alive with some minor lacerations and perhaps a broken rib. He is good to go. I think his fat ass actually saved his life. Let's get the fuck out of here before we end up on the receiving end of an RPG!" We reformed the convoy and continued north along Route Boardwalk until we reached the WTF a few miles ahead.

As we pulled away from the scene of the crime, I felt terrible for the man and for all the people in the village. Tribal members and family were rushing to the man's aid. Women were outraged, screaming at the convoy as we left them in our dust trails. It was a disaster. Our situation had been so precarious that we had no option but to leave, and while I felt bad about leaving the man there, our actions kept the insurgents from killing a platoon's worth of *jundi* sitting in the back of Leylands. We lost some hearts and minds this go-round. But now was not the time to dwell on this, as we were quickly approaching the WTF.

Establishing a Patrol Base

Recent HUMINT (human intelligence) reports had concluded that the WTF was a base of operations for insurgent activity. We went in expecting the worst but hoping for the best. We approached the main gate to the facility, which was surrounded by a six-foot-high wire fence that had not been serviced since the rule of Saddam Hussein.

The WTF was a small facility the size of two football fields placed side by side. From a tactical military perspective it was perfect as a defendable patrol base. The patrol base had a five-hundred-meter buffer that separated the compound's fences and the nearest residential areas, multiple exit points that allowed options from which to commence patrols, and a convenient location alongside Route Boardwalk that allowed us to maintain visibility on IED activity at all times.

We established initial security of the compound without incident. As the Marines secured the boundary, the *jundi* searched all the residential homes and informed the residents that we would be taking over their lives for the next few days. Amazingly, the residents of the facility were friendly to the *jundi*, inviting them to live in their homes for the course of the operation. I was not sure what to make of this kindness. It might have been old-fashioned Arab hospitality or it might have been the local's fear of telling a group of sixty-two soldiers toting machine guns "No."

By the time the *jundi* had settled into their basic defensive positions it was nearly 2100. We had one problem. In our efforts to ensure that the patrol base was established and the Iraqis were settled, we had forgotten to settle ourselves. "Jamal," Major Gaines said, "take Doc and find us a place to set up a COC."

Doc and I stumbled in the dark and tried to find a building that the Iraqis had not yet occupied. We decided to try the generator building in the center of camp. As we entered the building the drumming noise of generators running at full steam and the rusty taste of oil and gasoline in the air greeted us. Doc and I quickly realized that the fact the *jundi* had avoided the generator building should have been a warning. Nonetheless we wandered through the building in complete darkness. I felt that at any moment an insurgent would jump around the corner and stab me in the neck or blow out my brains. The building was nasty—plain and simple—but it was late and we needed to kick a patrol out early the next morning. The generator building was our only option until we could get a better assessment of the compound the next morning.

Combat Raid

We set up shop near the southern entrance of the generator building. We hurried to set up the radios, establish the basic security plan, and figure out the general scheme for the next day. By the time we finished it was 0200 and the first patrol would start at 0600. We decided to go on a staggered two-hour nap schedule split between sleeping, radio watch, and security.

Our nap plan did not last long. As I was half-asleep on the first radio watch of the night, a couple of semifrantic *jundi* came running up to our position yelling in Arabic, "Jamal, Jamal, as salama aleikum. Shifit erhabeen bil binaye!" (Jamal, Jamal, peace be upon you. I saw insurgents in the building!) I was in a semicomatose state. I answered them in sloppy Arabic, "IHchiet wiya inaqib Mawfood, awwal? Huwwa qaedek, mu anii." (Did you talk to Captain Mawfood first? He is your leader, not me.) The *jundi* responded, "IHchiet wiya inaqib Mawfood. Huwwa gillitna lazim niHchi wiyak." (We did talk with Captain Mawfood. He told us we needed to talk with you.) Great, I thought, the people who are supposed to be taking leadership of the Iraqi army are deferring to me for answers.

"Who's on your post right now?" I asked the *jundi* for fear they had abandoned their post. Fulfilling my fears, they responded, "Nobody." I rushed to wake Martin so he could help me with translation. I could operate without a terp, but when my mind was fried, having a terp made things much smoother and quicker. I told Martin, "Call Mawfood and figure out what the hell is going on. Also, tell these soldiers they need to maintain their post!" Martin reluctantly moved his cream-puff body off his rack, scratched his balls a few times, and fell back on his rack to sleep. I was furious. I shook Martin by the arm. "Get your ass up man—here is the radio—call Mawfood and see what is going on!"

Mawfood made his way over to our area. As he approached our position, he greeted everyone with "As salama aleikum." We all responded with "Wa aleikum salam" (And upon you, peace). Major Gaines, Captain Mawfood, and I walked to the southeast corner of the compound to listen to the Iraqis who had spotted the insurgents.

"You see that half-built house near Route Boardwalk?" Hussein, the *jundi* on post, pointed in the direction of a gloomy looking, half-constructed mud hut home 150 meters from their security post. He continued, "We think we saw seven or eight guys walk in there over the past thirty minutes. It looks as if they had shovels and weapons with them."

It was time to conduct Operation *Nimer's* first combat raid. I started to think back to Infantry Officers' Course, frantically digging for all the knowledge I had learned on the conduct of raids. It all came back to me as if I had just graduated. I developed a plan to raid the suspected insurgent hideout. I gathered Sergeant Kelley, Corporal Espinosa ("Espi"), and Nuts around the Humvee. With a red penlight in my mouth for lighting, I began to draw a sketch of the building and our plan for the raid. Meanwhile, in the background I heard a faint "As salama aleikum." I looked up and flipped down my night vision goggles to see who it was. I hoped my mind was playing tricks. It was Lieutenant Jaffer, the same guy who smashed a civilian the day before.

I had heard through Kelley and Espi that Jaffer was the "worst combat leader of all time and a flaming idiot." Despite Jaffer's poor track record, however, I stuck to my mission intent as a military adviser and said, "Jaffer, I'd like to hear how you want to go about doing this combat raid. I have a basic plan we can work from, but I'd enjoy hearing your ideas since I am here to advise and not command."

Jaffer proceeded to give me his basic plan. It sounded more like a poorly thought-out football play than a military operation. Essentially it was "send two guys this way, two guys that way, and then we will go in the front door and search for bad guys." I was not impressed; neither was I confident this operation would be successful.

I countered Jaffer's incompetence and presented a professional raid plan that involved setting an outside cordon, establishing a raid force, and establishing a support force. It was apparent my ideas were sailing over Jaffer's head. I knew I was not going to get anywhere with Jaffer; we would have to discuss raid planning later. I smiled, told Jaffer his plan sounded great, and told him to be ready by 0300.

Once Jaffer had left I grabbed Nuts, Kelley, Blanchard, and Espi. We went over our own internal plan. The operation had changed from a raid operation to a "protect-our-own-asses" operation. The biggest danger was not the insurgents in the building but the *jundi* under the leadership of Lieutenant Jaffer. The gist of my new plan was simple: let the Iraqis die first, watch out for *jundi* friendly fire, and take the lead in the operation only if it was a matter of our own survival. In my mind Iraqis should die for their country, not Marines.

Jaffer showed up with his *jundi* around 0330, thirty minutes late but respectable by Iraqi standards. The *jundi* who showed up, many of whom were from our battalion, greeted me with much fanfare. "Mulazim Jamal, as salama aleikum. Shlonek? Shlon sawtek? Shlon ahelek? Inta zien?" (Lieutenant Jamal, peace be upon you. How are you? How is your health? How is your family? Are you good?) It felt good to know we would have some familiar faces on this mission.

We pushed outside the compound gate and tactically moved in a squad-column formation to the building suspected to have insurgents. This was exciting. We slowly approached the abandoned building with our night vision goggles and watched as Jaffer put his so-called plan into action. Jaffer sent a few soldiers ahead to set up a "crap-tacular" cordon around the building. He next ordered two *jundi* with flashlights to search the building. I knew that if the two *jundi* entering the building encountered any resistance, they were toast. To make matters worse, from our position we would be unable to support them. Jaffer's plan was flawed but workable, so as an adviser cadre we were going to allow him to execute it.

I fully expected a gunfight. The abandoned building served as perfect terrain for insurgents who wanted to attack the WTF. But the gunfight never came. The *jundi* sent in to search nonchalantly walked back out of the building with their rifles slung and their flashlights dangling from their waists, swaying back and forth with the rhythm of their steps. They each fired up a cigarette and yelled to Jaffer, "All clear."

My heart rate dropped a good twenty beats a minute as my fear and excitement faded. So much for being Rambo and getting a chance to find some insurgents. I called back to the WTF, "Shadow One, there ain't shit in this building. What do you want us to do?" After consulting Captain Mawfood, Major Gaines responded, "Roger, Shadow Two, continue on with a normal foot patrol, we were going to push a patrol out in a few hours anyway." "Rog—," I began. But before I could end my radio transmission, Jaffer was already moving the Iraqis across Route Boardwalk to search a large Iraqi home.

We followed the remainder of the patrol across Boardwalk to ensure squad integrity. After examining the house and finding nothing except a family fast asleep, we continued east into the sleepy palm groves to search for stray command wires. The insurgents typically plant the IEDs on Route Boardwalk and string the copper command wires into the palm groves to maximize the concealment of the wires. By moving into the palm groves and walking parallel to Route Boardwalk, we would hopefully run into these command wires before the insurgents were able to use them to blow up a convoy the following day.

We stumbled across barren agricultural fields and moved eastward toward the lush palm groves that nestled against the Euphrates. As we bumbled along, each of us tried to look less idiotic than the other. I have always considered myself a coordinated person, however, throw eighty pounds of combat gear on your back, look through a P.S.-14 monocular night vision goggle, try to walk across mogul-like terrain for a few hundred meters, and see what happens. It's a humbling experience.

We approached the palm groves. Moving into the groves in the thick of night reminded me of classic war scenes from the jungles of Vietnam. While we did not need a machete to get through the thicket, it was damn close. I called for Jaffer through Martin's UHF radio, "Jaffer, let's talk about how we are going to move through these palm groves." Jaffer showed up and gave me his plan. His basic idea was for everyone to get in a line and start walking parallel to Route Boardwalk through the dense palm grove forests and the four-foot reed patches up ahead. This plan would cause him to lose control of his squad. We hacked on his plan and came up with something that was not perfect but could work.

The intent of sleuthing through the palm groves in the middle of the night was to run across copper command wires. After five minutes of falling on my face, untangling my gear from reeds, and ensuring I was not in the sights of an Iraqi Army AK-47, I realized that finding these damned command wires was going to have to take a back seat. It was hard enough seeing a foot in front of our faces, let alone being able to see a thin copper fishing wire on the ground. We made a collective decision to return to the WTF.

We returned to the WTF after four hours of trudging in treacherous terrain. Then we gathered everyone around for a quick debrief, which is SOP (standard operating procedure) for the Marines. I began my brief comments, which lasted all of three minutes. Jaffer responded, smiling gleefully, "Jamal, you are my brother, these *jundi* and these Marines are your brothers. Why do you make them suffer through a debrief?" I gazed into the empty faces of the forty-year-old Iraqi army soldiers on the patrol with us, many of whom had lived harder lives than I could even imagine. I replied, "Jaffer you're right. I'm sorry. Everyone get some rest. Great job today."

Insurgent Snipers Attack

After three hours of dreamless sleep, I awoke to the sound of roaring generator engines and the sight of an Iraqi civilian snooping outside the building. Instinctively I reached for my M-4. I notified Doc, who I found was tracking on the same man. Before we could figure out what to do next, Martin, who was sleeping outside on his cot, addressed the man, "Hey, what are you doing over here?" The man, who was scared out of his mind, timidly responded, "I am sorry, mister. I am in charge of the generators here and need to change the power circuits. Please do not hurt me. Captain Mawfood said it was fine for me come here." We calmed down the man and had him sit with us for a breakfast of MARES. The last thing we wanted was for the residents of the facility to fear our presence and cease to carry out their jobs at the WTF. I could only imagine how angry the locals would get if their primary source of clean water were to be halted.

I was to be the lead adviser on the next patrol and my crew was stellar. I would have my trusty comrades Sergeant Kelley, Espi, Private First Class Lynch, and Moody on my team. Kelley was the best of the best. He was an eight-year veteran Marine infantryman, a grizzled combat veteran, and had been on countless patrols in Haditha. If there was anyone I wanted to patrol alongside in Haditha, it would be Kelley. His partner in crime was Espi. Espi and Kelley both reminded me of John Wayne toilet paper—rough, tough, and didn't take any shit. It was a great reassurance to have these Marines on patrol with me.

We pushed the patrol in column formation outside the WTF main gate at 1000 hours. We headed across Boardwalk and into the same palm groves we had attacked the night before. As I left the gate Samir, the *jundi* operating the P.C. machine gun on the main entrance, said, "Targa bil salama" (Return in peace). I exited through the gate and replied, "Insha'allah."

Fortunately we didn't have Jaffer along for the patrol. In my mind this cut the probability of my dying enormously. Instead our patrol leader was Hussein, a forty-five-year-old Iraqi, with twenty-five years in the Iraqi army as an infantryman and special operations soldier. Hussein was as close to being a logical person as Iraqi people can get.

Hussein and I agreed on a basic patrol plan. It was sophisticated enough to accomplish the mission, but simple enough to ensure everyone's survival. We would sweep south through the palm groves for two kilometers and move west across Boardwalk into the villages. From that point we would push north back to the WTF through the villages, look for suspicious material, and ask the locals for information. While moving through the palm groves, we would split into two groups, one of four and one of six. Sergeant Kelley's group of four would trail closest to the Euphrates, looking for car batteries, generators, and triggermen who could be initiating IEDs. My group of six would travel along the western edge of the palm groves searching for the copper command wires along the ground.

We gingerly traversed the palm groves. As we commenced the movement south, I became furious. Daylight had revealed that if we had shifted our patrol from last night another hundred meters west, we could have completely dodged the reeds, jungle thicket, and mud pits that had caused us so much anguish. My resentment wore off quickly as I realized it was an amazing day to be in Iraq. The sun was shining, the temperature was hovering around seventy degrees, and we were on a long walk (okay, a combat patrol, but close enough). We came across farmers tilling their lands, sheepherders attending to their flocks, and kids playing games. I stopped to talk with everyone who would listen.

Suddenly the ignition of a single AK–47 round screamed in my ears. A symphony of gunfire followed. "Holy shit, how many fuckin' dudes are shooting at us?" I muttered to myself. My primal sensory abilities rose to a level I had never experienced. It was exhilarating. This shit was for real.

In the midst of the chaos it took me a moment to realize what was happening. It was likely that one sniper round had been fired in our direction and the remainder of the rounds were from the infamous "Iraqi fire blossom," a colloquial term for the phenomenon that occurs when Iraqi army soldiers are attacked. When under fire every *jundi* in the immediate vicinity starts firing all their rounds in all directions. The event creates a cloud of firepower that resembles a blooming flower. In many cases the biggest danger in Iraq is not the insurgents but the Iraqi fire blossom.

I took cover when the fire started and began to scan through my rifle scope for the attacker. I was staring into a palm grove thicket and could barely see thirty feet in front of me. Revenge was not probable, and it seemed the gunfight was over. I radioed to Sergeant Kelley, "We are gonna take cover here and lay down covering fire; you guys push south and try to flank this bastard." Kelley was excited to get in the action, as he knew we were in a perfect formation to catch the insurgents for once. He radioed back, "Roger, we are pushing south. Make sure the Iraqis don't shoot our asses." I replied, "Good to go. For your information, it sounded as though the fire was close range, maybe two hundred meters away. Don't push farther than five hundred meters if you can help it."

After my radio transmission with Kelley, I concentrated on the fight. I quickly realized a round aimed for my head had instead wasted the *jundi* who was patrolling ten feet in front of me. He cried in agony, flailing around as though he was on fire. Time to use some of Doc McGinnis's combat lifesaver knowledge, I thought, as my adrenaline kicked in and everything started to slow down.

Espi and I rushed to help the fallen *jundi* while everyone else posted security. This Iraqi was the luckiest bastard on the planet. The round had penetrated his leather gloves hanging from his flak jacket, and his two magazines and had gone through his entire SAPI (small-arms protective insert) plate. The round had stopped at the inside edge of his flak jacket, causing a small scratch and a silver dollar–sized burn on his chest directly over his heart. The pressure from the round had cracked his ribs, but he was going to live to tell the tale.

I radioed back to Major Gaines, "Shadow One, this is Shadow Two, we have one friendly routine casualty. Request QRF. Stand by for details." Following the transmission Sergeant Kelley radioed, "We are heading back to your position. We can't get through the brush up ahead—too fucking thick."

Within minutes Kelley and his crew had linked up with our force. We had a powwow with Hussein and decided that the best course of action would be to move back in pairs to a berm that was 150 meters behind us. Kelley's crew would go back first and we would follow. From there we would bound to the nearest home, where we could find and wait for the QRF. Once everyone got word of the plan, Kelley's Iraqi fire team began bounding back to the berm as we provided covering fire.

Kelley and his *jundi* sprinted to the earthen berm. I looked back to be certain everyone was okay and we had our sectors of fire covered. I gazed on the battlefield. All the *jundi* were hugging the ground, like cheese melted into a hamburger. These guys were scared shitless. In the midst of this, I saw Espi, snuggled up to a tree, trying to light a cigarette, seemingly oblivious to the immediate threat we had encountered. Perplexed, I hollered to Espi, "Dude, are you fuckin' Dirty Harry, man?" He replied, "Sir, I have seen this happen hundreds of time and it makes me go crazy. I have a new SOP—to light up a cigarette first thing after a firefight or I end up doing something stupid. I can put it out if you really want." I smirked and said, "Naw man, it's all good. Just keep your fucking head down. You can be my bounding buddy to the berm."

I wanted to hug Espi after his cigarette incident. His actions calmed me down and had me laughing aloud. My mind was thinking clearly again. "Espi, you ready to move out?" He responded, "Roger, Sir, I'm moving." I covered Espi as he bounded back to the berm where everyone else was taking cover. We continued to cover each other and move until we were the final ones to reach the berm.

Once at the berm Kelley grabbed four of the *jundi* and hauled ass to a large Iraqi home a hundred meters from the edge of the berm. After they established a foothold in the home, they waved the rest of us to move the casualty into it. Hussein and a couple of *jundi* grabbed the injured soldier. Hussein yelled to me, "Jamal, cover us." In response we provided cover fire while Hussein and his men moved the casualty to the home.

Another sniper round went flying over our heads, coming from the direction of Boardwalk. "Aw fuck, here we go again," yelled Moody in his thick Arab accent. We were facing fire from multiple snipers and they almost had us surrounded. Everyone took cover. I looked up and down the berm and everyone was clean. Before I could blink the Iraqis did what they do best under fire—get out of the area. The old saying "When in Rome, do as the Romans do" became immediately relevant. Bounding was a tactically sound idea, but we needed to get out of the kill zone—in a hurry. Everyone crouched under the berm and ran as fast as they could into the courtyard of the home Kelley and his men had under control.

Exhausted, Moody rushed to give me the bad news. "Jamal, my fuckin' radio is back at the berm!" I did the calculations in my head: a one-hundred-dollar UHF commercial Motorola radio or risk people's lives. The solution to that problem was easy—to hell with the radio!

Inside the home the family was courteous and understanding of our situation. Moody served as the "calm the locals" man, Kelley and Hussein set up security, and I coordinated for a QRF. Once things were settled I visited the casualty. A young boy had brought Ali, the wounded soldier, a large glass of water. I approached Ali and said, "Il hamdu Allah is salama!" (Thank God you are safe!) He grinned at me, blew a large cloud of smoke from his cigarette, and said, "Jamal, I am in fuckin' serious pain!" I laughed uncontrollably. Ali proceeded to show me the hole in his flak and his magazines. All of the *jundi* rotated through to see how he was doing and to hear his war story. Ali was now a living legend among mere men.

After speaking with Ali I went into the main room of the home. It was stunning. I am always impressed with what Iraqis can do with little means. I have a hard time keeping a film of dust out of my hooch back at the camp, yet these people can keep an entire home spotless. Moreover, the home had a spiral staircase with beautiful marble footings. At the foot of the staircase sat a two-person rocking chair. I walked up to the man of the house, who was sitting peacefully in the rocking chair, chatting with Moody. I introduced myself and told him he had a wonderful home. I apologized for our uninvited entrance. I think he understood our predicament; having a *jundi* with a bullet hole in his SAPI plate was more than enough to convince them we were in need of their help.

The QRF flew at sixty miles per hour down Boardwalk to our position, scaring every man, veiled women, and begging child in the area. It was obvious the *jundi* were at the helm. When they arrived in a fury of dust, we mounted the casualty into one of the Humvees and the QRF scurried out of the area and back to the WTF without incident. We were left to our own devices to get back to camp.

Without the burden of a casualty we cautiously left the home and headed across Boardwalk and into the village. The squad was uneasy. We rushed north with a focus on returning to base. We had seen enough action for the day. Our beautiful day in Haditha had turned into a game of Duck Hunt for the insurgents. To make matters worse, temperatures decided to rise past 100 degrees. The squad walked through the front gate of the WTF ready to relax. This was my first serious combat incident and I hoped it would be the last. Insha'allah.

Iraqi Interrogation 101

At the compound we had two new guests. The Iraqi QRF had managed to spot the two individuals running across the street at the time we were taking sniper fire. They detained them and brought them back to our patrol base for questioning. An Iraqi captain swiftly backhanded one of the detainees in the face as I approached. The bitch slap was followed by a rain of death threats and accusations. The scene was getting ugly. I sprinted to the scene, looking for hidden CNN reporters along the way. Dealing with a detainee abuse case was the last thing I wanted at this point.

Puzzled by what was happening, I said, "Captain Ahmed, let's first GPR [gunpowder residue test] these guys before you get too wild with your interrogation." He fired back in an emotional state, "Jamal, these men fired at you. They are insurgents. I know it. Let me take care of this the Iraqi way!" I replied calmly, "That might be the case, but let me test them first." I reached into my grab pouch and grabbed some flexi-cuffs. "Here; take these cuffs and secure their hands behind their backs." Ahmed snatched the flexi-cuffs from my hands while Espi went to grab the GPR kit.

"Owww!" The older detainee screamed in agony. I saw that his wrists were bleeding. Ahmed had decided to use the flexi-cuffs as a vice grip on the detainee's wrists. He had tightened them so snuggly they were cutting into the detainee's wrists, causing blood to spill on the ground. Captain Mawfood immediately yanked Ahmed from the scene to council him.

"Fuckin'-a, man," I said in a defeated tone, "now we gotta get these damn things off of this guy." I grabbed my Gerber all-purpose tool and went to work. I systematically tried to pry a knife under the cuffs, but because they were so tight, I only worsened the man's pain. He yelled again. I peered into his eyes and in California English said, "Dude . . . shut up!"

After five minutes of getting nowhere I came to an unfortunate conclusion: This Iraqi would have to endure some pain if he wanted to be free. The detained gasped, "Wallahhh" (Oh, God). As surgically as I possibly could, I got the knife blade under the flexi-cuff and ripped upward, cutting the plastic cuffs in half. The detainee cringed in agony but was relieved to have the cuffs removed. Espi reapplied the flexi-cuffs appropriately and we began the GPR tests.

The GPR tests were overwhelmingly positive. These kids had been playing in daddy's gun closet. The GPR was by no means a foolproof test, but given the circumstances, it was likely that these men had tried to kill me. After explaining to Captain Mawfood the GPR results, he ordered a group of *jundi* to take the detainees to the new U.S. COC, inside the security hut near the gate.

Major Gaines had us gather around. "Gentlemen," he said, "Nuts is taking out the next patrol, everyone involved in that group get ready. Jamal, you are the intel dude. Watch over these detainees and see if the Iraqis can get any information. Everyone else get some sleep." Everyone understood the order and went their respective ways. I stayed behind, wishing I could get some sleep too.

The makeshift guard shack that held the detainees was small, with a main room just big enough to hold a cot, a refrigerator, a bookshelf, and a side compartment room that acted as a sleeping post for the reserve guard on duty during Saddam's reign. The Iraqis liked the idea of taking the detainees into the compartment room. I waited in the main room on the cot and took the opportunity to take off my heavy load and rest after a hectic twenty-four hours of combat.

Thud, thud. A dense pounding sound came from the interrogation room. "Damn, I told them to play it cool with the detainees!" I said under my breath. I busted into the room and witnessed Martin, one of our terps, head butting the detainee and pounding him in the center of the back with his fist. "Martin, what are you doing man? You know if the detainee facility sees this all of our asses are gonna fry!" He looked up with a grin. "Jamal, this is how we always do it. Do you really want the Marines getting information from these guys? Gimme a break. The Marines suck at getting info! Plus the detention center never looks in the center of their back. The bruises in the areas where I am hitting these guys won't show up for weeks. Relax!"

I knew Martin. Any attempt to persuade him that torture was wrong would go nowhere. I addressed him anyway. "Listen dude, I don't care if you rough this guy up a bit and need to scare him to get some information, but you can't be pounding him in the back. That may be how you do it in Iraq and I understand Iraqis respond to this treatment, but I will be the one who goes to jail if they find out you guys beat the shit out of this guy and I knew about it."

Resgar, a Kurdish *jundi* and one of the few Iraqis I trusted, took me out of the room to explain the situation. "Jamal, I understand your concern. We do not want to hurt this young guy. We know he has a mother and a father who love him. But if we want usable intelligence, this kid needs to have a sense of fear and a sense that we are in complete control or he will not tell us anything." Resgar explained that he had done interrogations in the Iraqi army and for the U.S. government in the Kurdish regions for ten years before he became a communications expert. I believed him. The guy knew what he was talking about. Who was I to disagree?

I nodded in agreement and explained to Resgar that I agreed with his logic but felt for the young man's safety. I came up with a compromise. I knew it would be impossible for me to shield the prisoners from the Iraqis; there were many of them and only one of me. Yet if I could convince the Iraqis this guy had given us all the information he knew, maybe the *jundi* would be less likely to be violent with him. "Listen Resgar, I have an idea, let me go in and talk to the prisoner." Surprised, he responded, "You want to talk to him?" I said, "Yes, bring your electrocution prop and AK-47 into the room with me and follow my lead."

I barged into the detainee's room and yelled at the Iraqis to leave. I took the young man's blindfold off, looked him in the eyes, and said, "As salama aleikum." He responded in kind and swore he did not have any information. We continued to talk. He was surprised to see an American speaking Arabic. Through our conversation I learned the young man was in graduate school and had a family in the neighborhood. He even attempted to speak English in order to gain favor with me. As we talked Resgar fiddled with a small battery with exposed wires in the corner. He acted as though he was preparing an electrocution device. It was the ultimate "good cop-bad cop" interrogation routine.

I said to the detainee, "Listen man, I think you are an innocent man and

I hope you have told me everything you know . . . but I am not sure. I am going to give you five minutes to tell me what you know. If you don't I will let the Iraqis in here to do with you as they please. Please don't let this happen. I need you to tell me everything you know—please." The young man's eyes widened and he screamed in English, "Mister, no! Please, mister!" He continued in Arabic, "Rah agullek kullshi, wallah!" (I will tell you everything, I swear to God!) I smiled and reengaged the frantic detainee. "Listen kid, I am going to leave the room for one minute to grab a glass of water for you. You look thirsty."

In the one minute I stepped out to get a glass of water for the young man, Resgar played the bad guy. He blindfolded the detainee and said to him, "You better fuckin' tell the American everything you know." Resgar charged his AK-47 and pointed it at the kid's chest. The detainee screeched, "Jamal, he is going to kill me. Help!" I knew Resgar was trying to scare the shit out of the kid and had no plans to kill him. We understood each other's tactics without explaining them to each other. I sprinted into the room and yelled, "Get out of here, Resgar. If this kid doesn't speak, I'll let you have at him, but wait your turn." I took the blindfold off the detainee and handed him a glass of water. "Are you ready to talk?" He was ready. Tears gushed from the poor kid's eyes.

The detainee poured his guts out to me and Martin, whom I brought in for backup interpreter support. The guy told us everything he knew. He claimed to not be involved in the attack, knew those who were involved, and knew the location of an IED along Route Boardwalk one kilometer to the south of the WTF. His final piece of intelligence was a detailed description of one of the IED masterminds in Haditha who was responsible for numerous attacks.

At the end of the kid's information dump, Martin got more aggressive. "You are an insurgent," he insisted. "Don't lie. I will kill you." Thud. Martin head butted the detainee again. I pushed Martin to the floor and ordered him out of the room immediately. We were done at this point. I was willing to play mind games with the detainees, but my moral compass would not allow Martin to beat him senseless.

Dealing with the issue of torture for the first time in a real scenario made me think critically. I used to be in the "all torture is bad" camp, until I realized it would affect my survival. The issue is more complicated than simply saying torture is bad. This view is unrealistic and gets people killed. The argument I hate most is when people say torture is bad because there is a set standard of "ethics" in war. Wait a minute. War, at its heart, is about killing people until they agree with your viewpoint. Each side always has a different view of what is ethical and each side always thinks the other side is completely wrong.

To Iraqis torture techniques are a common sense approach to getting information. Iraqis feel that with torture they can ensure the prisoner will tell them everything they know and everything they want to hear. The positive aspect of this approach is you know you have exhausted the detainee's information; however, the negative side to this approach (and an argument Americans frequently cite) is that the interrogator now has to disentangle the true information from the information that the prisoner gave because he wanted to hear it. The Iraqis believe that getting information is the hard part and disentangling it is easy. For Iraqis it logically follows that torture makes sense.

Before we deployed our MiTT had received no guidance or training on what to do in a situation in which the *jundi* wanted to torture a detainee. My approach was to let Iraqis do what they needed to do while explaining to them that beating people and torturing them may only lead to false information. This was simple idealism. The reality was that no matter how much wasta I attained, I would never change thousands of years of history and culture. Torture, in some form or another, is part of Iraq. Those who succeed in Iraq learn to deal with Iraqi culture; those who fail in Iraq try to change Iraqi culture. I wish officials in the highest levels of our government would realize this.

In this particular detainee case, it seemed like the Iraqi's limited torture techniques worked, as we received outstanding information. We tried to get exact information, but reading maps is not a common skill in Iraq. Instead, the detainees gave us directions along the lines of "Go to the Hajji Mosque and turn a right at Abdul Azziz's house. Once you reach his place, head to the place where we play soccer. This is where the IED is." In the end the directions we received from the detainees were almost worthless. So instead we stopped by local homes to ask how to get to certain landmarks that they had mentioned.

Asking for directions from the locals ended up being fruitful. We had the chance to chat with the townspeople, hear their concerns, and learn about the local area. The stunning thing is that nearly every person in the village was either related to (or knew of) the detainees we had captured. How word of their detention traveled so fast is a mystery.

After a sluggish two-kilometer move south, we made it to the Hajji Mosque.

Finding a mosque is normally an easy task: look for the large minaret. However, the Hajji Mosque was unique, because a 500-pound MK-82 JDAM (joint direct attack munition) had destroyed the minaret during the initial stages of Operation Iraqi Freedom. The evidence that a mosque had ever existed was the rubble of the minaret and a village full of disenfranchised locals.

"As salama aleikum," I said to a heavyset older woman cleaning off her porch with the help of her kids. The women approached me to chat. I asked her if she was familiar with the name of the detainee. She went into a tizzy. "Where is my son? What have you done with him? He is a good boy, a college student, he would not hurt a flower! Please, tell me he is okay!" I explained to the woman, "Your son is in good hands and we are ensuring the Iraqi soldiers do not kill or harm him. If your son is innocent he will be returned to you within seventy-two hours."

The crying mother made me human again. This mother, who was as concerned about her son as my mom would be if I were in the same situation, touched me. She cried the same tears, asked the same questions, and professed the greatness and innocence of her child. I hoped she was right and her son was innocent. I am also thankful that I did not let the *jundi* go apeshit on her son. I would have felt like a real jerk if I told the woman her son was doing dandy but at the same time had watched the *jundi* beat him or electrocute him.

I heard a refined English accent come from a doorway. "Hello, what is your name?" A young, clean-cut man came out to see what was happening on the porch. "I am Jamal," I responded in Arabic. "I was explaining to your mother that we have detained your brother." He seemed content with this answer. "I am not worried. I know you will treat him in a fair manner. I work for a man named Scott. He is a Marine." The man's comments astonished me. I realized that this guy must be a Marine human intelligence source that provided valuable intelligence to the Marines. This was one family we didn't want to screw over.

"Sir, we gotta head south," Sergeant Kelley said. I bid farewell to the mother and told her that God would take care of her son. She released her death grip from my arm, wished me good luck, and we continued to press south to the suspected IED site. Twenty minutes later we reached the vicinity of the potential IED sites. We asked the locals if they had seen any activity in the area in order to pinpoint where it was located. We stopped by the nearest house on the other side of a wadi (dried riverbed).

Foliage surrounded the home. This house belonged to the second detainee we had captured—the one whose wrist bled from the flexi-cuffs. I could not believe it. Amazingly, out of the hundreds of shanty homes to choose in the area, we happened to pick the two that were the homes of the detainees.

The scene at this home was similar to that at the last one. The mother was frantic and wanted to know that her son was okay. The father, a former military man, was the only voice of reason present. After explaining the circumstances of his son's detention, he understood our situation and requested that we would take care of his son in a respectable manner. He followed up on the intelligence we had received from his son and elaborated on where he thought the insurgents had placed the IED.

We made our way through the thick foliage that surrounded the man's house. The man pointed to an open area and said, "That is where the insurgents have been recently." Kelley asked the Iraqi squad leader to gather some *jundi*-bots (Marine term for Iraqi soldiers who check potential unexploded ordnance and suspected IED sites) to assess the situation. While it seems insensitive to send a *jundi* to check on explosives, it makes more sense that a *jundi* rather than a Marine do this duty.

The two *jundi* searched around the suspected IED location for thirty minutes. They kicked trash piles, picked up metal fragments, and rummaged around in the dirt. This seemed to be a dry hole and we needed to move. We reformed the patrol and moved east across Boardwalk into the palm groves. We still needed to cover two and a half kilometers of ground to get back to the WTF. The last thing we wanted was to be in the palm groves in complete darkness—we had learned our lesson.

We arrived at the WTF with a mere glimpse of moonlight left. I had not slept in twenty-four hours, and it was time to hit the rack.

Special Forces Join in the Fun

I decided to convince Hussein, the Iraqi squad leader, to add a layer of deception on our next patrol. I thought our patrolling patterns were getting routine and we needed to change things if we wanted to keep the insurgents on their toes. We decided that for this patrol we would head south into the village as we typically did but would cut the patrol short and head north back to the WTF as it was getting dark. This would convince the locals we were done patrolling for the day. Once we arrived at the back entrance of the WTF, which was concealed by a small wadi, instead of calling it quits for the night, we would sneak out the western side of the WTF and make our way to an observation point (OP) five hundred meters north of the WTF on a barren hill that overlooked Boardwalk. The intent of the deception was to trick the insurgents into thinking our patrolling efforts were finished for the night and that they could freely conduct IED activities for a few hours before we sent out the early morning patrol.

Hussein agreed on our proposed plan. He decided to claim the deception tactic as his own idea and explained it to the *jundi* in the squad. I had no problem with him stealing my intellectual property; this is how the adviser gig is supposed to work. The *jundi* were excited.

We pushed south into the village area near the WTF at 1800. The sun would set in the next two hours. We patrolled though the village. Everything seemed peaceful and tranquil—something had to be wrong. Even so, we moved north toward the WTF, walking across the tallest hill in the village to ensure we were seen by all the townspeople. We reached the wadi west of the WTF and disappeared inside, covering our movement to the townspeople and insurgents who were certainly tracking our movements. I radioed our situation to Major Gaines. "Sir, we are at the back gate, over." Gaines responded, "Jamal, I got something for you. The Special Forces showed up and they want to send two of their snipers to the OP with you and the *jundi*. I'm sure you'd agree these guys are better marksmen than the *jundi* anyway, over." I confirmed. "Roger, Sir. Send them our way; we have to wait here in the wadi until it gets completely dark anyway. Out."

The thought of working with the Special Forces snipers was appealing. While the Hollywood appeal of Special Forces personnel had lessened since I had been working with them, I still thought it might be cool to have Special Forces snipers on our patrol. In fact, I knew this mission would be amazing. I would be the leading tactical adviser on a foreign military patrol in a war zone, speaking a foreign language and fighting alongside Iraqi soldiers as an equal. On top of that we were going to clandestinely move to a hill in the desert overlooking Route Boardwalk under the cover of darkness and hunt insurgents with help from a couple of Green Beret snipers. If this is not living the adventure, what is? I wondered.

The Special Forces snipers showed up at the west gate of the WTF. I sat them down with Hussein and had Hussein explain his plan to occupy the OP. It was a relief to work with the Special Forces. I knew I did not have to explain to the snipers why I was letting the Iraqis lead the show. They understand more than anyone that the role of being a military adviser is to advise, teach, and support—not to command.

Once the plan was in place we moved quickly and quietly into the desert under the cover of darkness. I felt a sense of peace in the silence. The footsteps of warriors walking in the desert broke the quietness. The *jundi* were not as graceful as I had hoped. On our way to the assembly area I counted five loud crashes caused by *jundi* who tripped in ditches and small holes in the barren landscape. Despite the racket we continued to push forward without notice. Route Boardwalk was a good six hundred meters away. If anyone had heard our commotion, the people would write it off as feral dogs thrashing around in the open desert.

We approached our tentative assembly area at the base of a small hill from which we would observe Route Boardwalk. From our position, we were not going to get close enough to the enemy to cut his throat, but we would have visibility on the road. At the assembly area the snipers and I had a U.S.-only meeting. We were carrying out a complicated operation and the last thing we wanted was the *jundi* to mess it up.

I addressed the Special Force snipers. "Listen, you guys know we are dealing with *jundi* here. I can guarantee that one of them is going to light up a cigarette while we are out here observing." Both the men nodded in agreement and I continued. "I'm going to have these guys sit at the base of this hill and get into a security posture beneath the hill. They can be the security element for the mission while you guys go up on the hill and observe with your thermal scopes and infrared optics. I'll be the middleman on the hill. If you guys need support or extra firepower let me know and I will signal to Hussein to rally the *jundi* cavalry." The snipers liked my plan. The plan allowed them to observe Boardwalk for enemy activity without having to worry about the *jundi* compromising our position and ruining the mission.

After explaining this plan to Hussein, we were set to execute. Hussein, a former Iraqi Special Forces soldier with vast experience conducting reconnaissance missions, was the perfect guy to have as the Iraqi squad leader. He set his men into a security posture and prepared them for their duties.

It became apparent that twenty-five years of service in the old Iraqi army was not helping Hussein. Marines know that while in a security position, weapons point outward, sectors of fire are assigned, silence is maintained, and movements are minimized. The Iraqi security posture is different. Their security involves small groups of three soldiers who sit in a circle talking about life and smoking cigarettes while one of the soldiers in the squad keeps a general eye out to see if anything dangerous is on the horizon. Suffice it to say I was glad I let the snipers push to the top of the hill alone. Sending the *jundi* would have compromised their position and ruined the mission.

Once the *jundi* were set in their "gaggle" (Marine term for something that isn't very organized), I crawled on my hands and knees up the hill to check on the snipers through my night vision goggles. I watched their left flank and marked the route back to the assembly area with infrared chemlights so they knew how to get back to the *jundi* without getting lost.

We sat, sat, and sat some more. I was annoyed that my first chance to live in a Hollywood movie scene was going to end so anticlimactically. All I wanted was to light up insurgents emplacing IEDs along Boardwalk, and we were in the perfect position to do just that. We sat for three hours and watched the villagers carry out their nightly rituals: evening tea with the neighbors, prayer at the local mosque, more tea with the neighbors, and then off to bed.

It was 2200—drop-dead time. I signaled to the snipers that it was time to move back to camp. We approached the Iraqi security circle at the base of the hill, praying they did not shoot us. Our worries were unfounded. Half of the *jundi* were fast asleep and the other half were smoking cigarettes and telling stories. Any hopes that this would be a clandestine mission were lost. The *jundi* still awake shouted to me, "Jamal, are we heading back to camp yet? We're tired and hungry." My only response was to laugh. These men were not military men, they were children. I found Hussein. He awakened his men and we went back to the WTF. The insurgents would live another day and we would go home empty-handed once again.

Who's Defending the Patrol Base?

We arrived back at the WTF at 0100 in the morning after patrolling for seven hours. I was beat. I went to sleep on the floor of the guard shack, which had become our makeshift COC. I was unable to sleep; bed bugs and mites crawled over my body and devoured my flesh. "Fuckin' fuck fuck, I'm going to kill these bugs," I complained. Unable to sleep, I did some rounds on the defensive perimeter.

In addition to continuous patrols in the town, the *jundi* maintain the defensive perimeter of the facility. Marine advisers are stuck in a "shit sandwich." Their problem is that they need to let the Iraqis lead operations so they can improve their tactics, gain leadership experience, and become a better army.

But in certain duties, such as establishing and maintaining defensive perimeters, how the Iraqis carry out their mission has a direct effect on Marines' chances of seeing their families again.

The Iraqi idea of a defensive perimeter means placing a few *jundi* at the corners of the WTF with their sleeping bags. These *jundi* stay up for a few hours, and when they get tired, they sleep and hope the insurgents do not attack. This is not defense. While the MiTT is selflessly willing to accept risks to our lives so the Iraqis can learn lessons the hard way and adapt, at some level we also need to look out for our own asses and step in. The last thing we need is an orange jumpsuit and a machete at our throats because the *jundi* failed to maintain a defense.

It was 0300, but I decided to snatch Captain Mawfood and show him how horrific his defense perimeter was on the WTF. He had promised Major Gaines that things were airtight. I didn't believe it. I went into the local residence where Captain Mawfood was sleeping. He was snoring on the floor in deep slumber. I had slept three hours in the past three days and the sight of him all cozy on the ground infuriated me. I nudged him with my hand and said, "Mawfood, we need to exercise some leadership and see how your men are doing on post." I was Mawfood's worst nightmare. After sucking down a glass of sugar-filled tea, Mawfood strapped on his boots and was ready to go.

The first position we examined, which guarded the entire west entrance into the WTF, was a perfect example of what not to do in a defensive position. I walked up to the abandoned PKC machine gun overlooking the western entrance. I questioned Mawfood in jest. "Captain Mawfood, is there a ghost operating this?" Mawfood smiled in embarrassment. I did not even have to add additional comments to get the point across to Mawfood. Instead, I pointed toward the ground where six sleeping bags were filled with Iraqis, dreaming about pork chops and unveiled women. If I wanted to, I could cut each of their throats before any of them even woke up. It was pathetic. The scene could have been yet another funny story about Iraqis being lazy, undisciplined, and selfish, but in this case the Iraqis' behavior was lessening the probability that I would come home to my wife. I was pissed.

Captain Mawfood, who was generally lethargic and slothful in everything I had seen him do, rushed to rectify the problem. He was professionally embarrassed. Mawfood roared, "*Jundi*, what the hell are you doing? Why are you sleeping on the job? In the old Iraqi army you would be beaten. What battalion are you from?" The single *jundi* who had the balls to speak up said, "Sir, we are from 3rd Battalion. We fell asleep. We are sorry." Mawfood was enraged. "Do you expect a ghost to fire this PKC? I expect more from men who want to call themselves Iraqi soldiers. You are an embarrassment!" Mawfood's tirade lit a fire under the *jundi*'s asses. They scurried like cockroaches. I was impressed. An Iraqi leader was actually solving problems and making things happen—absolutely, positively amazing.

Saved by a Six-Year-Old

Following a night of fixing the defensive perimeter of the WTF, it was time for yet another patrol. Thankfully, I was able to catch a few hours of sleep. The patrol would not leave until 1100. Our mission was to push south into the palm groves, clandestinely occupy a home along Route Boardwalk, and perform overwatch of the road in order to look for insurgents emplacing IEDs.

We pushed south through the palm groves. As we approached the location I had been sniped at the other day, my heart rate spiked. I suggested to the *jundi* we move toward the Euphrates edge and push past the position. Being fired upon for a second time was not my cup of tea. We moved into the thickest section of the palm groves. Ayad, a *jundi* from the battalion scouts and the Iraqi squad leader at the time, and I pushed forward of the patrol to determine which home we wanted to occupy. It was obvious none of the homes offered a clandestine approach. I told Ayad, "Pick your favorite."

"Clear." A *jundi* gave me the green light to cross an intersection adjacent to the home we were occupying. I darted across the intersection, jumped over a gate, and landed in a sheep pen where everyone else in the patrol had congregated. After a quick accountability check we knocked on the back door of the home. A young boy came to the door. Ayad explained the situation and the boy let us in. Once inside the boy introduced us to his father and four brothers. In accordance with the high standards of Arab hospitality, the father ordered his younger sons to bring us cold water and tea. Ayad ordered two *jundi* to the roof to establish overwatch on the road.

Mesmerized by the sight of an Arabic-speaking Marine, the boys attacked me with a barrage of questions. The eldest son greeted me and said, "Please, Jamal, come outside to the patio and we must talk. I want to learn." The four brothers escorted me to the front porch for a chat. I signaled to PFC Lynch to act as my bodyguard in case something happened.

One of the youngest boys was confused. "Jamal, are you Iraqi?" I laughed and told him I was from America, but that I would have been proud to be from Iraq. I pulled out my propaganda packet and showed them pictures of my family and my childhood. One of the other brothers asked me, "Can I see your rifle scope?" The sophisticated rifle scope on my M-4 assault rifle wowed the boy. I obliged and let the young boy look through the scope. He was bewildered. "Can we take a picture?" he asked. I replied, "Why not?" I gathered all the boys and gave the youngest boy my weapon so he could pretend he was Rambo. Ayad and Ali joined in as a *jundi* snapped the photograph. The kids clamored around me. "Jamal, you have to get us that picture. Whenever you come back, please bring us a copy." I told them I would do my best to get them the picture (see photo 15).

Perhaps in ten or twenty years, when Iraq is safe, I will stop by this home and drop them a picture. *Insha'allah.*

The young Iraqis realized I was a person with whom they could speak freely. The eldest boy asked a provocative question: "Why are the Marines going to stay in Haditha?" Puzzled, I responded, "How long do you think we will be staying in the area?" He shrugged his shoulders and said, "Thirty years maybe?" I laughed, praying to God that his estimate was inaccurate. I explained to the boys America's new strategy of helping the Iraqi Army stand up, so we could stand down. I reiterated my point and told him that the one thing the military wants is for Iraqis to solve Iraqi problems so Marines can go home to their families. I felt like the ultimate diplomat.

After bouncing between serious discussions of politics and local area security, the boys asked me about famous American cities, the Rocky Mountains, and Michael Jackson—their favorite performer. I spared them the details on Michael Jackson and told them we had to be on our way. Before we left Ayad asked one of the young boys, "Brother, can you run across the street and buy me a pack of cigarettes in the market?" The boy took the dinar bill from Ayad's hand and sprinted through the front gate. He was more than happy to help us. He opened the front gate, peeked for danger, and zoomed across Boardwalk to the neighboring market.

The boy returned dripping with sweat, obviously distraught. He sprinted to his eldest brother and whispered something into his ear. The eldest brother clutched my arm and pointed to Ayad to come closer. His younger brother had told him something important. He whispered, "Jamal, my little brother says the insurgents have an ambush awaiting you on the other side of the market. They are planning to ambush you when you cross the street!" Ayad looked at me. He hoped I would say there was no need to confront the ambush. I pointed toward the palm groves and said, "Ayad, La. Rah nrooh hinak" (Ayad, no. We will go there.) Ayad was relieved. As my brother, he was ready and willing to follow me into combat if I thought it was a good idea, but he did not want to die today. I agreed, today was not a good day to die.

Talk about real-time intelligence. We shit-canned the idea of crossing Boardwalk and moving through the village to the WTF. I was amazed that a little Iraqi boy had saved our lives. I will never say learning Iraqi Arabic was a waste of time. Without the ability to humanize myself with these young boys, I fear he would have viewed us as the occupier. I finally had the locals working for the good guys.

We moved with intensity. Ayad regrouped the Iraqis and gave them the hasty plan. We would return the same way we came, through the palm groves, and would scratch the plan to walk through the village. The Iraqi point man peered through a hole in the fence looking at the intersection. "Clear," he said. Like a group of deer crossing the road, the entire patrol started hopping the fence and running for the palm groves, quickly vanishing into the foliage, spoiling any insurgent attempt to surprise us. As I entered the dense foliage I looked back to see the young boys waving frantically in our direction. We owed that family our lives.

Comic Relief

Living at the WTF was the definition of rough. We were patrolling eight to ten hours a day, sleeping two to three hours a night (if we were lucky), babysitting *jundi*, and living on MRE's. The last night at the WTF, everyone was loopy from the lack of sleep, lack of water, and lack of chow. I was starting to approach my limit of sanity. We needed some comedy to break the monotony. Comedy came in the form of a portable toilet kit.

We had recently acquired a portable toilet kit so we did not have to bug the locals for restroom emergencies. The kit was a plastic version of a toilet with plastic bags strapped to the bottom designed to catch excrement. The kits were not fancy and worked a lot like five-gallon buckets. We always set our toilet kit directly outside the guard shack to maintain easy access. Whenever it was sunny the toilet area was exposed to the world to see. Every insurgent, village local, and donkey could see you taking a dump. But at night, because of the limited moonlight that would hit the area, using the toilet kit gave you a private moment.

Anyway, on our last night Major Gaines was out using the toilet kit. Meanwhile I was in the guard shack trying to find the light switch to the rear room. I sat there flipping switches up and down wondering why none of them worked. I continued going through the switches, but again none of them worked. I eventually found the right switch, very content with myself.

Major Gaines came crashing into the guard shack with his pants at his ankles. "Who the fuck is turning on the lights outside of the building?" he shouted. "I had a damn spotlight on me as I was taking a shit on the toilet kit! The whole village saw my white ass." I responded, "Sir, did you feel famous?" We all burst out into laughter. Then Gaines laughed. "Jamal, if I didn't love you, I'd kill you right now." We all laughed and started telling war stories of the past few days. We were excited to leave this hellhole.

Mission Accomplished

"Hallelujah!" Doc screamed the next morning as the MiTT convoy approached the WTF. Once the MiTT arrived to pick us up, we said goodbye to the locals, cleared our trash from the area, and checked that no sleeping *jundi* were left behind. On our way back Second Lieutenant Le Gette gave me the lowdown on the rest of the team's situation over the past week. Apparently, while we had been ambushed and shot at, their days had been filled with hanging out in the Haditha FOB COC and lifting weights. Le Gette said he was getting bedsores from sleeping too much.

I felt my first bout of infantryman angst. I now understand why the grunts are always angry and feel they are being shortchanged by the support units. I will admit that the noninfantry Marine Corps, while necessary, is not what the Marine Corps is about. God bless the Marine infantrymen.

On arrival at Camp Ali, we showered, slept, and ate to our hearts' content for the remainder of the day. We all needed to regain our senses. The best part about returning was finding the stack of packages from family and fellow Americans. My favorite piece of mail was a handwritten letter from my wife. It nearly brought tears to my eyes. I could only think about how shitty it would have been if I had been killed and never received her letter. Damn insurgents.

Chapter 15

Mo' Leave, Mo' Problem

September 2006

Jundi-bots in Action

One day in September we went cruising down Route Bronze on another leave run to drop the *jundi* off on vacation. The convoy was running smoothly until we reached checkpoint eleven, which is a Marine outpost with a primary mission to keep Route Bronze free of IEDs. They had not done a very good job.

We approached a bridge that crosses a large wadi along Route Bronze. Bridges are always likely areas for IED activity. Acknowledging this, the Iraqis stopped short of the bridge and conducted a sweep before the convoy passed through. We sat in our Humvee and watched Sermen and Juwad walk onto the bridge. They skipped along without a care. At the end of the bridge things changed. Sermen jumped off the ground like LeBron James preparing to dunk a basketball. Juwad ran over to Sermen's position and started frantically hopping in place. From their actions, I figured they had found a huge cobra or scorpion. If they had found an IED, they would be sprinting to the Humvee.

The Motorola radio screamed Iraqi Arabic, "Aku abu'at chebeera hna!" (There are huge IEDs here!) Major Gaines yelled to Martin in the backseat, "What the hell did they just say, Martin?" Martin responded in his sassy fashion, "They think they found some IEDs. I told them to get away from them; hence the reason they are sprinting to the Humvee right now." Gaines and I peered through our window and watched Sermen and Juwad clamoring to get back to the safety of their Humvee.

Sermen came sprinting to our Humvee after talking with the Iraqi convoy commander. Out of breath and sweating profusely, he described what he saw. "Jamal, holy shit, man. There are like ten to twelve artillery shells and a few propane tanks stacked on top of one another. The insurgents want to destroy the bridge, I think." Gaines interrupted. "Sermen, are you serious? We need to get the Humvees back. If that thing goes off we will all die from the blast overpressure." Gaines transitioned to the radio and requested the MiTT vehicle in the rear of the convoy help the *jundi* shift the convoy at least another four hundred meters away from the bridge.

Once we reestablished ourselves in a safer position, I drew up the nine-line EOD report while Gaines helped the Iraqi convoy commander organize the convoy. When Gaines returned he asked, "Jamal, you got that nine-line ready?" I replied, "Roger, Sir. One problem though. Our comm sucks balls here!"

We were sandwiched between two hills on both sides of the road and our communications equipment was unable to operate. As a workaround we sent a vehicle in the rear of the convoy farther up the road and had them relay the message to checkpoint eleven, which could relay the message to the 2/3 headquarters in the dam.

The response we received from checkpoint eleven was ridiculous: "Shadow, this is checkpoint eleven; expected time of arrival for EOD is at least four hours. How copy?" How copy? How about EOD get off their ass and help us out! We were stuck with 171 unarmed *jundi* in civilian clothes prepared to go on leave and sitting in the middle of the desert with a large bull's-eye on our chests. We were not waiting four hours for an EOD team. If one insurgent mortar attack landed near our convoy, it might destroy 60 percent of the Iraqi battalion.

We sent a message back to checkpoint eleven, highlighting our inability to wait four hours for an EOD team. We sat and waited for a response. Meanwhile, the Iraqis were getting restless. Garbled Arabic came over Martin's radio. Nuts asked Martin, "Martin, what did they say?" Martin responded, "Basically, the *jundi* are tired of waiting and have decided to go investigate the IED themselves." Gaines hollered, "What? Why would they   " Before Gaines could finish his sentence, we noticed the Iraqis were already sending out *jundi*-bots to investigate the IED.

Sermen and Juwad were halfway across the bridge. There was no convincing them to return to safety, and none of us was crazy enough to drag them back to the Humvees. This was an Iraqi solution to a problem—not a Marine solution. Was it the safest solution? Not quite. Could it work? Yes. So we let them go with it. Sermen, standing on top of enough explosive

Photo 1. Inside Al Faw Palace Major Gaines and Captain McShane sit in the chair Yasser Arafat gave Saddam Hussein as a gift.

Photo 2. Early morning view of the MiTT camp. The rest of Camp Ali, including the Iraqi soldier swahuts, are left of the picture (not shown).

Photo 3. The inside of the Iraqi chow hall at Camp Ali.

Photo 4. The author explaining to the Iraqi soldiers how Marines conduct cordon operations.

Photo 5. A destroyed bank in Bani Dahir, where the author chatted with a couple of Iraqi army medics.

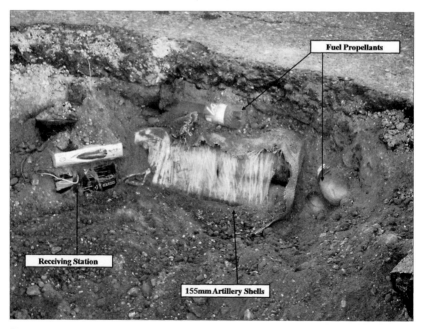

Photo 6. A discovered radio-controlled IED found along Route Bronze in the Haditha Triad.

Photo 7. Searching Iraqi soldiers for contraband, weapons, and military property before they are sent on leave to Najaf.

IED Blast Craters

Photo 8. Typical scene along Route Bronze, the main route between Camp Ali and Asad Airbase.

Photo 9. The standard operating procedure for the Iraqi army upon returning from leave: reunite with friends, tell war stories from back home, and wander aimlessly around the Iraqi brigade camp.

Photo 10. Iraqi soldiers jammed into the Leylands, excited about catching the leave buses in Al Asad.

Photo 11. [*left to right*] The author, Qatan, and Major Gaines fishing in the Euphrates to supplement the Iraqi diet.

Photo 12. The author enjoying the company of Iraqi soldiers during a meal.

Photo 13. The MiTT and the Iraqi army secure the Barwana market so the MiTT can purchase food to supplement the Iraqi soldiers' diet

Photo 14. The convoy prepared to carry the Iraqi army to war has a malfunction along Route Bronze and the Iraqi soldiers try to solve the problem.

Photo 15. During a combat patrol through Haditha, we stopped to conduct an overwatch mission in order to capture or kill IED emplacers along the main route through town. At the conclusion of our mission, a young boy [*second from left*] alerted us to an insurgent ambush awaiting us across the street. We quickly adjusted our patrol route and returned to base safely.

Photo 16. Iraqi soldiers express their excitement before they conduct their first independent convoy.

Photo 17. [*Left to right*] Ali Jabber, Mohammed, and the author on board a speedboat on Lake Qadisiyah.

Photo 18. Ali Jabber directs the island inhabitants to line up and show their identification to his Iraqi soldiers in order to determine who the Egyptian insurgents are.

Photo 19. The U.S. Marine embedded advisers and the leadership of 2nd Battalion, 2nd Brigade, 7th Division Iraqi army pose for a group photograph on Camp Ali.

force to turn him into a pink mist, relayed in colloquial English over the Iraqi radio net, "Cooool, man. Dis a really, really, really big one!" Major Gaines quickly asked Martin, "Did he just say, 'Wow, this is a really big one?'" Martin laughed and said, "I think so."

Talk about having a high level of risk tolerance. I wish I could say this was a sign of Iraqi bravery, but I think it was more a sign of dumbassery. All the same, his actions were not very surprising. To the Iraqis, when and how they die is a matter of insha'allah. Thus there is no problem with standing on an IED, because God is going to choose when to kill you anyway. There is no point taking precautions against death. I guess this could also explain why the *jundi* never wear their protective gear in combat.

After dancing on the live IED for a few minutes, Sermen and Juwad came to their senses and jogged back to the Humvee to give us their full report. Their estimate was that there were two propane tanks with three hundred pounds of PE-4 explosives per tank and fifteen 155-mm artillery shells set up to ensure the death of any vehicle that happened to stumble upon them. This was a huge IED and one that EOD needed to address. We decided to wait a bit longer for a response from checkpoint eleven on the status of the EOD team.

We sat, and sat, and sat. I drooped into the driver's seat of the Humvee, cranked up our defunct air-conditioner, and prayed EOD or a relieving unit would show up soon. I was about to go insane with boredom when I captured a glimpse of a sheep farmer walking through the wadi. He was slowly moving his way toward the IED.

I figured the sheepherder would not approach the IED. After all, it was likely he had played a part in providing the reconnaissance for the insurgents who actually placed the IED in the ground. I was wrong. The sheepherder slowly pushed his herd up the hill and headed directly toward the intersection of where the bridge met the road. He was about to turn his flock of sheep into one large shish kebab. I woke up Martin, who was in deep slumber. "Martin, dude, call Lieutenant Abass and tell him to yell at that herder before he blows himself up!"

After Martin's warning, Lieutenant Abass hopped out of the vehicle and hollered at the sheep farmer, "You are heading directly for an IED. Please move away. It will destroy your entire flock!" The sheepherder obviously did not get the message. He pushed his sheep to a small grassy area almost directly on top of the IED. Abass continued to yell to the sheepherder, to no avail. The herder was simply too far away to understand the message.

Thankfully, the man found out the news for himself. The sheepherder started running in circles. He realized he could lose his entire livelihood if the insurgents decided to detonate their IED. He jumped back and forth within the herd trying to get his flock to respond. The sheep were fixated on the grass. Every time the herder moved a few sheep away, they would sneak around him and run to get more grass. The scene was hilarious. Eventually, the sheep got the message after the herder smashed them on the face with a stick a few times and they exited the area. Phew, no shish kebab tonight.

Three hours later a unit from 2/3 arrived to relieve us. We regrouped the convoy and decided to create our own trail through the wadi so we could continue on the route. We had to go off road if we wanted to get through the three-hundred-meter-wide riverbed. For the Humvees this would be an easy task; however, our convoy had five Leylands full of *jundi* going on leave, a wrecker vehicle, an ambulance, and a BMW sedan we had confiscated from suspected insurgents the prior week. This was going to be quite a challenge.

We snaked the convoy down the steep edges of the wadi along a make-shift cart path. Things were proceeding smoothly. We reached the wadi floor and cautiously drove a few miles per hour, on the lookout for any command wires leading to the IED on the bridge. Suddenly Doc yelled, "Gents, you see that shit? I see it glimmering in the sunlight!" I replied, "What are you talking about Doc?" He replied, "Look twenty feet on your left." I glanced in the direction of where Doc mentioned. Sure enough, a thin bronze wire was on the ground, leading to the IED on the bridge. I slammed the gas pedal and crossed the wire safely. We were good to go.

The entire convoy had almost made it through the wadi when Mark frantically yelled over the radio, "IED! IED!" Because they were in the rear Humvee away from our view, we assumed something bad had happened. The Marine and Iraqi radio nets sparked to life and the convoy started moving faster. Mark had triggered everyone's survival mechanisms. Mark came over the radio again, "Uh, sorry. Actually, I just saw some command wires. Sorry about the confusion, I'm an idiot." Doc, Gaines, Nuts, and I all looked at each other and said the same thing, "God, I want to kill that terp!"

After some more drama the entire convoy made it along the bypass route and we continued along Route Bronze. We would make it to Al Asad, but we would be more than four hours late.

IED Jackpot

I called EOD to get a report on the IED the Iraqis found on the bridge. The EOD tech on the phone answered, "Sir, we didn't find much of anything. Granted, it was dark when we got there. All we found was a few strands of copper wire and that's it." I could not believe what I was hearing. I could still see the outline of the IED in the bridge when we were crossing the wadi the other day. I responded to the EOD tech, "Listen man, I know there is an IED out there. The longer it sits there, the longer it has a chance to blow up Marines. Ask your boss when you guys are free. We're going to lead you out there and show you the IED."

We convinced EOD to convoy with us to the IED location near checkpoint eleven. We arrived at the bridge around 0830, well ahead of the EOD team, which decided to convoy on their own because they were afraid of convoying with the *jundi*.

Whack! The EOD Humvee flew past my Humvee and took my left mirror with it. "What the fuck was that about?" I yelled to anyone who would listen. Major Gaines grabbed the radio to bitch at the perpetrator vehicle. "EOD, what are you doing flying by our Humvee? You took out a mirror." The young Marine driver answered, "Uh, Sir, we didn't want to get off the road for fear of pressure-plate IEDs." Gaines thickened his Texan accent and gave the kid an earful. "Listen, dumbshit, if you ever do that again I will personally kick your ass and a pressure-plate IED will be the least of your worries."

After things settled EOD sent their EOD robot to rig the IEDs for explosion. Meanwhile, we went into the wadi to collect the copper command wires so the insurgents could not use them again. We came across the wire I had spotted the day before. Doc got out of the Humvee with a pair of pliers and prepared to cut the wires. At the same time EOD called on the radio, "Shadow, get in the truck! Don't cut the wire by hand—it may be booby-trapped. Snag it on the back of the Humvee and break it." We all yelled at Doc, "Don't cut the wire!" He calmly opened the Humvee door. "What's all the fuss?" he asked. "I already cut it." We burst into laughter. "So much for listening to EOD," Gaines said.

After rolling up nearly a thousand meters of copper wire, we remounted the Humvee and drove up the side of the road to check on the Iraqis who were looking for wires farther into the wadi. We approached the crest of the hill leading into the wadi. An Iraqi Humvee was heading straight for us at fifty miles an hour. Chatter was streaming over the Iraqi radio net. Something was going on.

Lieutenant Abass sprinted through a cloud of dust that had billowed from his Humvee's immediate stop a few meters from the front of our Humvee. Frantically, he addressed me, "Jamal, Jamal, we saw the insurgents. We saw them." I replied, "Abass, calm down, man." Gaines ordered Martin, "Get out here and translate this so everyone knows what's going on and not just Jamal." Abass told the story to Martin, who relayed the news. Abass explained, "When we crested the hill, our gunner saw a four-door, white, Kia pickup moving toward the bridge location. The truck had a bunch of copper wire in the back. When they saw our Humvee on top of the hill, they immediately turned around and rushed to the village before we could even react. We were going to follow them, but we wanted to get your help in case there was an ambush setup."

We all digested the situation. Major Gaines concluded that it was time to play a little Cowboys and Indians. Gaines made the call to mount up; we were going insurgent hunting. Abass ordered his Humvee to start moving in the direction of the white Kia. We followed.

We piloted across the hilly desert terrain at fifty miles per hour; the ride was better than a roller coaster. Dust was flying, rocks were hitting the windshield, and Nuts was yelling more curse words than a sailor as he was bucked back and forth in the gunner's turret. Up ahead the *jundi* stopped at an odd-looking rock formation. We all got out to investigate.

The rock formation was in the shape of a triangle. Doc stood behind the formation, looking at it from the perspective the insurgent would have had. He proclaimed, "Holy shit, this is their aiming device!" We each looked at the top of the rock formation. It was angled perfectly in line with the end of the bridge almost eight hundred meters away. Doc was right.

We mounted the Humvees immediately. We were hot on the trail. Abass led us into a local village another thousand meters east of our current location. We figured we would run into the four-door Kia at best, and at worst we could find the insurgent's back entrance into the wadi. We cautiously moved through the town. All the civilians gave us the evil eye; we had spoiled all the fun. Unable to find the white Kia pickup, we pushed through the village until we found the route the insurgents were using to get into the wadi.

We found the mother lode. Every hundred meters a new copper command wire was strewn upon the ground, each of them going in different directions to various routes. This was the central hub of IED emplacement.

Sermen gave us double "hang loose" signs and yelled in broken English, "Fuckin' cool man. Fuckin' cool. We kick the erhabi [insurgent] fuckin' asses." He then showcased two different wires he had found. The guy was ecstatic. I laughed hysterically and threw him my wire cutters. "Start cutting, brother," I said.

We destroyed all the wires we could find. It was a great day to be with the Iraqi army and to be a Marine. We felt like triumphant treasure hunters. Our combined efforts had destroyed hours of insurgent work, found a key node of IED operations, and had probably saved lives.

Gaines got on the radio to EOD. "Listen gents," he said, "we have found the goldmine of IEDs down here. Request you copy the following grids." Gaines proceeded to send the grid locations of all the IED wires we had found to the EOD representatives so they could follow up on each of them and destroy the ordnance associated with each wire.

It was nearing 1300 and we needed to get back to Camp Ali to conduct a pay run. I radioed to the EOD team at the bridge and told them the situation. They suggested they return home with our convoy and told us they would return later in the afternoon to investigate the remaining IEDs we had found. We hoped they would actually do their job this time around.

The IEDs Come Back to Bite Us

Juwad came tearing through the MiTT camp in a Waz jeep. In broken English mixed with Arabic he frantically questioned, "Jamal, shaku maku [what happened] to all the people bil [in] Baghdad?" I was confused. Had the Green Zone been attacked? Had Al Qaeda attacked the capital again? I asked, "Juwad, I have not seen the news on Baghdad, what happened in Baghdad?" Perplexed, he responded, "No Baghdad—what happened in Baghdad?" Completely lost, I replied, "Juwad, treed ta'aroof an Baghdad loo Baghdadi?" (Juwad, do you want to know about Baghdad or Baghdadi?) He promptly responded, "Oh, yes, yes, yes—Baghdadi!"

I rushed into the MiTT COC and called 2/3's command center to see if there was any current action in Baghdadi. Sadly, there was action, and it involved our team. The team had been hit with an IED on their way to Baghdadi, near where we had found the IEDs.

I couldn't believe what I was hearing. Based on the location of the IED, it sounded like the same IEDs we'd found—the IEDs that EOD was supposed to have destroyed. If EOD caused someone in our Iraqi army or our MiTT to get jacked up, there was going to be some serious hell to pay. I rushed to call EOD to see if they had followed up on the IEDs from the day prior. The EOD clerk responded, "No. We did not have time."

I was furious. I called up to the dam hoping to get more information from 2/3. The watch officer on duty proclaimed, "Lieutenant Gray, the latest information we have is that the convoy was hit by an IED thirty minutes ago." "Great, that was really helpful," I said. I hopped into the Waz with Juwad. "Yalla, nrooh lil harakat" (Let's go to the Iraqi COC), I said. I knew that relying on the Marines for the latest information on the MiTT was not the smart choice. Getting information over the Iraqi radio net was the way to go.

Juwad and I ran into the S-6 and were greeted by a crowd of Iraqis who were all trying to get the scoop on the IED attack near Baghdadi. Abit, the Iraqi communications expert on duty, explained the latest to me. "Jamal, the convoy was heading north on Bronze toward Camp Ali when they hit an IED in the vicinity of the bridge we were examining the other day. Luckily it hit a Leyland, which by pure chance was filled with detainees the convoy was returning to the dam. No *jundi* or Marines were hurt, only detainees. I think one detainee is dead, and eight are injured. The convoy should be on Camp Ali any minute now."

The convoy came crashing into Camp Ali moments after I left the Iraqi COC. Staff Sergeant Donaldson, hanging outside his Humvee's window, yelled, "Get Doc!" I yelled back, "Why do you need Doc?" He quickly replied, "We have a Leyland full of bloody detainees!" I dashed for the MiTT camp to grab Doc.

Soon Doc and I arrived at the Leyland, the bed of which was full of crusted bodily fluids. Blood stained the detainees and the t-shirts that wrapped their injuries. As if the situation were not bad enough for the detainees, the *jundi* wanted to make it worse. They wanted to kill the detainees for causing the IED. They wanted to implement "Duke Nukem justice," which involves blowing everyone up and "letting God sort 'em out."

The logical progression of how the detainees caused the IED was not clear, yet one of the Iraqis on the convoy explained why it made sense to either kill or beat the detainees. First, these people were detained for a reason; they had not been picked up because they were on a Sunday stroll. It was likely the detainees were insurgents, and thus killing them now would probably eliminate a future problem. Second, the detainees were young males from the local areas and certainly knew what was going on in their streets. If the *jundi* were allowed to beat them, they could extract information on insurgent activity.

I replied, "If these detainees were insurgents, then why the heck would their insurgent buddies blow them up in an IED attack? You got a good answer to that one?" He didn't have an answer. He simply responded, "I still think we should beat them."

Iraqi logic is not always logical.

Chapter 16

Transitioning to Independent Operations

October 2006

As advisers we were not supposed to command the Iraqi army; rather, our mission was to advise Iraqis. At this point in the deployment, the MiTT controlled all Iraqi meetings, controlled all convoys, and conducted most of the planning for the Iraqi operations. The *jundi* did what we told them and gladly followed. In many ways the Iraqis were less prepared for independent operations than they had been with the previous MiTT. We had actually gone backward. This monumental failure annoyed me, and I decided to confront the problem myself.

Letting Iraqis Lead—A Novel Concept

My plan was to put together a convoy-training package that would transition the Iraqis to independent convoy operations, which made up 80 percent of our combat operations. The convoy setup involved three MiTT vehicles dispersed throughout the Iraqi convoy. We maintained the second, middle, and rear Humvee positions and kept control of the convoy at all times. The boss claimed that the Iraqis had free rein of the convoy, but that showed a complete lack of understanding. Every Iraqi officer who had conducted convoys had personally complained to me that the setup gave them no ability to control the convoy. Plus, with MiTT Humvees at the front, center, and rear of the convoy, it was difficult for the Iraqis to exercise any leadership without having their toes stomped on by our boss.

The three-phase plan I wanted to implement would radically change the way we did business as an adviser team. While the details of the plan were complicated, the basics of each phase were pragmatic and easy to grasp. The first phase would begin with a change in attitude. The Iraqis would not be looked upon as convoy participants but as convoy leaders. Additionally, the MiTT vehicle in the front of the convoy would be moved to the middle of the convoy and the other two MiTT vehicles would be in the rear of the convoy. By moving more toward the rear of the convoy, we would eliminate our ability to command and control the situation when things get hectic, which is the very time we want the Iraqis to work through the issues. Once everyone was comfortable with phase one we would move into phase two.

Phase two would take one of the MiTT vehicles completely out of the convoy. There was no reason to be risking four American lives and a bunch of equipment for absolutely no reason. In this phase, two American Humvees would sit in the rear of the convoy and merely provide communications support to call on American assets if the Iraqis needed them (calling up an EOD team to examine an IED would be an example). Also, the Iraqis would be required to give a full operations order before each convoy, which would cover all the aspects of the convoy mission.

Phase three of my plan was the gold standard. In this phase the MiTT would not even participate in convoy operations. We would merely coordinate movements and advise the Iraqis on COC operations back at battalion headquarters. The Iraqis would operate independently, make their own decisions, and learn from their own failures. There was no reason for Americans to die for Iraq when there were Iraqi soldiers to take on that risk. If we really wanted Marines to accomplish the mission in Iraq, we would kick out the Iraqi army, add an additional two hundred thousand troops, and implement martial law on the entire country. The tricky thing with the final phase was figuring out how to coordinate with other American units in the area and how to get support to the Iraqis if something bad happened.

Unfortunately, coalition forces have little to no Arabic-speaking capability. I also had a solution for this problem. I planned to translate various communications templates the Marines use, such as IED nine-line reports and enemy contact reports (SALUTE report). When the Iraqis needed support, they would fill out their template and send the message in Arabic back to the Iraqi COC. The terps would translate this message and hand it off to a Marine adviser, who would call on support from the Marines.

I pitched the plan to nearly everyone who would listen. I spent weeks going to every Iraqi officer's swahut to get advice on how to make the plan better. All of them were extremely enthusiastic about the opportunity to actually be free men and lead their own battalion versus being micromanaged by our MiTT. Everyone on the adviser team was enthusiastic with the plan as well. Sadly, the only person who had a problem with the idea was the boss—the one person we needed on board to make this work.

While I was not able to convince the boss, I had a good idea: Maj. Gen. Rick Zilmer, the Multi-National Forces West commander, agreed to help me out. The newest guidance required us to "make all efforts and accept more risk in order to ensure Iraqis are being given the chance to take the lead on operations." After seeing the general's new guidance, the boss gave me approval to kick my plan into gear.

The next day I woke up around 0630 after sleeping a few hours. Despite being tired, I was super motivated. I planned to sit down with Lieutenant Ahmed, the acting S3 operations officer, and start working on the convoy transition plan. This would be my chance to change the direction of our MiTT and do something that helped the Iraqis become an independent organization so we could get the hell out of this country.

Ahmed and I had an outstanding relationship. I sat down with him for about three hours discussing how we could implement the convoy transition plan. We accomplished in three hours what MiTT teams had been trying to accomplish over the past two years—transition security operations duties over to the Iraqis. We both felt like we had accomplished something. I took his ideas, he took mine, and in the end we had something that would make the Iraqi army more capable. At the end of our meeting I smiled at Ahmed and said, "We should be on a military advising brochure—that was too easy." Ahmed replied, "No Jamal, you make it easy. You understand how we operate."

It's amazing how critically important personal relationships are in Iraq. With good relationships you can manipulate an Iraqi to give you his only daughter; with poor relationships you would be hard-pressed to get an Iraqi to let you wash his dirty underwear. The system is a bit difficult to maneuver, but if you master it, the world is yours.

I am still on the fence as to whether I like the Iraqi system of relationships better than I like ours. On the one hand the Western system of friendship is much more efficient, timely, and facilitates our society's ability to have a great economy and get things done. On the other hand the Iraqi system, while arguably less efficient and more time consuming, is more user friendly. Iraqis are better at developing relationships that actually mean something. In Iraqi society you run into either "brothers" or people you have never met before; there are no "contacts." I respect the recondite friendships Iraqis develop. There is not that much to love about Iraqi culture, but every so often these people surprise me.

Release the Hounds

We finally cut the leash on the Iraqis. Lieutenant Abdulredha, a competent Iraqi officer, presented his convoy order brief flawlessly. We rehearsed the brief at 0600 so he would have confidence in front of his men. At the end of the brief Major Pyle was stunned. "Gentlemen," he said, "that was the best brief I have ever seen from the Iraqis. I am excited to see what you can do." I was even more impressed; I thought the brief rivaled some of the best briefs I had ever seen—Marine or Iraqi.

At the conclusion of Abdulredha's order to his men, I walked in front of the group of Iraqi warriors and addressed them in the best Arabic I could muster. "My brothers, this is your opportunity to lead the Iraqi army. We all know it is difficult to work with our MiTT, because many of the Marines want you to do everything their way. This time is different. You now have the chance to do it your way if you can prove to Major Pyle that you have the ability. I have confidence in all of you. I know you can operate independently." I paused, looking from face to face, before going on. "Gentlemen, I want to see my wife and family soon. I want the Iraqi army leading this country. I do not want the Americans leading your country. The next time I visit I do not want to be in a uniform but in my civilian clothes visiting you and your families in Najaf. I have great confidence in Lieutenant Adulredha and he has great confidence in you. Let's make this happen!" There was a roar of excitement in the room. I had given T. E. Lawrence a run for his money.

Lieutenant Abdulredha continued to motivate the *jundi*. Major Pyle leaned over and asked for an interpretation of what I told the Iraqis. I responded, "Sir, I just told them that this is their chance to operate independently and that they needed to prove themselves." Abdulredha released the *jundi* to go set up the convoy. As the *jundi* exited they showered me with hugs, kisses, and high-fives. Khalis hollered, "Mulazim Jamal, il Jeysh Iraqi ihebbek!" (Lieutenant Jamal, the Iraqi army loves you!)

The Iraqis were excited to be leading *their* convoy. While in the convoy staging area between the MiTT camp and the swahuts, *jundi* approached me and asked, "Why are the Marine Humvees in the rear of the convoy?" I responded with delight, "Because the Iraqis are leading now!" (see photo 16).

Things were off to an excellent start. The orders brief was good, the *jundi* were motivated, and the convoy was squared away. All we needed next was solid execution of the actual mission. And Lieutenant Abdulredha gave us just that   flawless execution. His actions were so proficient that the MiTT was getting bored sitting in the back of the convoy watching the *jundi* run the show. But they were about to be tested.

"Holy shit! Did you guys feel that?" Martin yelled. The 2/3 convoy half a mile in front of us was engulfed in smoke. They had been struck by a thunderous IED. I whispered to myself, "Oh God, why did this have to happen on the Iraqis' first time out the gate?" As the adviser convoy commander I immediately ordered the two MiTT vehicles to the front of the convoy so we could maintain better communications with the 2/3 convoy in case they needed our help. I said, "Koa, this is Shadow, what is your status? Over." The 2/3 convoy commander replied, "We are good to go. No casualties. The IED missed its target. Stand by for further word, over." I radioed, "Roger, Koa, Shadow standing by. Out."

While stationary, the Iraqis spotted a motorcycle buzzing along the palm groves near the river. Instinctively, Lieutenant Abdulredha ordered his lead Iraqi Humvees to chase the motorcycle. They were in hunter-killer mode. After an intense chase, the two Iraqi Humvees returned empty-handed. Abdulredha sprinted to my Humvee, out of breath. "Jamal, I'm sorry we had to run off like that without telling you. We tried to capture those guys, but they were too far away. What are we going to do next?" I responded, "Abdulredha, no problem. By the way, that was great leadership!" I paused to let him catch his breath then continued. "You don't need approval from me to do anything if you feel it is the right thing to do. The Iraqis are leading this convoy, not us—remember?" Abdulredha put out his arm with a balled fist and I met it midair with my fist. He said, "Ziiieeen!" (Great!)

After speaking with Abdulredha the boss started approaching my Humvee. I muttered to myself, "Oh God, here he comes to save the day." He asked, "Lieutenant Gray, what's going on? Why the hell are the Iraqis running off like that? Did you tell them they could do that?" I cut him short. "Sir, Abdulredha and I are in control of the situation. You can stay back here with the rest of the convoy and provide security." The boss responded, "Uh, okay, just keep me informed of everything that goes on." I replied, "Roger, Sir, will do."

Abdulredha and I hopped out of our Humvees and walked up to the staff sergeant I assumed was in charge of the operation. "Staff sergeant, how's it going?" I asked. "I'm Lieutenant Gray and this is Lieutenant Abdulredha. What's going on? You guys need our help?" He responded, "Sir, we actually could use your help. We called EOD and they aren't going to be here for at least three hours. The lieutenant and some of the Marines moved toward the small village to our east [Abu Hyatt] to search for the triggerman and any evidence. The problem is we cannot get comms with them. Can you go out there and see how they are doing?" I replied, "Roger, no problem. We'll be in contact via radio. If something goes wrong we will pop a green cluster." I looked over to Abdulredha, who understood English pretty well, and asked, "Fitihemita?" (Did you understand him?) He laughed and responded in English, "Of course, Jamal. I am wannabe American, you know!"

"Doc," I ordered, "make a path toward the village to our east and don't hit any IEDs." Doc immediately punched the Humvee across the desert toward the edge of a small hill that overlooked Abu Hyatt. The Iraqis followed. We approached the top of a ridge to get a better view of the small village. Abdulredha and I jumped out of our vehicles and met at the hood of his Humvee. He pointed. "Jamal, I see the Marines. Look about five hundred meters toward the river." I followed his directions. "Roger, I see them." Before I could even ask Abdulredha what he wanted to do next, he was in his Humvee burning a path through the desert to the Marine location.

We linked up with the Marines searching local homes. I approached the lieutenant in charge. "Dude, how's it going?" He replied, "We are good to go—no worries. We could use your *jundi* though. This woman came out of her home and pointed us in the direction of this home directly in front of us. I had my Marines go in there and check it out. They found weapons, washing machine timers, hollowed out 155-mm artillery shells, a book on the physics of electronics, and a bunch of copper wire. If that ain't fishy, then I don't know what is." Astonished, I responded, "No kidding? What do you need the Iraqis for? You need them to ask the homeowner what's up or something?" The lieutenant replied, "Yep, exactly." Abdulredha, who had overheard our conversation, said, "Roger, Jamal, I am already sending soldiers to check it out."

I approached the *jundi* and asked, "Shaku maku wiya il biet?" (What's up with the house?) Abdulredha came to explain the situation. "The women of the home said all of the men were gone for the day and that she didn't know how this stuff arrived in her home," he said. "She said it is the male's property and that she has nothing to do with it. This is an insurgent home, I know that." I replied, "Roger, well, we will cause more problems by detaining the lady. I guess all we can do is confiscate the illegal material and be on our way." I jumped in my Humvee and waited for the Iraqis to wrap up their business.

Abdulredha radioed over the Iraqi radio net to Martin, relaying the message they were ready to move. Martin, in uncharacteristically honest form, looked at me and said, "You need to look in the Iraqi Humvee before we leave. They took that woman's antique shotgun. I think they are trying to steal it." I knew Martin was not being honest for honesty's sake, since he was the shadiest bastard in Iraq. I also knew that Martin did not get along with Abdulredha and that this might be a false alarm. Nevertheless, I investigated.

I looked in the back of the Iraqi Humvee, which had the woman's shotgun, a legal weapon for Iraqis to have in their home. I approached Abdulredha, disappointed, and asked, "Why did you guys take this weapon? These people are authorized one weapon and this one obviously isn't meant to kill people." Abdulredha grinned and said, "Jamal, the lady already has an AK-47, so we took this shotgun." I laughed. "Listen, this is an antique shotgun that would have a hard time killing a bird. You can take it if you want, but I'll tell you this, you had better be able to justify this to Colonel Abass when we get back to the camp. If you don't think you can justify this with Colonel Abass, I recommend you return the lady's antique."

Abdulredha knew he had been caught red-handed engaging in some Ali Babba activities and decided to choose the path of righteousness. He ordered one of the *jundi* to return the antique weapon to the lady. He smiled at me. "Jamal, you know what that thing is worth in Baghdad? Big money, man, big money." I replied, "Well, I think you did the right thing. Good work."

We returned to the main convoy body, which was still sitting on Route Bronze. I arranged to bypass the 2/3 convoy and we continued on our mission to Baghdadi. A mile from Baghdadi, Abdulredha stopped the convoy and ordered his *jundi* to search the bridge ahead for IEDs. The Iraqi *jundi*-bots got out of their Humvee and screened the path. Ayad, one of the searchers, sprinted back to the convoy, flailing his arms in all directions. He had found an IED. "I looked in one of the old IED craters and saw copper wire coming out of it," he explained. "I didn't stay to check for details, but I'm sure there is an IED there." We immediately cordoned off the area and set up security. We all knew we would be here for a while, waiting for EOD to come to our position and clear the IED.

I started transmitting my EOD nine-line. "Checkpoint twelve, line one: 151300 Zulu, line two: grid, thirty-eight Sierra—" I could not transmit another word because my jaw had dropped. An American convoy was heading right for the IED Ayad had located. The *jundi* in the front Humvee were all out of their Humvees waving frantically to get the Marines to stop before they crossed the bridge. I quickly switched frequencies to contact the convoy that was about to run over an IED. I was too late. By the time I contacted the convoy commander, their Humvees were already past the kill zone of the IED. Even so, the IED never detonated. Either the convoy coming our way knew something we didn't or they had Allah on their side.

I addressed the Marine convoy commander, who stopped to chat. "You guys know there is a suspected IED on that bridge and your convoy just drove over the top of it, right?" The lieutenant convoy commander replied, "Hey man, EOD took care of that IED last night. I was here when they did the controlled detonation. It looks like they didn't pick up all the wires in the detonation pit, hence the reason the *jundi* thought there was an IED in there." I was speechless. EOD had already screwed us over, and this was just another addition to my long list of EOD complaints. I replied to the lieutenant in a sarcastic tone, "So what you're telling me is we have been sitting here for an hour, calling in the nine-line, setting up the cordon, setting up security and making traffic wait, because EOD is too lazy to pick up the wires?" He responded bluntly, "Yep, pretty much." I couldn't help but laugh. "Well, shit, at least we're all alive, right? Oohrah. Be safe, dude."

Our Iraqi-led convoy finally made it to the Baghdadi Iraqi army compound. We were greeted by Nuts, Lieutenant Adams, and Captain McShane, who had spent the past four days in Baghdadi helping 3rd Iraqi Company prepare for their move to Camp Ali. Nuts chided us. "Hey, thanks for leaving us down here to help the *jundi* organize their mountains of trash," he said. "We really appreciate it, guys. I hope you all die tomorrow." McShane replied, "Yeah, it pretty much sucked down here, but what can you do? Let's get this convoy rearranged and get the hell back to Camp Ali!"

We followed up on McShane's suggestion and approached the problem of forming a new convoy with all of the equipment, personnel, and Humvees from 3rd Iraqi Company. The situation was daunting. Somehow

Abdulredha and I needed to organize sixteen vehicles in some sort of convoy order. And all of this had to be completed inside the Baghdadi FOB, which was about the size of a baseball field. Faced with the complex problem, I realized why being an adviser could be a great job. I walked up to Abdulredha and asked, "You got a plan for getting this convoy together? If you need any help, just let me know. I don't want to get in your way." Wanting to impress me, Abdulredha replied, "Watch me make this happen. This is a difficult operation for the Marines, but an easy operation for the Iraqi army."

Abdulredha came through on his claim. Somehow he was able to put together the finest piece of Iraqi army planning I have ever witnessed. Within an hour the convoy was on Route Bronze heading north to Camp Ali. If this excellent performance by the Iraqi army could not convince the boss they were ready to do independent operations, then nothing would. The sooner the MiTT worked itself out of a job, the sooner America could quit wasting time and resources in Iraq.

Chapter 17

The Combat Operations Center Is Launched and the Mission Changes

Late October–Early November 2006

O ur lives changed for the rest of our deployment. The Iraqis had shown an ability to conduct successful independent convoy operations, so we shifted our focus from training the Iraqis on the intricacies of combat operations to training them on higher-level functions like centralized command and control. To this end the first Iraqi problem we planned to address was the defunct Iraqi Combat Operations Center.

In addition to a change in the advising agenda, the MiTT attitude changed. From here on out, if work needed to be done, the Iraqis would be doing it. If a problem required initiative to solve, the Iraqis would deal with it. In addition to a shift in attitude, half of the team was pulled away to focus on advising 3rd Iraqi Company, which had moved to Camp Ali a few days earlier. Meanwhile the rest of the MiTT, including me, would be in charge of maintaining and developing the Iraqi COC. From this point forward, our only chance to get outside the wire would be if a quick reaction force were needed. I was bummed I would not be heading outside the wire as often to take part in the action, but I thought I could serve the Iraqis better by staying back in the COC and working with their staff officers to facilitate better command and control. If it all worked out, the Iraqis would be running everything and we would go home.

After a week of sleepless nights, we finally got the Iraqi COC into operation. Its setup was not complicated. In one corner there was a desk for a MiTT watch officer, who advised the Iraqi watch officer on COC operations, and in the other corner was a desk for an Iraqi watch officer, who monitored all combat operations for the battalion. But the new COC was a complete shit show. Nothing worked, communications were abysmal, and the Iraqi officers were not happy about actually having to perform watch officer duties. The Iraqi leadership was accustomed to their cushy jobs. They essentially did nothing except collect a paycheck, chain smoke, and order Iraqi soldiers to do all the work.

An attack on an Iraqi foot patrol in South Dam Village illustrated how poorly the system worked. Upon hearing news of the attack, the entire MiTT converged on the Iraqi COC to see how they could help. Captain Mohammed, the Iraqi watch officer at the time, was on his two-hour lunch break. Fighting the urge to take control of the situation, I talked to Abit, the radio clerk. "Abit, you need to get Captain Mohammed to the COC. We are not gonna do his job for him." Mohammed responded on his radio. "Abit, just have the Marines take care of the situation—I'm on break." I grabbed the radio from Abit's hand and said, "Mohammed, inta mejnoon? Ta'al il harakat, hessey. Il doriya yehtajek!" (Mohammed, are you crazy? Come to the COC, now. The patrol needs you!) Surprised that I had grabbed the radio or understood what he told Abit, he promptly replied in broken English, "Okay, okay, no problem. Now I come COC. No problem, Jamal. No problem." By the time Mohammed made it back to the COC, the patrol that had been attacked and needed help had already returned to Camp Ali. Way to go, Mohammed.

If Mohammed's ineptitude wasn't enough, Lieutenant Kusay, the 3rd Iraqi Company commander, piled on the problems. He walked into the COC around 1300 to talk about his upcoming patrol operations with Lieutenant Le Gette, who was advising him. Acting as an interpreter for Le Gette, I asked Kusay, "Brother, can you tell me what is going on right now with the Iraqi patrol schedule? I don't even see a schedule posted anywhere." Kusay explained, "Jamal, our patrol plan is working out so well right now we don't even need a schedule." Le Gette and I laughed.

I knew a patrol was outside the wire and I wanted to test Kusay's knowledge of his own operations. I asked, "Kusay, when is your next patrol leaving?" He confidently replied, "A patrol should be leaving in thirty minutes." I snapped, "Kusay, there is a patrol outside as we speak, how can there be another patrol leaving in thirty minutes? You don't have enough men to run simultaneous patrols." Captain Mohammed, feeling the urge to help defend Kusay, chimed in. "Jamal, I am not sure about what is going on at the moment, but Kusay is the company commander and knows his operations very well." Le Gette and I gave up. I said, "Kusay, Mohammed, I'm glad you guys are on top of it."

We followed up with a question about the future of patrolling efforts. Le Gette explained his basic plan to run three patrols every twenty-four hours to keep the insurgents on their toes. Kusay bagged on the proposal. "I think we only need to do one patrol." Le Gette snapped in return, "But that would leave the insurgents twenty hours a day to conduct operations?" Kusay replied, "Yes, that is true, but my *jundi* will get very tired if they do three patrols a day."

Le Gette was stuck. He wanted to let the Iraqis run the show, but we also had to worry about our safety and the safety of other Marines in the area. If he let Kusay do his one-patrol-a-day plan, the insurgents would place IEDs all along the routes frequented by the Marines from 2/3. If an IED were to kill the Marines along our assigned routes, their blood would be on our hands. He was stuck in a catch-22. If it became the Iraqi's initiative, they would gladly go back to their lazy ways and let him do all the work, and if he let the Iraqis take control, it would put Marines in danger. Le Gette opted to compromise and insisted that they do at least two patrols a day.

Because the new Iraqi COC and the push to let the Iraqis take the initiative had all but failed, I asked Ahmed Ali, one of the few Iraqis I still respected, how we could make the Iraqi COC more proactive. "Jamal," he said, "here is how I would do it. First I would get the lowest ranking *jundi* on camp and put him in a chair with a radio. Everyone else would go to their swahuts and sleep or watch television. When something happened with a unit outside the wire, the *jundi* on duty could run and awaken the officer. This system is what we used during the fights against the Americans in the old Iraqi army. Everyone gets more sleep and we still accomplish the mission. It's a great idea, isn't it, Jamal?" I wanted to say, "Ahmed, you want to know how we kicked your ass during previous wars? Because your COC operations rely on the lowest ranking *jundi* in your military for success," but I replied more cordially. "Ahmed, I'm not sure I agree with that idea, but I'll take your word for it that it's great."

Chapter 18

Chasing Egyptian Insurgents

December 2006

D id a wild hare get up your ass?" I had heard this question countless times in the Marine Corps and I still wasn't sure what it meant. All the same I thought it aptly described my sudden burst of motivation to do something that didn't involve sitting around in the Iraqi COC any longer. I was ready for another combat mission.

2/3 needed some folks for a special operations type mission. They had asked us if we could take the Iraqi army scouts on speedboats to a remote island in Lake Qadisiyah. Our mission was to clandestinely approach the island, find some Egyptian insurgents, and bring them to the dam so the HET (Human Exploitation Team) could interrogate them. Moreover, because we were short on terps, it looked like I would be assigned as the interpreter for the mission. This was as close to being James Bond as I would ever get in my life.

Sightseeing around Lake Qadisiyah

Once the mission plan was finalized between the MiTT and the Marines driving the boats, we stopped by the scout swahut and told them to get their gear together for a special mission. After their gear was packed we marched up to the dam and jumped in the back of a Marine troop transport vehicle that was heading for the top of the dam.

On the drive to the launch point I slowly translated the intelligence material I had in the best Arabic I could muster. The Iraqis absolutely loved it. I couldn't speak fluent Arabic, but I could motivate the hell out of

Iraqis with the Arabic I did know. By the time I was done explaining the situation, the *jundi* were ready for the mission.

At the launch point we boarded the speedboats and sprinted north over the horizon in search of a particular remote island. The cold wind off the lake shot through our combat gear. Corporal Jackson looked to me and said, "Sir, we are going to freeze our asses off, I'm afraid." I smirked. "Yeah, pretty much. Good times ahead!"

Fighting the frequent splash of freezing water hitting me in the face, I yelled at Abdulhaddi, "Sadeeki, inta zien? Khallis?" (My friend, are you good? You ready?) Abdulhaddi, one of the rare "glass half full" Iraqis, responded in terrible English, "Jamal, very good, very good. I kill Ali Babba with you!" Shaking from the thin coat of freezing water over my body, I responded with a huge smile. "Insha'allah," I said. Abdulhaddi, Salah, and Ali Jaber, the three Iraqis on the craft with me, all responded in unison, "Insha'allah, Jamal. Insha'allah" (see photo 17).

The excitement of flying across the water in speedboats came to a sudden halt. The Marine operating the boat yelled, "Fuck! Boat down." We looked across the way to see the other craft stalled. Nuts stood up and punched his hands in the air, obviously distraught. Sgt. Jamar Bailey whispered to me, "Sir, it looks like Staff Sergeant Chesnutt is pretty pissed." Smirking, I replied, "Yes. Yes, it does."

Forty-five minutes later, well into our special operations mission, we were still sitting a thousand meters from the dam trying to fix boat engines. The lead boat operator said, "Gents, I know you don't want to hear this, but we need to squish everybody onto two crafts instead of three. It's gonna be a little cramped, but we will need to make it work." Grudgingly we piled onto the two boats. Within minutes we were once again galloping along the waves of Lake Qadisiyah. Our path took us on a typical patrol route, which would not arouse any suspicion among the insurgents who lived on the islands scattered throughout Lake Qadisiyah.

We approached our objective. "Hold on, gentlemen," bellowed the Marine staff sergeant controlling the raft. "We are gonna make a sharp turn and charge into the island, stand by." Before we could react to the announcement, the momentum of quick change in direction created chaos. The *jundi* tumbled on top of me and we formed a human layer cake in the bottom of the craft. I looked at Ali Jaber, who had fallen on top of me, and said, "Uh, as salama aleikum, shlonek sadeeki?" (Uh, hello, how are you my friend?) Ali Jaber smiled. "Jamal, hatha Marine mejnoon!" (Jamal, that Marine [who is driving] is crazy!)

We zipped toward the island, attempting to maximize the element of surprise. The way the island was originally described to us in the intelligence reports, it was supposed to be a hundred meters long and have one hut that housed the Egyptians. The island we were approaching, though, was the size of a small college campus with rolling hills, ten to twenty primitive huts, maybe a hundred inhabitants, and a slew of donkeys and wild dogs. Human intel had once again gotten it wrong.

A hundred meters off land the boat operator yelled again, "Shit. Gentlemen, it's too shallow here—you aren't swimming in this stuff!" He slammed the brakes and all of us cannonballed along the belly of the speedboat for the second time. We continued to try to find a potential landing site, but to no avail. After six attempts at landing it was getting so ridiculous I felt as though we were playing a role in a spoof movie. To make matters worse, witnessing the entire escapade was a group of Iraqi fishermen, who were huddled outside their stone hut drinking tea. They waved in our direction. Our element of surprise was dead.

Sergeant Bailey pointed in the direction of a small peninsula jutting from the island. "That place looks good," he said. We agreed with Bailey's suggestion so we could offload. We hopped out of the boats and immediately secured the area. The *jundi* and I were the first team off the boat and pushed ahead to recon the area.

What Next?

Nuts walked up to me and said, "Sir, what the hell are we going to do next? This island isn't exactly as small as they told us it was going to be." During my Marine Corps officer training the instructors always mentioned there would be a moment where everyone looks at you and says, "What next, lieutenant?"

This was my opportunity to shine or falter. Perplexed, I relied on some common sense. "Well, we know they probably aren't those dudes over to the east, since they watched us try and land our boats for the past hour. And to the south is the lake. We don't want to go swimming. That narrows it down to either going north or west. Let's head west. We'll patrol to the top of the hill, get a better vantage point, and work from there." I paused then said, "But before we do anything, let's ask Ali Jaber what he wants to do, since he is the Iraqi squad leader and in command of this operation."

I confronted Ali Jaber, who was happy to let me lead the group. "You are the squad leader so I will let you make the decisions on what we do next,"

I said. Ali Jaber looked at me with a puzzled expression and said, "Jamal, I don't know what to do next. What do you want to do?" I said, "This isn't my country, what do you want to do?" Luckily, a couple of young Iraqi men started approaching our position. I leaned over to Ali Jaber and said, "How about you ask those guys if they know where these Egyptians are located." He replied, "Good idea. Let's do it."

Ali Jaber and I jogged over to the young men. The men stopped in their tracks and their eyes widened to the size of eggs. It was obvious they had never seen a Marine or *jundi* on this island. Ali Jaber spoke with the men for a few minutes. When the conversation ended, he addressed the squad. "Well, they gave me the directions to the Egyptians. All we have to do is head west over the hill and look in the hut closest to the shore." I slapped Ali Jaber on the shoulder and told him, "Inta qaid doriya kullish zien!" (You are a great squad leader!)

We patrolled to the suspected dwelling on the other side of the island. I was convinced I had landed on another planet. The island was lifeless, aside from a handful of primitive stone-built huts the size of a one-car garage. The only signs of activity were three wooden boats and a line of fishing nets scattered along the shore. Nuts said, "Sir, I bet we are the first Americans to ever touch this land in the history of the world." I looked around. "I think you're right."

At the objective, we found fifteen men hovering around a steaming cauldron of baked beans. In unison they welcomed us, saying, "As salam aleikum." Ali Jaber replied on our behalf, "Wa aleikum salam." He immediately got down to business, lined the men up single file, and started frisking them for contraband. Meanwhile, Nuts and I explored the detainees' shack for weapons or booby traps (see photo 18).

The inside of their living quarters was atrocious. Trash was everywhere, blankets were strewn about the floor, breadcrumbs were scattered along the floor, and the rat shit was so thick it felt like we were walking on a bag of rice. Before we could investigate further, Ali Jaber cried, "Jamal, ta'al hinah. Shasowwi hesse?" (Jamal, come here. What should I do now?) I had some simple advice for him: find the Egyptians.

Ali Jaber and his *jundi* immediately went to work. He ordered the detainees to pull out their identification cards. He made quick work of the situation, approached me, and whispered in my ear, "Jamal, these two men are the Egyptians. It says so on their identification cards." I replied, "Are you sure?" He snuck a little closer. "Yes, Jamal. What should we do with them?" I pondered, then answered, "Hrmm, tell them we need to take them back to the dam for some questioning. Tell them we do not believe them to be guilty of anything, but believe they may be able to help us find some insurgents and that they will be rewarded for their efforts." Once we had attained our "prizes," the next step was to explore the immediate area for suspicious activity. I grabbed a small group of Iraqi scouts and went to search some abandoned tents along the coast.

A spring from an AK-47 rifle came flying out of a shredded tent and directly into my face. "Ow. Shit, dude, watch out!" I blurted out in English to Mofak, one of the *jundi* with me. Mofak looked at me puzzled, not understanding what I had said. "Jamal, shaku maku? Inta zien?" (Jamal, what happened? Are you okay?) Still flinching from the pain, I replied, "Anii zien, bess shtisowwi wiya AK?" (I am fine, but what are you doing with the AK?) Mofak would not respond, so I entered the tent.

Mofak decided to dismantle the AK-47 inside the tent. "Mofak, what are you doing, man?" I asked. "Nothing," he responded. "I am destroying this AK-47 so they don't attack us with it when we leave." Despite my desire to agree with him, I had to explain to Mofak that the Iraqi people were allowed to have one AK-47 per household, even if their household was a shitty tent on some island in the middle of nowhere.

Mofak understood and begrudgingly tossed the rifle on the ground. "Jamal, you know everyone out here is an insurgent, don't you?" I responded, "Yes, Mofak, that may be true, but we have to respect these people. Here's a deal. If they fire on us when we leave, we will come back here and take them all back to the Iraqi camp for interrogation. Will that work?" He nodded in agreement. "Okay, that is good. However, I will kill them if they shoot at us so we won't even have to worry about bringing them back to Camp Ali."

At the conclusion of our search efforts, we rallied everyone together, including our two insurgent detainees, and patrolled back to our landing zone for extract. Our mission, despite its chaotic beginnings, had been a complete success. The Marines operating the boat hollered, "Sir, how was it? You got the insurgents?" Excited, I answered, "Oh yeah, we got them. Now let's get the hell out of here!" They shouted back, "Oohrah, Sir. Roger that." We loaded onto the speedboats and dashed for Haditha.

Part 4

BETWEEN IRAQ AND A HARD PLACE

Chapter 19

Contending with Iraq Culture

November–December 2006

"**R**esgar, do you want to run with us?" Adams and I were on a jog and wanted to see if our resident Kurd, who speaks five languages, was interested. "Jamal, I am so sorry," he replied. "I cannot run with you. I have too many bullet holes in my legs." Never hearing this excuse before in my life, I asked again for clarification. Resgar elaborated. "Jamal, I have five bullet wounds in my legs from snipers in the Iran and Iraq War. I have shrapnel in my body and hands and I have a bullet wound on my head from a friendly Iraqi aircraft round that ricocheted off my head. I have a hard time moving my body."

What can you reasonably say to an excuse like that? I laughed. "Resgar, my brother, no problem. We don't want you running with us anyway—you will probably make us run too fast!"

Iraqis operate in an environment unimaginable to outsiders—and it is reflected in their unique culture.

Iraqi Sex Education (or Lack Thereof)

Most of the MiTT hates sitting on Iraqi COC duty. I particularly love it because it is a great opportunity to speak with the Iraqis. One day the Iraqis and I discussed everyone's favorite topic—sex.

The Iraqis receive little to no sex education and are naturally curious. Our first conversation was on the fabled clitoris: what it was, how to find it, and how it can give a woman pleasure. In what was very awkward conversation, I explained to the *jundi* the basic concept of the organ. I tried to explain everything to the serious-faced *jundi* in Arabic without bursting into laughter but had a difficult time. I think the Iraqis understood the gist of what I was trying to tell them, even if they got half of it wrong. I was amazed at how sexually illiterate they were. I felt like I was surrounded by a bunch of teenage boys who were frothing at the mouth for the opportunity to learn the basics of female anatomy. I didn't claim to be any sort of expert on sexual matters, but even my rudimentary knowledge put me in a class above most Iraqis.

The conversation lit a fire under the *jundi*. Lieutenant Colonel Ali asked, "Jamal, how do American men last so long in bed and how do you grow your penises so large?" Baffled, I replied, "What are you talking about, man?" He responded, "On all the movies I see the man humping the woman for over an hour and they always have a penis the size of a baby's arm! What cream or medicine are you guys taking?"

I shook my head in disgust, hiding my laughter. "Listen, you understand that in the porno movies they always hire the guys with the biggest dicks, right? You also gotta understand that the reason those movies go on for hours is because they cut scenes and take breaks—none of it is reality!" Ali wasn't buying it. "Jamal, you are full of shit. I know there is a medicine you can take. I've seen these things on the Internet. I have also heard that to increase your penis size you guys inject some sort of jelly substance into your cock."

Sometimes I wondered where Iraqis get their information. I continued, "Oh, so you saw it on the Internet and now it must be true? Guys, let me tell you, everything you see on the Internet or on television does not reflect the reality of America." I paused. "Trust me, my penis is only nine inches long and I usually only last an average of thirty minutes in bed." The sarcasm in my comment didn't communicate to the *jundi* I was joking. They looked at me with a sense of reverence. "Guys, I'm joking. Lighten up."

I was tired of being the *jundi*'s sexual education teacher and instead turned the conversation over to them. I addressed Ahmed and the others. "Ahmed, tell me about sex in Iraq. What do you guys do that I would find surprising?" Ahmed turned to his fellow Arabs and they conversed in Arabic for a moment, then Ahmed turned to me. "Jamal, have you heard of the Shia custom of 'enjoyable marriage?'" Perplexed, I replied, "Enjoyable marriage? Naw, never heard of it. Explain this one to me."

Ahmed explained, "Jamal, the concept is very easy. If you are a widow you are allowed to pay a man to be your temporary husband. The temporary husband's job is to have sex with the woman, protect her, and take care of her." I smirked and asked, "What does Allah think of all this?"

"Well, it's a tricky situation," Ahmed replied. "Allah doesn't really see this as a true marriage because there is no love involved. It is purely a pragmatic solution to a common problem." I replied, "Uh, you're going to have to explain a bit more for me, Ahmed." He obliged, saying, "Sure, I will give you an example of when an enjoyable marriage is legal and not legal in the eyes of Allah."

Ahmed began to lecture. "Okay Jamal, let's say a widow wants to have an enjoyable marriage. She will market herself or other men will come to her to make a proposal. Let's say they agree to a six-month agreement. The man from that point forward is able to have sex with the woman and is obligated to take care of her." I asked, "Okay, why doesn't Allah see that as having sex outside of marriage?" He responded, "Well, here is the catch. At the end of the six-month period, the agreement must end. If the two individuals actually love each other, or want to continue the contract, they have to get married. If they are caught having sex after the agreement, they will be punished as any other sexual offender would be punished."

Astonished, I replied, "Isn't that cheating the system? It almost seems like prostitution." Ahmed retorted, "Well, Jamal, you need to realize that the woman will be distraught when she is a widow and may be driven to kill herself without a man in her life. This is a solution that allows the woman to maintain some sort of sanity while she gets back into her life."

"Tell me this Ahmed," I asked, "can the woman do this multiple times? Like can she do multiple contracts? Also, how many guys come clamoring for deals like this hoping to get some sex?" Ahmed laughed. "Jamal, I will be honest with you, I think the woman can legally do this multiple times, but I do not know the official religious law for this. And yes, men do come clamoring to sign on for these enjoyable marriage deals."

I replied, "The Sunnis hate this idea—right?" Ahmed quickly responded, "Oh yes, they think it is against Allah's wishes, but we disagree with them on many things so that is natural."

After learning about the enjoyable marriage concept, I sparked a flurry of sex-related stories that all the Iraqis wanted to share. My favorite was of this famous man in Fallujah who wanted to have sex fifteen times a day with his wife. The nickname for the man was "Horny Hameed." For obvious reasons, Horny Hameed's wife wasn't so keen on the idea and took her husband to the local equivalent of court, the local sheikh.

Typically, in an Iraqi marriage the woman has to do what her husband wants; however, because of the absurd nature of her husband's request, the local sheik was willing to hear her concerns. The final judgment from the sheik was that Horny Hameed would be limited to having sex with his wife only three times a day. And if he broke this rule, his wife would have the legal right to separate from him. The wife, without a real choice, agreed to the ruling. Horny Hameed and his bride left the sheik's presence to live happily ever after—or so everyone thought.

A few months passed and Horny Hameed's wife returned to complain to the sheik. Her husband was once again forcing her to have sex fifteen times a day. Standing by his word, the sheik ruled that this was grounds for a legal divorce and that the woman could part ways from her husband because of his unnatural demands. Thank God, there is some sense of reasonableness in Arab society.

One evening, during my Iraqi COC duty, Imus, the terp working with me, showed me a talent I never knew he possessed. "I can swoon any women with the stroke of my pen or the sound of my voice," he told me. I've always thought Imus was a blowhard: he is thirty-seven years old and relatively wealthy, yet unmarried. Any male in Iraq with these characteristics has no excuse not to be married. While I had my doubts with regard to Imus's abilities, this evening Imus proved to me that he is a "ladies' man."

Imus typically set up his computer next to mine on our table in the Iraqi COC. While on duty with me he spent his nights chatting on the Internet, since I only occasionally needed his terp services. This night was no different. Imus booted up his computer and started chatting online. Imus usually spoke with his friends and relatives, but this time he claimed to be chatting with a married American woman who wanted to marry him.

To call his bluff I sat over his shoulder and watched the conversation between him and whoever was on the other side of the chat session. While the chatter between Imus and the person on the other end seemed to corroborate Imus's story, I found it hard to believe that a married American woman could be swooned by an Iraqi with no hope, no future, and living a world away. Imus was likely dealing with a pedophile searching for his next victim.

Imus managed to prove me wrong. He put on his headphones and told the lady to turn on her webcam so he could see and speak with her. I called Imus out. "You are so full of shit," I said. "I guarantee the person you're talking to will not show their face." I returned to my desk to continue my work.

Within a few minutes I heard a thick West Virginian accent say, "Imus, baby, I love you. I want you to come to America so we can live together. I will leave my kids and my husband." I sprinted to Imus's computer screen. I couldn't believe what I saw.

I was looking at a woman in her mid-forties sitting in what appeared to be her study. I shook my head in disbelief and went back at my desk. Imus began speaking with the woman through his microphone. The conversation was mundane: They asked each other about their families, the weather, and made general small talk. After my astonishment wore off, I stopped eavesdropping on the conversation and went back on my work.

"I am putting my tongue on your hard nipples now. I am slowly moving my way down your body so I can lick your beautiful flower." I popped out of my chair. "Imus, did you just say what I think you said to that lady?" He ignored me and continued spewing graphic sexual speech to the woman on the other side of the computer. I couldn't handle it. I had to see what was going on. I witnessed the unthinkable. The housewife had her top off, she was caressing her breasts, and was obviously pleasuring herself out of the webcam's view.

The absurdity of the situation was too much. From a swahut in Al Anbar Province, in the middle of a war zone, Imus was conducting phone sex with a married woman. Even so, this homemaker, a world away, continued to enjoy what Imus had to offer. I guess this was her release from what I can only assume was a lame duck life she had with her husband. Imus continued his Casanova tactics on the lady. I was still not completely convinced. I told Imus, "I need to talk to this woman and make sure she isn't some chick from some sort of paid service."

Imus wanted to prove to me that this was the real deal. He spoke with his Internet lover. "My friend just came in the room here. He is a U.S. Marine and wants to talk with you to see how you are doing. Would you mind speaking with him for a few moments?" Imus handed me the headset. I introduced myself and started asking the lady basic questions that only an American would know. She responded effortlessly. We spoke about West Virginia, her family, and the weather in the States, and she thanked me for my service in Iraq. This was the real deal. Scared about what I had stumbled upon, I handed the microphone back to Imus. I was in shock. I had witnessed an unshaven, 130-pound weakling, living thousands of miles away from America, have phone sex with a married West Virginian with three children and a steady job. I couldn't imagine anything more mind-boggling.

After handing the microphone off to Imus, I went back to my desk to get my head around what had just happened. I then heard the lady crying over the microphone. She moped, "Imus, I love you—so much! How can I get you to America? I want to be with you forever. Just tell me when you come here and I will leave my husband for you. We are meant to be. I pray everyday that you will show up on my doorstep." Imus smirked in my direction and then redirected his attention to his psycho friend, saying, "I love you too, darling. You are my flower, and my joy in life. Everyday I am without you is another day I wish I were dead." I simply rolled my eyes at the crap he was spewing.

The Romeo and Juliet soap opera conversation went on for a good ten minutes. Eventually, the woman's husband came home and she needed to cease the webcam conversation before she was caught. Imus gave her his best wishes and more words of his undying love for her. After this experience I never questioned any of Imus's stories. I had witnessed with my own eyes the absurdity that can occur over the Internet. While there was a general lack of sex education throughout Iraq, a few Iraqi men had done their research. ¡Ay, caramba!

Laziness, Lack of Initiative, and Militias

Sometimes working within Iraqi culture is fascinating and provides a front-row ticket to a comedy show; however, most of the time it is simply frustrating. One morning it seemed like there needed to be five Mulazim Jamals at one time. Everyone on the adviser team liked to task me to deal with their *jundi* problems. Now even the boss was getting in on the action.

Major Pyle grabbed me and said, "Jamal, I need some help with the Iraqis." I replied, "Sure, Sir. What do you need?" He said, "Jamal, I need you to address Lieutenant Seif and ask him why the hell he didn't wait for me to attend his convoy brief this morning. We had a deal last night that he would wait for me. I thought you had these guys squared away." I knew why the Iraqis didn't want him to attend the briefing—they hate him. Even at this late stage in the deployment the boss insisted on controlling everything the Iraqis did. The *jundi* wanted no part of him.

We caught up with Lieutenant Seif. He addressed me in Arabic before we were able to utter a word. I interpreted what Seif said to the boss. "Sir, in a nutshell, Seif says he started his brief early so his men could prepare their trucks and be on time for the convoy departure." Once the boss left the area, I addressed Seif to get the genuine scoop. The reality of the situation was that Seif started the convoy brief ten minutes early, went over the basics, and cut everyone loose. They didn't want Major Pyle attending because they knew he would drag the meeting out forever and make them do their convoy brief according to the Marine standard I taught them a few months prior.

Major Pyle, like many U.S. military commanders, always wanted to add complexity and extra bullshit to the Iraqi equation. In the Marines we can accept longer meetings that go over things in more detail. We can accept more attention to detail. We can accept time-consuming measures that lower risk. In summary, Marines are Americans, and Americans are typically risk averse when it comes to life or death situations. We do everything we can to mitigate risk, despite the fact the mitigation efforts will cost us in lost time.

But the Iraqis are completely different. They are much more willing to accept risk if they can waste less time in meetings and on mission preparation. The Iraqis will never accept the Marine way of doing things as the right way of doing things. Sure Marine methods may save someone's life every so often, but every second spent pontificating and addressing risk factors is time wasted to Iraqis. The cultural acceptance of death makes the *jundi* lazy. For Americans being labeled as "lazy" automatically carries negative connotations. Paradoxically Iraqis will think of positive connotations associated with being lazy. In their mind, lazy people are wise people.

I was starting to follow the Iraqi logic, despite how obtrusive it was to our mission in Iraq. Being lazy made perfect sense in the Iraqi environment. Imagine being raised in a Bedouin tribal culture, immersed in a searing desert environment where the next fight for survival could be at any moment. For any chance at survival you would make sure you didn't waste time or energy on frivolous activities. Wasted effort meant more water lost, more resources expended, and less readiness for an inevitable conflict. This attitude, I began to realize, pervades everything Iraqis do. Their laziness is an adaptation, a survival mechanism they use to cope with an extreme environment.

To get a better understanding of why Iraqis are so lazy, lack desire, and have no initiative, I approached our terp, Moody, whom I considered a sage on Iraqi politics and culture. "Jamaaaalll, come on in!" Moody shouted, as I entered the terp's swahut. Lebanese music videos were blaring on the television, and the smoke from Moody's hookah pipe engulfed his head. "Jamal, sit down, chill out, stay a while my friend."

After a round of small talk I started my interview. "Moody, I'm going to be frank here. Why in the hell are the *jundi* so lazy?" Moody smiled and said, "Jamal, the answer is simple. Their country is at war, their families are in constant danger, they are not paid much, they live in Al Anbar, their work sucks, everyone is corrupt, they don't get a chance to see their families often, their relatives and friends are dying everyday, and there is no real incentive to even be alive. Would you be very motivated in this situation?" Before I could even answer Imus mysteriously popped out from under his bed sheets and said, "Jamal, if I already live in hell, why does it matter if I live or die? I do not care. Why would I put effort into anything?"

"Thanks for your two cents, Imus," I replied. "You can go back to bed now." I turned toward Moody again. "Moody, seriously, how can these guys be so lazy? Do they not have this same sense of patriotism or pride in their work as Americans? How can we get them motivated? Colonel Abass told me that in the old Iraqi army soldiers were more motivated."

Moody broke things down like an economist. "Jamal, American soldiers are idiots when you think about it. Americans use pride, patriotism, and all that shit so they can pay their soldiers less money. And at the same time, the government is able to get them to do a very dangerous and crappy job. Think about it." Moody looked at me then continued. "Colonel Abass is correct—at some level. In the past there was a lot more pride and sense of patriotism in the old Iraqi army, but let me tell you that Iraqi soldiers were still lazy back then. It's just that at that time Saddam was able to use fear to motivate the *jundi*. If they didn't perform their duties, they were pummeled or their families were beaten."

I asked, "What's the solution?" Moody said, "Solution to curing Iraqi laziness? Ha!" He paused. "You want more soldiers? You want them to work harder and get more done?" He raised his voice and proclaimed, "Pay . . . them . . . more!"

I laughed aloud. Moody was spot on. "While I think there may be five idealistic patriots roaming the Iraqi countryside," he ranted, "my guess is that the rest of those who join the Iraqi army don't believe in the government or the country. All they care about is getting a paycheck, feeding their families, and being a respected member in their tribal community. The Iraqi army is nothing more than a mercenary force made up from local tribes who are hired by the central government to do its bidding. The way to encourage mercenaries to do a better job is to pay them more money. It's pretty simple."

"Militias? What about militias?" Mark stumbled from his rack and into the conversation. "Mark, what's going on, brother?" I said. "We weren't talking about militias, we were talking about how the Iraqi army is made up of mercenaries." Mark replied, "Oh . . . well, I feel stupid." I comforted him. "Sit down, man. Let's talk about militias, I guess it's related and you seem excited about the topic." Mark eagerly jumped up to join the conversation.

"Mark, Jeysh il Mahdi [the Mahdi army], what's their story?" Mark replied, "The Mahdi army? Oh, it is run by our good friend Muqtada Al Sadr in the Sadr City district of Baghdad. I love those guys!" I sneered at Mark and said, "You love the Mahdi army? The same guys who are causing many of the problems in Iraq?" Mark retorted, "Problems? Man, those guys kick ass. In my neighborhood in Baghdad they are the only reason my family is still alive! They walk around my neighborhood and make sure no Sunni or other troublemakers are in the region. If someone from outside the local area is in town and can't explain why they are there   they are shot."

I immediately asked, "Well, what happens if I just want to hang out or check out your neighborhood." Mark replied, "Jamal, there is no 'hanging out' in Baghdad these days. Anyone who says they are just visiting is a terrorist."

The talk of militias got me thinking: How many of our *jundi* on leave go back home to moonlight as militia members? Are we simply training the Mahdi army? I asked Mark, "Dude, what percentage of our battalion is Mahdi army or part of a militia? I see Muqtada Al Sadr pictures on the *jundi*'s cell phones all the time." He responded, "Well, I do not know the exact portion, but my guess is there are many. I have spoken extensively with Qatan, Sermen, Ayad, and Badr on the subject and its seems the general assessment is that at least half of our battalion probably moonlights in a Shia militia when they go home on vacation."

I retorted, "Mark, there is no way, man." He replied, "Jamal, there is a way—think about it. You are a young military man, strong, trained, and so forth. How can you not join a militia when you get home? Your family and tribe would be ashamed if you did not help the local militia. You think it is coincidence that all the militia members on television look just like *jundi* in civilian clothes?" Defeated, I replied, "Yeah, you are right. I guess I just haven't connected the dots until now."

Mark continued to describe the militias. His basic point was that the militias did a good thing for the communities because they provided security and kept outsiders from causing problems in the neighborhood. In effect, they were the neighborhood watch with AK-47s and RPGs.

After gaining insight into why the militias were so revered by the people in Iraq, I understood why it would be difficult to get rid of them. From the local Iraqi perspective, when the central government told the militias they needed to disband, they were effectively telling the local citizens that they were taking away their security and letting them be slaughtered. The central government's claim was that the Iraqi security forces would take care of the job, but this was nonsense or the militias wouldn't have been needed in the first place. It appeared that part of the final solution in Iraq would involve accepting militias in Iraq.

Somehow our conversation started with why Iraqis are lazy, moved to militias, and ended up on the discussion of oil. Whoever coined the phrase "It's all about oil in the Middle East" was a genius. It is all about oil. Mark, unlike other Iraqis, spoke about oil in a positive light. "Jamal, we have the ability to produce three million barrels of oil a day and have over one hundred billion barrels in the ground," he told me. "If we can produce three million barrels a day, 333 days a year, we are pumping out one billion barrels a year. If oil stands at eighty dollars a barrel, that equates to eighty billion dollars in revenue a year for Iraq." He explained further. "Let's say it costs twenty dollars a barrel to get it out of the ground. In the end, Iraq has sixty billion dollars in profit. Iraq only has a population of around twenty-three million these days. What this means is that we could pay every single Iraqi almost thirty-five hundred dollars per year. It is insane that we continue to fight and bicker."

"Dude," I said, "that is insane. These *jundi* make four thousand dollars a year [outstanding pay in Iraq] and their life sucks. Now tell me this, are you saying that if everyone in Iraq just stopped fighting, went to their homes, and engaged in a national oil effort they could double the average Iraqis wage [perhaps two thousand dollars a year]?" Mark replied, "That is exactly what I'm saying. Pretty crazy isn't it? The problem is I'm a Kurd. We understand this logic. The Arabs, not so much. They will never trust each other to do something like this."

Regrettably, I think Mark's assessment is correct. In the midst of everyone trying to get their fair share, they will forget to share.

Iraqi Bloodlust

There are no days off in Iraq. Some 122-mm mortars hit the Iraqi army side of the Barwana FOB on one of our supposed days off, liquidating one *jundi* and mutilating another. We were immediately dispatched to retrieve the body and calm the *jundi* at the Barwana FOB. We mounted the trucks and prepped our gear.

I was furious that the insurgents had killed the *jundi*, but my anger was contained. In contrast the *jundi* were hell-bent on revenge. On the trip to Barwana they engaged two vehicles because they "looked suspicious." In both cases it was obvious the *jundi* were acting out of character. Normally they respected civilians and granted them the benefit of the doubt, but when they were wired, everyone was an insurgent and deserved death.

The return trip home was no less heated. Immediately after loading the angels into the Kraz and exiting friendly lines at the Barwana FOB, radio traffic spewed over the Iraqi net: "We are taking fire." The Iraqis quickly engaged a vehicle on the side of the road. Doc, the world-class Navy corpsman he is, lunged from the side door of our Humvee as it was still rolling to a stop and sprinted to the scene to administer first aid. The *jundi* had fired indiscriminately into a vehicle and three rounds had shredded an older man's legs. Despite the patient's profuse bleeding, Doc promptly stabilized the civilian and saved his life.

The event happened so quickly it was hard to decipher the situation. Luckily, at the time of the incident another group of Marines were watching over the scene. The squad leader radioed to our truck, "Shadow, what the hell are your Iraqis doing? The lead Humvee just started firing on a vehicle." Major Gaines replied, "They told us they were being fired upon." The Marine on the hook responded, "Negative, Shadow. They fired at vehicles on the west side of the road with civilians. Unprovoked. We've been watching the entire incident."

I looked at Gaines. "Sir, these guys are insane." Gaines nodded in agreement and replied on the radio, "Roger, we'll address the issue with the *jundi* when we arrive to Camp Ali. Report the incident as you saw it to your higher headquarters. Sorry about the mix up."

We did a quick turnover with the Marines on location and forced the *jundi* to get out of the scene. At this point they were just loose, loaded cannons on the road. The longer we had them outside the wire in an emotional state, the better chance we had at landing a headline on the CNN nightly news.

As if the Iraqis hadn't caused enough chaos on the convoy, the excitement continued. While on Route Raptors, a military-only route along Lake Qadisiyah, the convoy came to an abrupt halt. Before I knew it the *jundi* were on their feet chasing down a vehicle. By the time we got to the scene the *jundi* had five young Iraqi males lying flat on the desert floor with their hands tied behind their backs. I addressed the situation with Captain Natham, the convoy commander. "NaQeeb Natham, Shaku Maku? Leysh nugof hinah?" (Captain Natham, what's going on? Why did we stop here?) He responded irrationally. He and the *jundi* felt these kids were responsible for firing the 122-mm into the Barwana FOB. In my mind these kids were obviously a group of brothers who had been fishing throughout the day and were on their way home. Nevertheless, after a long discussion it was determined that the young men would be taken back to Camp Ali for further interrogation. We were completely against the idea, but sticking to the adviser code we let the *jundi* carry on with their actions.

Upon our arrival to Camp Ali the intensity and emotions were electric. The battalion mosque was playing martyr music over the loudspeakers and everyone in the camp came to see what was left of the bodies. I looked at Staff Sergeant Haislip and said, "Good God. I didn't even know this many *jundi* existed on the camp!" Amid the mourning I was tasked with transferring the innocent detainees to the detainee questioning area. This was not a trivial task, as we had to wade through a hundred revenge-minded *jundi* who needed a scapegoat for their anger. We gingerly made our way through the traffic. Without my presence I'm sure the detainees would have been beaten on the spot.

Once at the questioning area I addressed Natham. "You guys will treat these detainees fairly, right?" Natham smiled. "Of course, Jamal," he said. "We will take care of them." I usually trust Natham, but this was one case where I was not convinced. I left the questioning area for a few minutes, planning to return to see what had transpired between the *jundi* and the detainees.

I returned to see the young boys with two by fours resting across their backs and the *jundi* yelling at them to give them information. At the beginning of my deployment I would have gone crazy and done something useless, like tell the *jundi* to stop what they were doing. Instead I simply spoke with Riath, one of the *jundi* involved in the questioning, to see how he was doing. My intent was not to actually have a conversation but to let the *jundi* in the area know that I was watching them and that they would need to refrain from being violent.

After the angels were transported to Al Asad, emotions died down. The detainees (who had no information) were released and received full apologies from Natham. Everyone was back to being friends. It was as if a light switch had turned off. Uncontrolled emotions can be dangerous.

Religious Matters

I've told the Marines on the MiTT that regardless of their true beliefs, while they are in Iraq they will appear to be Christians who believe in God. Period. Apparently 2/3's Fox Company Marines were never sent this memo. While in Barwana today a group of *jundi* approached me, obviously distraught, and asked me why the Marines don't believe in God—truly the ultimate sin in the eyes of Iraqis.

I was caught off guard. "Uh, minu gilitek hatha?" (Uh, who told you this?) Ali, one of the *jundi* in the concerned group, answered, "Huwaya Marines gilitna hatha" (Many Marines have told us this). The hamster wheel started spinning in my head. I needed to think of an excuse, and fast.

Then it came to me. Deny, deny, deny. I told the *jundi* that they were having translation issues with the Marines and what the Marines were really saying was that they believed in God, but that they were having a difficult time figuring out how He fits into their lives. None of the Iraqis seemed to understand my fabricated explanation. Instead they asked me another question: "Jamal, where do you think children come from?" I refrained from telling them they came from a sperm and an egg meeting in the womb and then cells dividing multiple times until it formed into a functioning organism. Instead I told them, "From God, obviously." Ali replied, "See Jamal, you understand. Why do the Marines not understand?"

I couldn't think of what to say next. I was stuck between a rock and a hard place. I wanted to be honest and tell them that not everyone in the world believes in God, but I also didn't want to destroy any relationships or positive feelings the *jundi* had toward the Marines or the West in general. I decided to go the Arab route—I lied. "Well, I think a lot of the religious beliefs get lost in the translation," I said. "I know all Marines believe in God. Sometimes, it just doesn't translate perfectly when they are speaking with you and it appears that Marines have doubts in God. I would not hold it against them, because they are all believers."

The Iraqis seemed to like my explanation. As long as the Marines believed in God, they were decent people. I left the scene quickly and immediately wrote in my notebook: "For commanders: before you come to Iraq, you need to have a plan for how you will communicate your religious beliefs. The trick is to not tell these people the truth, but, rather, tell them what they want and expect to hear so it doesn't take away from your ability to accomplish your mission. Iraqis lie all the time to ensure relationships run smoothly. Do the same. One of the ways you fight fire is with fire itself."

T. E. Lawrence, a British military officer famous for rallying the Arab tribes against the Ottoman Empire in the early twentieth century, summed up this lesson nicely in article eleven of his "Twenty-Seven Articles" (Arab Bulletin, August 20, 1917): "The foreigner and Christian is not a popular person in Arabia. However friendly and informal the treatment of yourself may be, remember always that your foundations are very sandy ones. . . . Hide your own mind and person. If you succeed, you will have hundreds of miles of country and thousands of men under your orders, and for this it is worth bartering the outward show."

Beggars Everywhere

There is one English phrase that every Iraqi knows by heart: "Give me." The MiTT and I have come to realize that living on Camp Ali is a lot like being stranded on an island where two hundred beggars surround you and demand your only coconut on a daily basis. During training the culture classes always mentioned that Iraqis are into gift giving and are generous people. The instructors told us that if an Iraqi gives you a gift, you should give him something in return as a sign of respect. Likewise, if you give an Iraqi a gift as a friendly gesture, he will give you a gift in return. Newsflash to future advisers: the gift-giving classes are complete bullshit. Iraqi soldiers want everything you own and have zero intention of ever giving anything to you in return. They are glorified beggars. For some reason the begging problem kept getting worse as we got closer to leaving. People only seemed to demand things; they never wanted to give anything up.

One experience exemplified begging in Iraq. I was on my way to the Iraqi COC for duty when one of the civilian cooks came galloping to me. Somehow the guy knew my name, and he addressed me as if we were life longbuddies. "Jamal, how are you doing, my brother? How's life?" Before I could respond he butted in and asked, "Can I have your camera?" I laughed at the audacity of his request. "No, you can't have my camera. I need it. Sorry, I have to go to work." The begging didn't stop: "Can I have your hat?" I told him no. "Can I have your computer?" Again I said no. He asked, "Can I have the t-shirt you are wearing?" Flabbergasted, I replied firmly, "La! Iimshee!" (No! Get out of here!)

After continuing along his laundry list of absurd requests, he blurted out, "Can I have your socks?" I stopped in my tracks. "Are you asking me for the socks I have on my feet right now?" The guy smiled, thinking I had finally caved to his requests. "Yes. Can I have them? Please give them to me." Angry, I replied, "Listen, I am not here to give you things. And no, you can't have the socks I'm wearing, you idiot. What the hell is your problem? You'll have to excuse me, I must go to work."

Later I experienced a begging incident that was the straw that broke the camel's back. I invited Sa'ed, a young, hardworking *jundi*, to my hooch so I could give him some things people from America had sent me that I did not need. Of course, Abdulrachman, the leader of the admin shop, ordered Sa'ed to tell him where he was going when he set out to visit me. Abdulrachman, and some of his *jundi* buddies, sensing they weren't going to get their fair share of whatever Sa'ed might be receiving, followed him to my hooch.

Sa'ed knocked on the door and I heard him say, "Jamal, shlonek? Anii Sa'ed." (Jamal, how are you? This is Sa'ed.) He sounded like something was wrong. I quickly opened the door, and immediately the uninvited Abdulrachman greeted me. "As salam aleikum, sadeeki. Shlonek? Shlon sahtek?" (Hello, my friend. How are you? How is your health?)

I was disgusted. Sa'ed looked at me, shrugged, and defended himself in terrible English. "Sorry, Jamal. He come, Jamal. Me no stop." Abdulrachman said, "Can I call my family? Can I have some of your food?" I shot him a nasty look but showed him Arab hospitality nonetheless, saying, "Abdulrachman, sit down, please. Unfortunately, the satellite phone is not working so you will not be able to call your family [a total lie]. If you want some food you can have whatever you would like on my shelf."

As soon as Abdulrachman sat his ass on the corner of my bed, he started eyeing my food supplies. He dug into everything I owned like a starved raccoon. I stopped him. "Abdulrachman," I asked, "what's up man? Are you going to take everything I own?" He responded, "Sorry, Jamal. I will only take a few." Before the last words could leave his lips, he had dipped his paw into my can of cashews and grabbed a massive handful, spilling half of them on the floor. Corporal Salazar, my roommate, said to him, "Hey, Iraqi dude, get the hell out of here. You are causing too many problems!"

My proposed meeting with Sa'ed, which was my attempt to award a *jundi* who did good work, ended up as a disaster. I pushed everyone out of the room. Everyone slowly left the hooch, grabbing at various articles of clothing and food like professional pickpockets. Everyone except Abdulrachman, who was still loading up on supplies of food. I peered at him. "Abdulrachman, what are you doing? Get out of my stuff! Are you a thief? What is your problem?" He said, "Oh, sorry, Jamal. I am leaving."

I turned around, expecting Abdulrachman to exit. He didn't. I turned back around to witness him grabbing one last massive handful of cashews and stuffing his mouth full of jerky. I raised my voice. "Abdulrachman. Out—now!" He sprinted for the exit, flipped a 180, and turned toward me. "Jamal, I want to talk to my family. Give me the satellite phone, okay?" I contemplated grabbing my M-4 and shooting him in the head, but instead I maintained my cool. "Abdulrachman, you will have to speak with Major Pyle about this or ask Colonel Abass."

Sa'ed realized my frustration with the situation and, risking a beating later on, yelled at Abdulrachman, "Seyidi, Jamal ma yreedna hinah. Yalla, rooh!" (Sir, Jamal doesn't want us here. Let's go!) Abdulrachman replied, "Sa'ed, leysh tiHchi illi? Rah arooh shwakit areed. Iskut. . . . Yalla!" (Sa'ed, why do you talk to me? I will go when I want. Shut up. . . . Let's go!)

Abdulrachman was not an aberration. I'd seen similar behavior in the local kids, the local adults, the Sunni Iraqi contractors on our base, and the Shia *jundi* throughout our battalion. Everyone wanted handouts from the Americans, but nobody wanted to do anything for the handout. Iraqis are survivors. If they can get something for nothing they will latch onto the opportunity. My fear was that on a micro-scale, and probably on a macro-scale, we had become Iraq's "sugar daddy."

The begging problem became such an issue for the team as a whole that I began turning away the generosity of Americans back home who had been sending boxes upon boxes of toys, candy, and clothes for the Iraqis. While their gestures were sincere, if they knew how little the Iraqis appreciated their generosity, they would cringe.

Tribalism Strikes Again

"Jamal, help me. Ayad need you help. Ayad need you help, bad. Tigder tisai'edni? "[Can you help me?]" Ayad, a soldier in our battalion, blurted in a mix of English and Arabic. Ayad was in a cold sweat upon his arrival. Floored by the chaos, I replied, "Ayad, calm down, brother. I'll take care of you."

I sorted out the situation. Ayad needed to contact his family immediately because a *jundi* in the battalion heard that Ayad's family was in serious trouble. Ayad pleaded with me to let him use the satellite phone so he could call his family. At first I thought this might be another Iraqi trick to get something out of me for free; however, Ayad was a good Iraqi and had never begged from me before. I had to help. I grabbed the phone from the MiTT COC and handed it to him.

The story that unfolded was shocking. I understood chunks of the conversation Ayad had with his grandfather, but couldn't quite believe what I was hearing. I had Ahmed (who escorted Ayad to my living space) fill me in on the details after the conversation was finished.

Ahmed recapped, "Jamal, essentially, every male in Ayad's family is in jail. Ayad's eleven-year-old brother, Abdullah, was playing soccer in Najaf against some other kids on the neighborhood soccer field. At some point in the game Abdullah got in a huge argument with a kid on the other team, who happened to be from another tribe. During the game the kid on the other team did something to infuriate Abdullah. Abdullah took matters into his own hands, went home, grabbed the family's AK-47, and sprinted back to the soccer field. Upon his arrival he unloaded a magazine of 7.62-mm lead into the kid who offended him, killing him in cold blood."

Astonished, I looked at Ayad and asked, "Akhuek iktelit il waled?" (Your brother killed the boy?) Ahmed interrupted, "Jamal, let me finish the story here." I said, "Okay, sorry, Ahmed, continue." Ahmed went on. "So after the killing, the kids all scattered and the local police showed up immediately. When the local police arrived, they immediately apprehended Abdullah and marched directly to his home. The police arrested all of the male relatives at the home and brought them directly to jail."

I interrupted, "They sent everyone to jail?" Ahmed said, "Yes, Jamal, in Iraq the standard procedure is to put not only the perpetrator in jail, but to put all male relatives of the perpetrator in jail until the situation is solved among the tribal sheikhs. While the males were in jail, the tribal sheikhs representing Abdullah and the kid that was murdered got together to figure out the appropriate blood money to ensure continued peace and harmony between the two tribes."

I looked at Ahmed, bewildered. He paused a moment then continued. "If no amount is agreed on, the tribe that had the member killed is obligated to conduct a revenge killing against a member of Ayad's tribe or their honor would be disgraced." I asked, "What happened?" Ahmed replied, "Thankfully, the tribes came to an agreement—seven million dinar [forty-five hundred dollars]. Ayad's family will pay four million, and the tribe will pick up the three-million-dinar tab, using the funds received from the tribal taxes. The tribal sheiks have also agreed that once payment is complete, the males in Ayad's family will be allowed to walk free from jail and the tribes will never talk of the incident again. Great news, isn't it?"

I wasn't really sure how to respond and simply replied to appease my Arab friends. "Sure, that sounds . . . awesome," I said. "I'm so happy for your family."

Great news? Were these guys serious? This was the most insane story I'd ever heard in my life. I was still trying to get a grasp on it. At the most basic level, I was convinced that a baby born in America and a baby born in Iraq were the same people, but Iraqis, who live in a complex and demanding environment alien to our own, have developed perspectives on life and society that bear no resemblance to those of Americans. I had learned many things from my experiences to date, but there was one overarching theme: Iraqi culture is not Western culture and never will be. My Uncle Richard, a retired Navy man, sent me an e-mail that says it all:

> People ain't people the world over after all, are they? They sure ain't like us, and for any ignorant person here to even suggest using an American style of problem solving is ridiculous to say the least. The people of the Middle East or Southwest Asia are more of a feudal society than anything else. Yes or no? In other words, their allegiance goes to the path of least resistance or harm and that knows no government. Honestly, I believe individual courage is a rarity in their society unless you are a religious zealot. They fear being out of the mainstream, which is essentially forced upon them by thugs, warlords, and religious fanatics. There is no overarching rule of law such as we have in the United States, even though Iraq is where the rule of law actually started with Hammurabi. But trying to change their minds under that premise, is just plain ill informed and incompetent.
>
> The smile of a child is a wonderful thing in any civilization. It is as if they have something in common with us after all. That is until they have been tainted by the idealism of their supposed adults. I hope you have spent more time with some of the elders there rather than passing candy or toys out to children. You must win the hearts and minds of the elders in order to help change the future lives of those children you encounter. Not to burst your bubble or anything,

but even the cutest of puppies can grow up to be a raged dog if not properly raised by a competent trainer. Hopefully that is what you will take home with you.

Stay alert, be smart, and learn every day. You are in the best college available. My dad told me, "There is a lesson to be learned from everyone, thing, or situation. The goal of the truly intelligent is be able to see what that lesson is." I am proud of you, Wes. As proud of you as if you were my own blood.

Chapter 20

Violence Spikes

November–December 2006

"They cut their heads off and mailed them to the families?" I asked Corporal Shlessinger, a member of the Police Training Team (PTT) working with Colonel Farooq, the Iraqi Police leader in Haditha. He replied, "Yes, it's completely fucked up. Ten of our Iraqi police members were going on leave just north of Barwana to a town called Beiji. The insurgents caught them in a vehicle check point, chopped off their heads, and sent the heads to each of the respective families with a note telling the families to never cooperate with American or Iraqi government security forces."

I asked, "What did Colonel Farooq do about this?" Shlessinger replied, "Well, he actually collected all the heads from the families and gave them a proper burial during a ceremony held the other day. I mean, what can he say? All he cares about is getting revenge." Taken aback, I replied, "Yeah, sheesh. This country is warped."

After hearing about the bad news for the Iraqi police, I was in no mood to hear about more chaos. Nobody listened. Captain McShane came sprinting onto the MiTT COC patio with the bad news. "The leave convoy returning from Najaf was just attacked with a massive IED," he said. "Captain Hasen is missing half his torso and is presumably dead. Lieutenant Leif cannot even be found. Lieutenant Ahmed and Lieutenant Abass are both seriously wounded—it isn't looking good. I'm still trying to get details from brigade."

I couldn't believe it. Captain Hasen was dead? He was one of my best Iraqi friends and the best officer in the battalion. Hasen was a family man with two young daughters and a beautiful wife. He was not supposed to die. Losing Hasen would be a huge blow to the morale of the battalion and the country of Iraq. He was one of the few true Iraqi patriots in the country. Tragic. Doc said, "Dude, we are fucked." I responded, "Yeah, that is some seriously bad news, man. I can't believe we were sitting on this same patio a week ago eating popcorn with Hasen. Things aren't looking up these days."

War was indeed hell. Just a few weeks earlier we had lost some of our top Iraqi officers to an IED attack near Fallujah. A few days earlier Capt. Rob Secher, a fellow MiTT member in Hit, had been killed by a sniper bullet. During Captain Secher's memorial service 122-mm mortars came crashing into the ceremony with pinpoint precision. Someone within their Iraqi battalion had likely snitched to the insurgents. The initial estimates were five *jundi* killed, thirty-two seriously wounded, and one Marine adviser seriously injured. The insurgents didn't even have the decency to allow us to mourn our dead.

Baghdad on Fire

There was huge news out of Baghdad in late November. A massive attack on Sadr City, a primarily Shia area of the city dominated by the Mahdi army, had caused over 160 dead and anywhere from 200 to 300 wounded, with perhaps many more dead. At first glance a massive attack in Baghdad shouldn't have had an effect on our operations in Al Anbar Province. Unfortunately, we were feeling the effects.

The attacks prompted a countrywide vehicle curfew, which meant that the leave runs from Najaf had to be delayed yet again. And that meant that we would lose our fresh soldiers coming back to the battalion. The other consequence was that all the *jundi* were extremely concerned about their families and knew that they would not be going home anytime soon. Morale, already low, was sure to plummet.

To get further insight on how the recent violence in the country was affecting the *jundi*, I went directly to the source. I made my way to Sermen's swahut to get the inside scoop. Sermen, who had just returned from vacation in Baghdad, greeted me at his door. "Wasup, Jamal? Come on in, let's drink tea." I obliged and followed him into the rustic swahut. "Jamal, Baghdad is pure chaos," he said. "You wouldn't believe it. There are no longer rooms in the hospital to care for the wounded and people are being left in the streets to rot and die. Shit is disgusting." I urged Sermen and his mates to tell me more.

Sermen went on to describe a harrowing incident he had experienced at one of the sectarian checkpoints set up all around the country by various Sunni, Shia, and tribal militia groups. "Jamal, it's crazy. Just last week on my vacation, my buddy and I, who are both Sunnis, were actually stopped at a checkpoint on my motorcycle. We tried to divert our path, but their cars barricaded the road so fast we couldn't run away. Before Mohammed and I could figure out a getaway plan, the militiamen approached us." Sermen paused briefly then continued. "Mohammed, the dumbass he was, thought the men were Shia, so he pulled out his Shia version of identification [many *jundi* carry a Shia version of their identification and a Sunni version of their identification so they can present the appropriate version at militia checkpoints, which are scattered throughout Iraq]. I knew they were Sunni, so I pulled out my Sunni ID. In the end I was right. They were part of a local Sunni militia."

I asked, "What did they do to you guys?" He replied, "Well, for the next ten minutes I had to beg for Mohammed's life and try to convince the men that he was trying to cover as a Shia because he believed they were Shia. These guys were not having any of it. They gave me a proposal and said I had to accept it. The lead man told me, 'Kill your friend—now. If you do not, we will shoot him in the head and then shoot you in the head.'"

Taken aback, I said, "Whoa, fuck. Are you serious?" He answered, "Dead serious. I was in shock at the moment. I couldn't figure out what to do next, but by the grace of God a U.S. Army convoy started heading to the checkpoint. I thought for sure I was saved. Of course, the stupid Army guys just kept on driving and didn't notice that a militia checkpoint was underway and we were about to die. My heart sank again."

"Wait, the Army dudes didn't stop? Why not?" I asked. "Man, Jamal," he replied, "I have no idea, but I will hate the U.S. Army for the rest of my life. Anyway, so I had to think fast. I told the lead man, 'I will shoot my friend.' I then grabbed Mohammed—who yelled, 'Sermen, are you fucking crazy?'—and quickly drug him over to my motorcycle so I could grab my pistol. I winked to Mohammed and whispered, 'one, two . . .' I cranked my motorcycle, slammed the accelerator and we peeled out of the scene. Bullets were flying everywhere past us, but none hit us."

Gasping, I said, "Good God, man. Were you afraid or what?" Sermen peered downward, grasped his Jack Daniels cowboy belt buckle in both hands, and proclaimed, "Naw, it was cool, man!"

After hearing Sermen's amazing story of survival, he told me more about the situation in Baghdad. "Jamal, I'll tell you what I think the biggest difference is in Baghdad these days. It is not the Iraqis hatred for each other—this has been around forever and always will. It's the newfound hatred for Americans. Everyone hates you guys these days: old, young, Sunni, Shia, male, female—everybody. Hell, I have even heard of kids in Baghdad shooting RPGs and AKs at Americans because of the mess you have created."

I said, "Wait a sec, this is all our fault?" Sermen, a remarkably sensible Iraqi, replied, "You and I both know this is everyone's fault; however, one thing is true: if America wants to win Iraqis hearts and minds, they need to kill every Iraqi in the country. Then, they need to transplant new people in the area, because I doubt the current society will ever forget the pain and anguish America has put them through. Personally, if I was America, I would just bring in nuclear bombs and kill everyone."

Typically I took Sermen's assessments with a grain of salt. I also tried to get other Iraqi opinions on the matter and I talked to the terps to get the update on the sense of the Iraqi people. Unfortunately everyone I'd talked to was singing the same tune. I was even seeing reports in the Triad that validated some of the crazy comments made by Sermen. Recently I'd seen multiple human intelligence reports of little kids carrying guns and helping insurgents conduct attacks in Haqliniyah and Haditha.

It seemed the strategy of "winning over the younger generation" had all but failed. The perception in Iraq was that America was responsible for the chaos, ethnic cleansing, and tribal bloodbaths occurring throughout the country. Our designation as the ultimate scapegoat in Iraq may have laid the foundation for a whole new generation of people that hate our guts. *Awesome.*

It appeared that with the added children and with those who used to be fence-sitters, the supply of insurgent labor had gone way up. Now that we had effectively pissed off all of Iraq, we had more insurgents who were willing to accept lower wages to conduct terrorist activities. Our policy in Iraq sucked.

Business in Baghdad

My newest neighbors were Salah, Mostafa, Younis, and Qutaiba. All four of these Sunni men were highly educated, English-speaking engineers from Tikrit who were the leaders of the Iraqi construction company that was building new facilities on Camp Ali. To say they had lived tragic lives was an understatement.

Qutaiba invited me into his trailer to speak about his own struggle with the violence in his country. Qutaiba, an elderly man, "not a day over sixty" in his own words, was quite impressive. He was fluent in English and Arabic and conversant in Russian from studying advanced physics. His degrees included a bachelors, a masters, and a Ph.D. in civil engineering from the top universities in Iraq and the Middle East. If Qutaiba had been sent to America and dropped into the professor role at any university, nobody would have been able to distinguish him from any other highly educated university professor. Even so there was one distinguishing feature that made him different from your average university professor: twelve bullet holes in his body.

Qutaiba invited me to sit down. "Jamal," he said, "we have not spoken much, but I hear you are a legend on this camp." I replied, "Who told you that? Do you talk to the *jundi*? Actually, here is the important question: did people tell you I was legendary in a good way or a bad one?" Qutaiba laughed. "Jamal, it was all bad, my friend. I am sorry."

After looking with curiosity at Qutaiba's arm, which was surrounded in a metal contraption with medical pins penetrating his flesh, I had to ask him about it. "Qutaiba, what the heck is on your arm? You look like Robocop." He replied, "Jamal, are you sure you can handle this story? I know you Marines are squeamish." I smiled and said, "You think you're funny, don't you? Let's hear your story."

He went on to tell me his tale. "Jamal, six months ago, a group of men approached my corporate headquarters in Baghdad dressed in U.S. Army camouflage uniforms, spoke fluent English, and told me that they needed to set up a meeting to talk about a future construction job. Because these men were U.S. Army soldiers and I knew they had money, I quickly agreed to meet with the gentlemen, thinking it would be a great way to tap my business into the American money that was rushing into construction projects. The men requested that at the meeting I bring all of my top employees for the discussion. Excited about the opportunity, I agreed to set up a meeting for the following week."

The old man continued. "The following week the gentlemen I originally met came to my offices at the prescribed time, this time dressed in civilian clothes. Everything seemed perfectly normal. However, the lead U.S. Army soldier had an odd request. He asked me to bring all of my employees outside and put them in a line so they could search them for weapons. I thought this was a fair request, since these men were U.S. Army soldiers. I followed the request and marched all of my employees outside the building and had them form a line."

Qutaiba looked down and shook his head, obviously saddened by where the story was heading. He raised his head and continued. "Well, Jamal, my fourteen employees and I stood in a single-file line. We felt like we were being set up for an execution. We stood still for five minutes, trying to figure out why the men would not search any of us. Then the lead man commanded, 'Turn around and face away from us.' We obliged." I was stunned by what I was hearing. "We waited for another five minutes," Qutaiba continued. "I turned around, and to my horror there were five men dressed in U.S. Army fatigues pointing AK-47s and RPK machine guns in our direction. The men transitioned from speaking fluent English and began chanting in fluent Arabic with a Persian accent, 'Allah akbhar, Allah akbhar.' [God is great, God is great.] They opened fire on us, mowing us down like weeds. This was not a meeting for business, it was an execution mission set up by sophisticated Iranian terrorists."

I gasped. "Whoa! How did you survive?" Qutaiba replied, "I am not sure how I survived, Jamal. I felt rounds entering my body multiple times and blood was everywhere. I thought for sure we would all die. The terrorists finally left the scene, assuming everyone was killed. I was the only one still alive. Me, the oldest person in my firm. I crawled back to my office to call for help. Luckily the commotion roused the suspicion of people in the area and people came running to see what had happened. Il hamdu il Allah [Thanks be to God]."

He paused before continuing. "They told my family that I would die, but somehow I made it. I now have twelve bullet holes in my body and for the next two years of my life, I must wear this metal contraption so my arm can function in the future. Pretty wild story, isn't it?" I was in shock, but was able to respond, "Yes, you could say that."

Qutaiba scooted his chair closer to mine and came within six inches of my face, just close enough so I could feel his warm breath on my cheeks. "Jamal, my entire company staff was murdered, my business was shutdown, I had both hip bones replaced, and I underwent ten surgeries on my chest and arms. The terrorists took everything from me. But do you know what they did not take, Jamal? My fighting spirit. They can never take that from me. I will never give in to the terrorists."

Chapter 21

Wayn Jundi? (Where Are the Soldiers?)

November–December 2006

I finally got a grasp on the numbers coming back from the leave run. The situation was truly dismal. We had a grand total of 197 soldiers on hand, and I wasn't even sure that number was correct. More important, our battalion was left with a total of five officers, which meant that Iraqi leadership was nonexistent. Additionally, half of the 3rd Company *jundi* who operated out of Camp Ali were AWOL (absent without leave). We barely had enough people to run a platoon-sized patrol operation, yet we were still considered an Iraqi battalion on all official records.

The Battalion Comes Apart at the Seams

The reason for the complete lack of personnel was very simple: The Iraqis had decided to go on "extended" vacation, probably because of the recent violence in Baghdad and the spike in sectarian warring that had curbed the *jundi*'s desire to fight in Al Anbar when they had plenty of fighting to do near their homes. Of course, the Iraqis had been taking extra vacation throughout our deployment, so I wasn't sure this was the complete answer.

There was nothing we could do about the extended leave except report the issue up the MiTT chain of command and hope disciplinary action was eventually taken at the MOD level. But I was highly skeptical MOD would do anything about the situation. They were on their knees begging for more soldiers and couldn't afford to lose any more. Any sort of crackdown on the current *jundi* who decided to take extended leave would only have worsened the personnel crunch. The MOD had already had to rehire every soldier who had been fired due to disciplinary actions.

As if the actual numbers weren't bad enough, to make matters worse, none of the S-1 administration section had returned from leave. Ironically, the people who were supposed to count the *jundi* weren't even here. It looked as though I was now the S-1 clerk for the Iraqi army. Of course, at this point I was not too concerned about the problem. I had given up hope on the Iraqi army being anything more than a bunch of thugs, beggars, thieves, and desperate men with uniforms and AK-47s. There was no use stressing over the reality of the Iraqi army.

Let me be perfectly clear and state up front that my morale at the time was sky high, even though I hadn't seen my wife in four months. If I hadn't had a wife and a mother who were losing sanity every minute I was in Iraq, I seriously would have contemplated taking some of the *jundi* up on their offer to provide me shelter, security, and an Arab wife. It might have been cool to hang out in Iraq for a few years to learn more about the fascinating culture.

Nevertheless, I was highly disappointed with the progress we were making with our Iraqi army unit. I knew that some of our battalion's failures were due to some foolish actions by advisers on our MiTT. Even so the vast majority of the failures were the fault of the Iraqis: they did not give a shit about anything the Iraqi army did and they put more effort into figuring out how to avoid work than they did into actually working. As the saying goes, "You can bring a horse to water, but you can't force him to drink."

The biggest issue with the *jundi* was that they didn't show up for work. We had been on the brink of a personnel crisis the entire time we had been in Iraq. We had started with about 300 soldiers, which was less than 50 percent of what we were supposed to have in an Iraqi army battalion, and we now sat at fewer than 200 soldiers and had no key personnel or leadership resident to the battalion. We could have moved forward with 200 soldiers—if the leadership had been here. It would have been ugly, but we could have accomplished some basic objectives. But with 197 soldiers on hand, no leadership, and nobody willing to step up as a leader and make decisions, we effectively were left with 197 bums collecting a paycheck.

In Haditha the 4th Iraqi Company was representative of the crisis we faced. Out of the original 59 *jundi* we had there at the beginning of the deployment, 16 were injured, 10 were AWOL, and 19 had quit—leaving us with a grand total of fourteen. Fourteen soldiers? Were the 250 Marines in

Haditha going to turn over security duties to these 14 derelicts with AK-47s? If that was the plan, we wouldn't be leaving Iraq for the next hundred years. The situation was ridiculous, and if Colonel Abass and the rest of the key officers didn't return from this next leave period, our MiTT would no longer have a job.

Every time I hear a speech by President Bush touting the progress of the Iraqi army, I wonder if he has looked at any of the data from Al Anbar Province.

Running for the Exits

Poor morale among the *jundi* had been growing and was finally reaching disastrous levels. One day the buses from 3rd Iraqi Brigade (based in Rawah, which is west of Haditha) stopped at our camp to rest and refit. A slew of our *jundi* saw the buses parked outside the camp and immediately packed their bags. In their minds this was their opportunity to quit the army and get out of the area as soon as possible.

The scene at the buses was straight from a comedy movie. *Jundi* were tripping over themselves trying to transition from their uniforms to their civilian attire so they could get on the bus. I asked Abdulrachman, the nefarious S-1, to determine how many people we would lose. "How many *jundi* are leaving?" He replied, "Jamal, I don't know. The number is changing as we speak."

Although I knew the situation was futile, I called the boss to tell him the news. I knew he would be in a complete tizzy and want to come fix the situation himself. Predictably, Major Pyle came running to the Iraqi COC to get an update on the situation. When he arrived he noticed that the Iraqi leadership was doing nothing to stop the *jundi* who were trying to flee from Camp Ali. He walked up to my desk and began one of his heroic speeches. "We can't let this happen. I can't let this happen. I am going to go out there and stop the *jundi* from leaving." He turned to Martin, the terp on duty, and said, "Martin, let's go. By God, we are going to stop this shit!" Within seconds he was waddling out the door in the direction of the buses. He looked like a puffed-up rooster on his way to a cockfight. I mumbled under my breath, "Good luck, dumbass."

Why the boss wanted to stop the *jundi* from leaving on the buses is beyond me. We already knew there was going to be a huge number of *jundi* quitting after the next leave run, which would occur in seven days. I figured we should let the quitters go early so we could save on food and supplies. More important, we would give the quitters less time to think up schemes to steal shit from the camp as their parting gift.

Not surprisingly Major Pyle was unable to stop the buses before they could leave. I just didn't think the guy got it. What was the point of wasting everyone's time to keep a few *jundi* from quitting when they were going to get on a leave bus in seven days and quit anyway? I guess common sense is not a common virtue in the Marine Corps.

With the runaways on the buses and the rumors of an additional thirty *jundi* quitting after the next leave run, we stood to lose an additional 30 percent of our battalion, bringing us to a grand total of 150 soldiers—for a battalion that was supposed to have 755. For all intents and purposes, our battalion no longer existed. There wasn't even a unit to advise. The concept of standing up what is effectively a "Shia militia" in Al Anbar had failed.

Chapter 22

Disaster Strikes

December 2006

J ust as a game of poker started in the MiTT COC, Corporal Castro, an embedded Marine adviser who worked with 3rd Iraqi Company, came rushing into the COC. He addressed Doc with an odd request. "Doc, do you have a long plastic glove that goes up to your shoulder?" We all turned around and simultaneously said to Castro, "What did you just say?" I said, "Castro, I don't really care about what goes on over there in the swahut you guys live in, but what sort of kinky stuff are you guys doing these days?"

Castro, embarrassed and smiling, said, "Gentlemen, I lost the Surefire light that goes on the end of my rifle." Doc said, "Ouch, those are like five hundred bucks. But why do you need one of my long plastic gloves?" Castro, hesitating, responded, "Uh . . . well . . . I was in the Port-a-John [outhouse] and I was using my light to find the toilet paper so I could wipe my ass. The light fell out of my hands, everything went pitch black, and I heard a loud splash." We burst into laughter. Adams summarized the situation. "So you lost your Surefire in the shitter? Wow, now that is a shitty deal." Castro responded, "Sir, that is probably the worst joke I've ever heard." That night Castro went fishing for his Surefire light.

The Worst Day in Iraq

One day in December was definitely the worst day of the deployment. The first piece of bad news came from brigade. They reported that the leave convoy had been hit once again with an IED—in nearly the same

211

spot it had been hit the last time. Sixteen *jundi* were seriously wounded or injured. Thankfully, nobody had died this time around.

I was now very much on the side of the Iraqis. They had constantly bitched and complained that they shouldn't be taking the same route and traveling with the American convoy on the leave runs because it made them an obvious target for the insurgents. We needed to change the road or change the route—at a minimum. I did not want to see any more of my Iraqi friends die for no reason.

A second piece of bad news came by way of an email I received from Dan Ballard, a friend from Okinawa, Japan, whom I had worked with at 3rd Marine Division before going to Iraq. The e-mail subject was "Did you see the news on Nate Krissoff?" Oddly, there was no information in the body of the e-mail. Concerned, I immediately sent an e-mail to Krissoff, my roommate in Okinawa and my best friend in the Corps, to see what the news was all about. Unfortunately, the email to Krissoff was never answered.

Within minutes of receiving the e-mail from Dan Ballard, I got a phone call from Lt. Jeff Brewer, a good friend, and the assistant intelligence officer (S2-A) for 2/3. I knew something was not good the minute I heard Jeff's voice on the phone. He relayed the news. "Dude, Krissoff is dead, man. He died in an IED attack today." The words sucked the life out of me. I responded calmly, "No fuckin' way, dude. How the hell did that happen? I was just talking to him yesterday and he said he rarely even got the chance to go outside the wire. Are you sure?" Jeff responded, "I don't know, man. I just got the information and figured you should know." I hung up the COC wire-phone and sprinted to my SIPRNET computer to send another e-mail to Ballard. Ballard responded immediately with the details on what had happened to Nate.

He was definitely dead. There was no denying the fact I would never see my best buddy again. He had been on a convoy mission in Fallujah when his truck hit a pressure-plate IED that detonated directly under his seat in the back of the Humvee. He was the only one to die in the accident. The other Marines traveling with him were seriously injured, with shrapnel and burns, but they survived. Krissoff was apparently jammed in the backseat, knocked unconscious, and unable to get out of the vehicle before it burnt to the ground. May his soul rest in peace.

Nate Krissoff, or "Natedawg" as I called him, was one of the best guys I'd ever met, and it just plain sucked that he was dead. I wasn't mad for myself, but I was furious for America as a nation. Nate was a guy that was going places way above and beyond the Marine Corps. I had been around Ivy League kids, successful hedge fund managers, Wall Street types, Nobel Prize winners, and many other highly successful and accomplished individuals in my life, but I could honestly say that Nate Krissoff was going places none of them had been before. He was that good. Even if his death meant we would save the entire country of Iraq and make it a democratic beacon in the Middle East, I still didn't think it was worth it. He had a charisma and charm that were the best. He was a water walker.

I will never forget my times with Natedawg in Okinawa. We lived in the Bachelor Officers Quarters (BOQ) together and were roommates in a house that took us two painstaking months to find. I also got to share wild and serious times with him in the Philippines during the Leyte mudslide disaster and in Kumomoto, Japan, during the Yama Sakura bilateral military exercise. Natedawg and I were inseparable when we arrived at Okinawa in late 2006. We even got tagged to go to Iraq at nearly the same time. The only thing that really separated us was that he went to Fallujah and I went to Haditha.

As I write this I am still trying to get my head around the fact Krissoff is dead. Remarkably, I feel no self-pity. I know that warriors die so other men can live in peace, and that's just how it is. I am proud and feel privileged to have known such a great warrior, a great Marine, and a great friend. His soul will live forever in my mind. Gunnery Sergeant Hartman put it best in the movie *Full Metal Jacket*: "Always remember this: Marines die. That's what we're here for. But the Marine Corps lives forever. And that means *you* live forever." Nate Krissoff will live forever in the minds of warriors of the present and the future. Semper fi.

The Marines Encounter More Tragedy

Tragedy befriended the United States Marine Corps in December. In addition to Krissoff's death, a CH-46 helicopter missed the landing pad on top of the dam and landed in Lake Qadisiyah. Lance Cpl. Elliot Weeks and Lance Cpl. Michael Goble, two of the Marines working with our MiTT, had been on top of the dam at the time of the incident and witnessed the entire thing. Weeks recapped for me. "Sir, the bird was lifting off, and as it was moving past the edge of the dam structure, it just nosedived into the lake and then floated on the water's surface. We ran to the scene, jumped in the water, and started pulling people to safety. It was crazy."

Weeks and Goble's immediate and selfless reaction was admirable. They were both heroes.

A rule of thumb in the Marines states that initial reports are always incorrect. But the initial reports we got on the helicopter crash were way off the mark. The 2/3 had one confirmed Marine KIA and three missing in action (MIA) but presumed dead. A horrific day for the U.S. Marine Corps. One of the MIA was the 2/3 operations officer, Maj. Joseph Trane McCloud. Losing him was a huge blow to the Marine battalion. This was terrible news to receive a few weeks before Christmas. My prayers were with their families.

The night after the helicopter crash I lay in bed and listened to the rescue helicopters searching for our fallen comrades in the lake. They began moving search efforts to the Euphrates River, thinking the bodies had gone through the dam. It was heart wrenching and surreal to listen to the helicopters buzz overhead as we tried to sleep, but it was also comforting. We knew the Marines would recover the fallen no matter what the cost or inconvenience.

When they couldn't find the bodies from the air, the Marines took some very drastic measures in order to find them: they shut down the dam and drained the Euphrates. The site was breathtaking. There were a few things I was sure I'd never witness in my lifetime: the parting of the Red Sea, Africa taking over the world economy, and the draining of the great Euphrates River. To see the two-hundred-meter river, the lifeblood of civilization, driven to a small stream was a spectacle. I'm sure there were quite a few Iraqis in Fallujah and Baghdad who were wondering what was going on upstream.

The helicopter crash story had even made the news on CNN. The official report noted four confirmed dead and ten survivors, which jibed with what we had been hearing from the Marines in the dam. While it was absolutely tragic for the four men who died, I was very thankful ten men had survived. When I first heard of the crash, I thought for sure there would be no survivors given the unforgiving conditions of Lake Qadisiyah.

Later I got a firsthand look at how ridiculous the Arab media is—and at the same time I realized that our own media was not that far ahead. The Arab media reported that there was a possibility the helicopter had been shot down by insurgent gunfire and that thirty Marines may have died in the incident. Their evidence came from some Haditha resident who claimed to have seen a flyer posted on a Haditha mosque by a member of the Islamic state of Iraq. What a bunch of bullshit.

Our media reporting wasn't much better. Our own highly respected newspaper, the *Washington Post*, published buffoonery. In a press release dated December 5, 2006, Nancy Trejos, a *Washington Post* staff writer, wrote a couple of absurd things. First, she claimed that the mayor of Haditha, Ibraheem al-Bayati, said the helicopter had been shot down by insurgents with machine-gun fire as it was taking off from town. This was impossible because before the crash the mayor of Haditha had been sent to Abu Ghraib for being an insurgent. I guess Trejos interviewed him from prison to get his expert opinion on an event that happened in Haditha. Ridiculous.

Trejos then made another absurd claim—that an Iraqi army officer named Lt. Hussein Muslih was making the same claims as this Ibraheem al-Bayati character. This was equally absurd. I was the S-1 adviser to our Iraqi battalion and I have asked every Iraqi officer and looked through every administration roster for the past year—there is no evidence that anyone with the name Hussein Muslih ever existed. Moreover, I had the Iraqis check with the brigade, and they said there was no such officer in the entire brigade. This means that this *Washington Post* writer either made stuff up or cut and pasted propaganda from the Islamic State of Iraq's website and claimed the site's work as her own. The amount of lying, misinformation, and false claims in the Arab media—as well as in our very own—is appalling.

As if all this weren't bad enough, one day in December I woke up to a group of bomb sniffing dogs searching around the MiTT camp. Apparently Colonel Abass had heard rumors that many of the *jundi* were also in the Mahdi army. He had been catching *jundi* bringing in bits of explosives. Perhaps he thought that they were assembling some sort of explosive device piece by piece and that it would be wise to investigate the camp for safe measure. I swear this place gets crazier and crazier every single day. Tension just fills the air.

The Icing on the Cake

When it seems things cannot get any worse, they sometimes do. I knew my wife had been struggling during my absence. I spoke with her on the phone and found that she was officially clinically depressed. I was proud of her for telling me the truth and proud of her for going to the doctor to get drugs and counseling, but her timing was not impeccable. Her news came when Marines were dying all around me and big issues were at hand. I wished I was there to help her out. Or at minimum, I wished things weren't quite so terrible in Iraq so I'd have more time to talk to her. It was just one more thing to add to the list of shit that was going wrong around me.

Chapter 23

Light at the End of the Tunnel?

Late December 2006–January 2007

Things had to change. All I seemed to see and hear was bad news. I wanted to see something positive, but it just wasn't happening. I was curious to hear what the news back home had to say about the situation. Actually, I already knew without even watching: Fox News thought things were going great, and CNN thought things were falling off a cliff into oblivion. At least our media had their bets hedged.

Today we came together as a MiTT and decided on the future of our Iraqi battalion. Everyone agreed that because our numbers had dropped so dramatically it made sense to consolidate. Major Pyle agreed to ask higher headquarters if we could consolidate all the *jundi* in the Triad and bring them to Camp Ali. I thought it was a good short-term solution. Longer term, the only way to be successful was to get more soldiers.

The MiTT members were not the only ones thinking strategically. 2/3 had been drawing up some dramatic plans in an effort to stop the rampant violence in the area. It planned on digging huge trenches and building earthen berms around the Triad cities. Also, they intended to outlaw all nonessential vehicle traffic and create single entry and exit areas into each of the Triad population centers. Once the villages were contained, they would systematically purge each area of insurgents. In essence they were implementing martial law.

At face value the 2/3 plan seemed like a great idea, at least for the short term. 3/1, the Marine battalion that was caught up in the so-called Haditha Massacre, did the exact same thing during Operation River Gate and ended up having a relatively peaceful deployment.

Signs of Hope in the Triad?

2/3's counterinsurgency-control measures were working wonders. The vehicle traffic ban, entry and exit checkpoints, and the berms around the towns caused insurgent activity to plummet. On the flip side these rules also made normal life in the Triad a near impossibility. Teachers could no longer get to school, the cost of everyday goods like food and gas went through the roof, smuggling rings popped up throughout the Triad, and visiting relatives in a nearby area became impossible.

While all the Triad villages showed progress, Haditha's success was the brightest. Haditha had been the hottest place in all of Iraq, with an average of thirty to forty attacks a week. Now there were one to two a week. Additionally, Haditha's all-girls school was back open, women were now walking around the streets without burkhas, shops were reopening throughout town, and there was a renewed sense of hope in the area. All of this was compelling. Only two weeks earlier we had been living in complete Armageddon. The reduction in violence was the best Christmas gift we could ever have received.

Political Reconciliation Stalled

Despite appearances it seemed the Iraqis were not on track for success (at least as the West sees it). They probably never will be successful. Not until their entire culture changes. I wish I could say something more positive about the situation, but I can't. I've seen the man behind the curtain pulling the strings.

I had been living at the FOB in Barwana and had had the opportunity to mentor Lieutenant Ahmed, the 2nd Iraqi Company commander. His actions before an important meeting with all the Barwana area leaders, including local sheiks, the Iraqi Police commander, and the 2/3 Fox Company commander, were a perfect example of how Iraqi cultural traits of laziness, poor leadership, and selfishness lead to poor outcomes. Unfortunately, I wasn't allowed into the meeting because they wanted the meeting to have a primarily Iraqi face. Instead, I was to make sure that Ahmed, the Iraqi army representative in the town of Barwana, was ready to attend.

About thirty minutes before the 1030 meeting, I went to wake up Ahmed. He was conked out. He looked like a dead body. I tried to wake him. "Ahmed, you know the big meeting is going in thirty minutes. You have to wake up!" He grumbled something in Arabic that I didn't understand. I gently grabbed him by the shoulder and said, "Ahmed, you are the leader of the Iraqi army in Barwana, you must go to this meeting to represent the army!" Ahmed replied, "Jamal, I was on a patrol last night until 0200. I'm tired. I'm hungry. Who cares about the meeting? Nobody will agree on anything anyway." Trying to appeal to his anti-Iraqi police stance, I said, "Ahmed, if you don't go, the only representative for Iraqi security forces will be the Iraqi police commander. Do you want him speaking on the Iraqi Army's behalf?" Ahmed just turned over in his rack. "Jamal, tell them I am not going. Have one of the *jundi* go if they need somebody."

Stunned, I looked as him in disgust as he rolled over on his rack. I thought about how, when I first came to Iraq as an adviser, I would not accept this behavior and would make the Iraqis get up and go. But now, if Ahmed, the leader of the Iraqi Army in Barwana, didn't have the motivation to help win the war and foster political reconciliation in his small area of Iraq, why the hell should I? America wasn't in Iraq to win the war for the Iraqis. The Iraqis were here to win the war for the Iraqis—with our help if need be. We could win the war for them, or at least attempt to, but the minute we left, the country would revert to the way things have always been. What is the point of us even helping in the first place, if when we leave the place, it is going to revert to an ass-backwards tribal society in the desert?

Political bickering was evident at not only the local level in the Triad. While the drop in violence was especially promising for the Triad's future, the continued rhetoric in Baghdad among the Sunni and Shia powers was having direct effects on our ability to accomplish our mission. One day Colonel Abass and Qutaiba, the lead Iraqi construction contractor, received calls from the Ministry of Energy (MOE) and the Ministry of Water (MOW). Their message was direct: all of the contractors and all of the current construction already underway needed to be stopped and moved elsewhere because the land Camp Ali rested upon was officially the property of MOE and MOW and not the property of the MOD. According to the MOE and the MOW, the MOD had not been cleared to commence construction, even though construction had been given the green light many months ago during the project's planning phases. Talk about a complete waste of money and time. To make matters worse, the Iraqi contractors on base (who were exclusively Sunni) had gone on strike. Now we didn't even have the personnel to fill in the holes that had already been dug around camp.

It seemed there was a sectarian contest going on between the various ministries that was keeping the project from continuing. I could not pinpoint the reason for the bureaucratic bullshit, but I could pinpoint one direct effect—huge waste. The Iraqi and American governments were going to lose millions of dollars over this because a few guys at the Iraqi ministries couldn't get along and make a decision that was mutually beneficial to everyone.

When ridiculous bureaucratic decisions are made at the higher level of government in Iraq, the *jundi* always know what is going on (or at least, they think they do). The most common conspiracy theory I heard from the *jundi* is that the Shia ministers who dominated power in Baghdad did not want the government spending any more money in Al Anbar and would rather it was spent on projects in support of Shia interests around Baghdad and southern Iraq. I wasn't sure if their theory was correct, but I imagined there was probably a kernel of truth to it.

Marine Lance Corporals Have All the Answers

Lance Cpl. Andrew "Mac" McMonigal, at the ripe old age of eighteen, summed up the general assessment of our adviser team. We had been sitting on a security cordon in our Humvee for twelve hours during a mission to rid the northern part of Haditha of insurgents. Mac yelled from the Humvee's turret, "Sir, you want to see my moto [motivational] tattoo?" Tired of listening to lance corporal stories for twelve straight hours, I replied halfheartedly, "Sure Mac, whatcha got?"

McMonigal quickly dropped down into the cab of the Humvee and folded out his bottom lip. He mumbled, "Sir, this is my moto for life. What do you think? Pretty cool, eh?" I glanced at the inside of his lip. Tattooed in thick black ink was "fuck it." I responded, "Mac, you've got to be kidding me. You had 'fuck it' tattooed on the inside of your lip? What is wrong with you, man?" Lance Corporal Morgan, the driver, chimed in. "Sir, we're infantry grunts. Our lives suck. 'Fuck it' is our moto." I laughed. "Yeah, I guess you have a point."

Part 5

ALL GOOD THINGS
MUST COME TO AN END

Chapter 24

Civil War and Democracy in Iraq

December 2006

I had a chance to sit down with Colonel Abass while I was fixing his computer. I asked him some deep questions about his thoughts on Iraq's future, the invasion, and the current state of conflict in the country. Speaking with Colonel Abass was always an eye-opening experience. He had been an Iraqi military commander for twenty-four years. He had lived all over the country and survived, which was a testament to his intelligence and ability to understand his environment.

I listened intently to Abass's insights. "Jamal, the Americans say they have come to our country to help," he said. "I believe in their hearts this may be true. But this help reminds me of when the British came here in the sixties and seventies to fix the problems with our palm grove trees, which were infested with disease. They told us that we needed to treat our trees or they would all die of infestation. The Brits convinced us, but the problem only got much worse. All of the palm groves were destroyed. They didn't help anything, they just made the situation worse."

Abass shuffled around in his chair, sat upright, and continued. "I believe this second attempt of Westerners to help Iraq is similar to the so-called help the Brits gave us forty years ago." The room was silent for a moment. I then asked Abass a fundamental question. "Do you think we caused the current crisis in Iraq?" His response was crisp and clear: "Yes, of course."

Before I could ask him to elaborate on his bold assertion, he ranted about the idea of freedom and why it would never work in Iraq. "The Iraqi people have not known democracy—ever," he said. "How can we just let them have it? I see democracy and freedom as vaccinations. If you give someone vaccines who has never had any exposure whatsoever, the medicine that is meant to help them will actually kill them. A better method would be to give this medicine slowly and in small chunks so the people could adapt to it. Over time the vaccine would be much more effective." I sat and thought about his analogy, and it began to make sense.

Colonel Abass elaborated further on what America calls freedom. "Let me just tell you that freedom is not a healthy thing in Iraq," he declared. "You must remember that Iraqis are like caged lions. Imagine if you had a lion in a cage all of its life and then you let it out of the cage without any guidance or rules. This lion will do whatever it wants and wreak havoc. This is the mindset of the Iraqi people. The Americans dropped freedom in their laps and they acted like freed lions. The Iraqis have never lived with freedom or lived as a civil people. They have not had the chance to learn how to do it."

I reflected on Colonel Abass's statements. "Jamal, you know, the freedom Americans have granted Iraqis is not the same freedom Americans have," he continued. "Americans are not free like Iraqis are free. Americans cannot kill their neighbor for stealing their goat, cannot shoot an enemy because of a tribal feud, cannot kill their daughter for ruining the honor of her family. Americans do not have our freedom. They are simply free to operate in a highly constrained civilized system. The freedom granted to Iraqis is the truest of freedoms. It allows everyone to do anything they want without repercussion. In one word, anarchy. The only true freedom. Anarchy is what America has granted Iraq."

Still processing what the colonel had said, I responded, "Sir, what do you see happening? How do you see all of this playing out?" Abass paused to think for a bit. "Are you familiar with the civil war that occurred in Lebanon?" he asked me. "I see our crisis working very similar to theirs. I see America leaving soon after they realize they are only exacerbating the problems in our country and their dream of a democratic Iraq becomes hopeless. Once they leave there will be civil war and a struggle for power within Iraq. This struggle may last one year or it may last fifteen, as it did for the Lebanese, but eventually people will get tired of fighting and the leaders will sit down at the negotiating table and work out some sort of deal. The end game here is very predictable and has been played out many times in this region."

I hate to admit it, but I think Colonel Abass is a man to be listened to, even though everything he says spits in the face of the logic and rhetoric that comes from the Bush administration. His description of the Iraqi people as caged lions may sound as though he is saying the people act like wild animals and have no sense of civility without a cage around them. Unfortunately, his assessment, in a general sense, is correct. The Iraqi people are completely different because they live in completely different circumstances. All they know is violence as a means to an end. All they know is dictatorship and power as a means to control the population.

In hindsight it seems foolish for George W. Bush to claim that we are granting the Iraqi people freedom. What he really means is that we want to grant Iraqis the freedom to act in a society that constrains the actions of citizens. What we have given them is freedom in the truest sense, or in other words, anarchy. The questions Iraqis rightfully ask us are simple: how can America grant us freedom and then all of a sudden expect us to conform to the many rules a free society inherently accepts and abides by? What if we don't want to have other people practicing other religions here? What if we want to practice two-thousand-year traditional tribal practices of stoning women who commit adultery? What if we want to implement Islamic Sharia law? What if we want to implement honor killings? You gave us freedom, right?

I think America has made a huge strategic blunder in assuming that Iraqis would perceive freedom and democracy in the same way Westerners do.

Chapter 25

America Never Looked So Good

January–February 2007

O ne morning in January I went into the MiTT COC to catch up
on the latest news. It was not happy. Once again I was reminded
of just how dangerous and volatile Al Anbar Province could be. A
massive IED had struck a Marine Humvee, killing Navy corpsman Mat-
thew Conte and Marine gunnery sergeant Terry Elliot. In addition, two
other Marines had to be evacuated for urgent surgical wounds and their
survival was questionable. I just hoped that their families had the strength
when they heard the news.

Sickened by the news of more Marines dying, I went to turn off the
Internet. Suddenly an instant message window popped onto the screen.
It was a college fraternity friend of mine who worked and lived in New
York City. He, like most Americans, wanted to thank me for my service.
While I really appreciated his concern, he inadvertently said something
that showed his ignorance. He asked, "Wes, has your wife had time to visit
you out there in Iraq?" I didn't really know how to respond. Here I was
chatting with an Ivy League-educated Wall Street investment banker and
he didn't have a clue about the situation in Iraq. Ridiculous.

I wasn't mad at him for his comments, but I feared that his ignorance
was representative of many Americans who were never forced to deal
with the realities and costs of war. Unfortunately, these same people also
vote for what happens in war. Any time decision makers aren't forced
to recognize the costs of their decisions, they are destined to make poor
decisions.

We All Want to Escape Iraq

The final days at Camp Ali were some of the best I'd had in Iraq. Now that things were winding down and the few *jundi* I still advised were taking care of their own respective functions, I spent my time learning about Iraqi culture and experiences.

One afternoon I stopped by the terp hooch—my favorite destination for good conversation. Mark, Moody, Imus, and Martin were all available for discussion. Because the end was so near for me, and the terps would have loved to be in my shoes, the topic for the day was how to escape from Iraq. Mark's story had to be the most captivating. He told us the tale of his brother's harrowing escape from Iraq and into Sweden.

Mark's story began after the Gulf War (1990–91). Because of the security situation in Baghdad and turmoil after the war, Mark's family fled to Iran. After a few years they caught the "Kurdish pride" bug. This disease forced them to return to Kurdish lands in northern Iraq, where they would be surrounded with their family from generations before. Everyone was keen on the idea except Yasser, who felt there were no opportunities for him in Iraq. He had his eyes set on Europe.

Despite the impossible odds Yasser commenced his mission to escape Iraq in mid-1993. The first stage of his journey involved attaining a fake Iranian passport and sneaking into Iran. Once in Iran, the next stage for Yasser was to make his way north into Russia. Typically, the cost needed to bribe people along the way was prohibitive, but Yasser had saved the appropriate amount of money from selling Persian rugs on the black market in Iraq over the previous couple of years. In mid-1994 he made it to Moscow.

While in Russia Yasser rented a studio apartment and dated a local Russian woman who could show him around the city and teach him the language. Life was good—for the time being. In 1995 economic turmoil struck the country. A survivor by nature, Yasser saw the turmoil as an opportunity to escape to Europe, his final destination. As soon as it was possible Yasser jumped on a train to Lithuania, which had recently opened a policy to accept Iranians into their country. Bribery and Yasser's fake Iranian passport were going to come in handy for a second time.

Once in Lithuania Yasser scoured the country for work, but with no luck. After spending six months living on the streets, the situation was dire. Thankfully an opportunity finally came knocking: A new black market transport operation had opened for business and was offering to smuggle individuals on a cruise boat that traveled between Sweden and Lithuania.

The smuggling operation was not comfortable for refugees. The kitchen workers on the boat were involved in the operation to pad their poor incomes. The operation was simple: store refugees in the meat cooler away from the ship's security and then smuggle them off the boat in the garbage containers once they reached Sweden. Although it sounded chaotic, Yasser wagered his last funds on the opportunity.

Cruise liners typically attract many nationalities. The black market cruise line, it seemed, would do the same. On Yasser's trip inside the meat cooler, he was smashed in between 150 other people from Pakistan, Russia, Iraq, Iran, Afghanistan, and most other countries within a five-thousand-mile radius of Lithuania. All of these people had the same story: they were fleeing their countries and wagering their last funds on the chance for freedom. And the stakes were high. If the Lithuanian or Swedish government found them on the boat before they had entered Swedish waters, they would be returned to a Lithuanian prison where they would starve to death.

The boat ride during the cruise was horrific. The exiles shivered uncontrollably, meat carcasses slapping them in the face with each wave. What made the situation worse was the lack of oxygen in the refrigerator. The operators of the smuggling business had gotten greedy and had tried to fit twice as many refugees as was possible given the oxygen content of the cooler.

Stuck in the meat cooler with no oxygen proved a disaster. People started dropping like flies. Unfortunately, there was no way for the refugees to open the door from the inside to allow more oxygen into the room. Yasser, assuming the role of the leader for the group, decided on a plan. They would form a human pyramid that was tall enough to reach a small opening at the top of the meat locker. Hopefully, someone could fit in the opening, crawl through it, and eventually make it to the outside to open the door and save everyone inside. If this person was unable to open it, the meat locker would gain 150 additional carcasses.

The strongest individuals still able to function created the human pyramid. Yasser crawled along the human ladder to the small opening at the top of the cooler. He met face to face with the small opening that would save everyone's life.

Yasser attempted to squeeze through the opening but failed miserably. But he couldn't give up. He stripped naked to make his profile slimmer. He tried again to force his body through the opening. He eventually became stuck and thought for sure he would die in the meat locker. With no hope, Yasser corkscrewed his body through the shaft. As he moved he felt blood slowly trickling down his body as his exposed sides scraped against the screws along the passageway walls. The pain was excruciating, but this was a matter of survival.

Eventually Yasser popped out on the other side of the shaft. Unaware of his surroundings, he immediately started running around the ship, buck naked with blood soaked over his body. He yelled for a doctor or the captain of the ship. Miraculously, he ran into the captain's quarters on the ship. Trembling and in extreme pain, he began yelling in Arabic, hoping the captain would understand what he was saying.

Yasser failed to communicate but was able to convey that there was a dire situation somewhere on the boat. The captain called on a doctor to attend to Yasser's wounds. When the doctor arrived Yasser was able to explain to him the situation. Yasser and the doctor sprinted for the meat locker hoping to save those inside.

Once at the door to the meat locker, Yasser sprinted to open the door. He pulled on the levers. An Afghan man yelled at him from inside, "If you let us out of here I will kill you, and so will many others!" The Afghan, and a concerned crowd inside the locker, were afraid they were still over Lithuanian waters and believed that even if they survived this ordeal they would be sent to a Lithuanian prison to die.

Yasser was then faced with a decision: save these people now or wait a bit longer to fully explain the situation and hope they were in Swedish waters. Yasser explained in confidence to the doctor the situation they were facing. The doctor looked Yasser in the eyes and told him that if he did not open the door, the people in the locker would die very soon. Yasser continued to hear the cries of the Afghan man and a large crowd inside the meat locker who begged him to reconsider. Yasser decided to follow the wishes of his fellow refugees.

Yasser told the doctor his decision and the doctor sprinted to the captain of the ship to explain the situation. The captain of the ship, a kind-hearted man, called the office of the king of Sweden to ask for a solution to their predicament. The decision was quickly reached by the king: everyone on board would be granted green cards, guaranteed safe passage, and would not be handed over to the Lithuanian authorities.

Upon hearing the news the doctor streaked to the meat locker, where he met Yasser. "Open the hatch!" he cried. "The king has saved you." The two men tugged on the doors with all their might and cranked them open. A crowd of very cold but very grateful refugees poured from the cooler. The immediate exposure to oxygen-filled air saved everyone in the nick of time. They were all going to be given another chance at life in Sweden.

To this day, according to Mark, Yasser thanks God and prays for the king of Sweden on a daily basis. He has also found out about the finer things in life, such as drinking wine and hitting on Swedish woman, things that he dreamed he would be doing in Europe five years before he began his journey.

Showing the New Guys around Campus

Il hamdu Allah! The day the new MiTT arrived at Camp Ali was quite possibly the best day of my life. At the time I thought that if I died right then and there it would not matter, because in the past twenty-four hours I had felt more joy than most people feel in a lifetime.

The Iraqis decided to make the new team's first experience outside the wire way more exciting than we had hoped it would be. Within five minutes of leaving friendly lines, as we crossed into South Dam Village, the lead Iraqi vehicle had spotted an enormous daisy-chained IED, set up to destroy multiple vehicles in one shot. On finding the IED we conducted our immediate action drills, secured the area, and waited for the EOD teams to arrive.

As we were waiting on EOD there was even more excitement to be had. The *jundi* starting firing their massive Dushka (a 12.7-mm antiaircraft machine gun) in the direction of the palm groves. A hundred meters away each of us in the Humvee could feel the thunderous boom of the machine gun's rounds leaving the barrel. The young captain in the rear of my Humvee yelled, "What the fuck is going on? Are we in a firefight?" Suffering from combat complacency, I calmly replied, "No, Sir. I'm not sure what's going on. Iraqis like to shoot things. I wouldn't worry about it. There will be radio traffic any second now explaining what is going on. Just stand by." As I had suspected, the *jundi* firing into the palm groves was a knee-jerk reaction to nothing.

Eventually EOD arrived on the scene. We handed over the situation to them and proceeded to take a bypass route through the western desert. Typically, such a bypass operation was not a problem. However, Bill, the new terp, had forgotten his Motorola radio. Without a radio to communicate with the Iraqis, the scene escalated into pandemonium. The new team was witnessing the most unprofessional and pathetic showing of military efficiency and effectiveness the world had ever seen.

After bypassing the IED through the open desert, we continued on our way to central Haditha. A few miles away from the Haditha FOB, we entered an Iraqi police checkpoint. As soon as we arrived at the checkpoint, bursts of AK-47 fire spewed in front of us. We were in the rear of the convoy and did not know what was happening. It turned out that the Iraqi police had opened fire on a vehicle that was speeding toward their checkpoint. The captain and the sergeant from the new team immediately looked toward me and asked, "What the fuck is going on up there? Does this shit happen all the time?" I attempted to calm them down. "Gents, listen, this is not normal. Past month has been dead silent. I'm not sure why everyone got antsy on your first time outside the wire."

After showing the new team the operations in Haditha, we returned to Camp Ali. On our arrival the boss ordered, "Gents, we're going to turn around and do the same convoy, but we're switching in different members from the new MiTT." Doc sneered at me. "Sir, is he serious?" I answered, "Doc, would you expect anything less from our fearless leader?"

On our second trip to the Haditha FOB, we assumed we would field fewer questions. We had a Navy corpsman who was on his fourth combat tour and a Marine gunnery sergeant who was on his third trip to Iraq. Our assumption was false. The Navy doc acted like a puppy the entire time. First, he bitched about Staff Sergeant Haislip's driving and told him he was "swerving and juking around on the road trying to play games." I tried to explain to the doc that you couldn't drive in a straight line because you have to dodge potholes and suspicious areas along the way. This explanation sailed over his head. In his mind the drive to Haditha should be like a drive down the Pacific Coast Highway in California.

The new doc's other gripe was that we didn't immediately turn on our Chameleons on leaving camp. I tried to explain to him that there was no radio-controlled IED threat in the area and that the insurgents don't plant IEDs just outside the gate of Camp Ali because it is under surveillance at all times. He dismissed my answers and then threatened to kick all our asses if the next time around we didn't turn on the Chameleons the exact second we left the wire. Doc McGinnis replied to the new doc's threats for all of us: "Doc, quit being a pussy. You are with the Marines now. Plus, the Chameleon is not a force field that saves your life. Grow a pair of balls, dude."

The new team was running scared. I understood being motivated when you are in a combat zone and training hard, but I also understood that this was a marathon and not a sprint. If these guys planned to survive the deployment they needed to take a "chill pill" or they wouldn't survive the tour. I got tired just watching them.

The absurdity of the new team was exemplified on our convoy to Barwana. On the way the Iraqi water truck overheated and died along Route Phoenix. Somehow Sermen and his crew of Iraqi mechanics were able to get the thing running just long enough so that we could make it to the entry/exit checkpoint that sits on the outskirts of Barwana. With the malfunctioning water truck, we made it into the safety zone. We were relieved. If we had been stuck along Route Phoenix in hostile territory, the situation would have been much worse. The new team seemed to have a different assessment of the situation, however. They still thought we were under enemy fire. Once the Humvees stopped at the checkpoint, the new MiTT rushed from their vehicles, posted security, and searched for the enemy.

Doc McGinnis and I, still sitting in the safety of our bulletproof Humvee, looked at each other in amazement. Doc blurted out, "Sir, are these guys crazy?" I had no reasonable response. They were crazy. Here we were, in a Marine-controlled checkpoint surrounded with ten Marine amphibious assault vehicles mounted with 50-cals and MK-19 grenade launchers. What the new MiTT guys were going to accomplish by exiting the safety of their bulletproof Humvees was beyond me. I wondered if we had acted like this when we first got here. I remembered being nervous, but not stupid.

Chapter 26

An Assessment

January–February 2007

Turnover to the new MiTT was officially complete. We were no longer on the hook for anything. The new team was definitely a different breed, and I hoped they would be successful. I thought they would realize over time that their overconfidence, strictness, and motivation were useless on adviser duty unless they formed relationships with their Iraqi counterparts. I knew it had taken our team at least a few months to understand that Iraqis do not take orders from Marines.

I was happy our duties were over, but I was also very sad that I was leaving the battalion. I had formed amazing friendships with the Iraqis and gone on some amazing adventures. Sure, they were selfish, lying, untrustworthy, backstabbing, begging bastards for the most part, but they were my friends. I had to survive alongside these men. They were rough around the edges, but I knew that if it came down to protecting me in a firefight, every *jundi* in the battalion would have taken a bullet for me (see photo 19).

We were bound by a warrior ethos, and that is something I will never forget.

Final Observations on Camp Ali

I made some observations my final day at Camp Ali. Around camp we had half-built foundations for a group of buildings that were supposed to have been erected months ago, fifteen tractor and heavy equipment machines collecting dust and at the same time costing Iraqi and American taxpayers large amounts of money, a group of Iraqi contractors sitting in their hooch watching television and sleeping all day, and an ongoing fight within the MOD and the MOE/MOW over whether or not building can continue at Camp Ali. Hordes of wasted efforts and resources because the central government could not agree on issues.

We also had a battalion that had gone from about 500 soldiers to a unit of roughly 185 with low morale, no initiative, no desire to protect the Iraqi foundations of democracy, and a strong desire to collect their paycheck.

I witnessed six different occasions on that last day in which Iraqis, both *jundi* and the civilian contractors, came up to MiTT Marines to beg for coats, gloves, computers, iPods, memory sticks, and food. All of this begging despite the fact that many of the Iraqis already owned many of these items. The root of their begging stems from their perception that Americans have all the money in the world because the Jews stole it from the Arabs and stashed it in American banks.

In addition, I asked one of the Sudanese engineers on camp how he was doing as he walked back from his morning shower. He replied, "Kosey" ("Good" in African Arabic dialect). I then looked around and noticed that out of the fifteen generators on camp that this guy was supposed to be maintaining, only two worked. This begs a few questions: who from the Iraqi government is overseeing these contractors? Why can't somebody just tell these guys they aren't cutting it and rehire someone who can get the job done? And why is the Iraqi government hiring Sudanese engineers when they have a population of unemployed Iraqi engineers?

Another observation: this afternoon Howyi, a *jundi* squad leader, slapped an insurgent detainee in the mouth, which caused the detainee to bleed from the lip. The MiTT Marines were then under the gun from the 2/3 lawyer. He wanted them to explain what was going on and why they allowed the incident to happen. What kind of question is this? How long is it going to take American policy makers to understand that we are never going to change Iraqis and make them Americans? Iraqis are going to get rough with their detainees and there is nothing we can do to change this until they decide it is a bad idea.

The lawyer's next request from our MiTT Marines was to see the latest copy of the Iraqi SOP for interrogation. Is the U.S. military clueless enough to assume that the Iraqi army has a written SOP for all aspects of their operations? Are you kidding me? Iraq doesn't even have a functioning legal system that outlines what the rules are in society (aside from the local tribal law that rules most areas). How can they create an official document on their interrogation techniques when there isn't even a base-line body of law? I guess the "solution" we will use is the same one we always resort to: copy our documents, translate them, hand them over to the Iraqis, and tell them this is how they should do business. We can even tell them that detainees are to be given food and water, they need to be treated humanely, should never be intimidated or in fear, and should be handled with extreme care. The very idea that we can dictate any ideas—from democracy all the way down to how to do interrogation—is a grade-A example of dumbassery.

My take on the observations above is that the main reasons Iraq continues to falter is not because the U.S. military isn't trying its best but because of Iraqi culture, which sets them up for failure (or at least failure as defined by Americans: no democracy, not an ally in war on terror, not integrated into global economy, and so forth). Moreover, the American failure to understand Iraqi culture is encapsulated in my observation of the insurgent detainee. Even if Iraqis weren't destined to fail due to their tribal-based customs, Americans, because of our desire to control and influence every situation, would never allow the Iraqis to do things the way they would like to do them, which would stymie their ability to operate effectively.

One Marine's Perspective

There is a now-defunct theory held by war cheerleaders that if peace and security come to Iraq, the people will somehow magically come together and want to sing "Kumbaya" in unison. This is far-fetched for a number of reasons. After studying the Iraqi people for years and working with them every day for seven months, I doubt any Iraqi in the near future will ever trust another Iraqi when money, power, or resources are at stake. I was exposed to a real-life experiment (Operation Al Majid) in the Triad that allowed us to test the war cheerleader hypothesis that bringing security to areas in Iraq would foster agreement and somehow sprout democratic institutions.

Operation Al Majid was a great success by all military standards. After it, attacks went from forty to fifty per week to a couple attacks in an entire month—more than a 90 percent drop in violence. Along with that drop in violence there was a great increase in the number of people who seemed to view coalition forces positively. There also was a steady increase in normal activity throughout the Triad: shops were opening, people were finding ways to attend schools, and more and more people were out on the streets doing normal things. In effect, Al Majid created an environment of security and relative peace and quiet.

The way the theory goes, that security and peace should foster agreement, the formation of local governments, more respect for the national government, and the sprouting of democratic institutions. But I did not see or hear of any of this happening. What I heard was that all the local sheiks continued to fight among themselves, that sheiks were trying to broker deals with the Marines to get more resources and benefits at the American taxpayer's expense, and that people still had a complete distrust of the central government.

Nothing really changed—except who the sheiks supported. Before the sheiks had favored the religious zealots, but after the American sugar daddy came to the table, they supported us instead.

Regardless of who the sheiks support, the key factors are still the same: The Sunnis have no reason to believe in the central government, the sheiks want to maintain their little fiefdoms, local governments continue to bicker and fight amongst themselves, and nobody is willing to stand up for the nation of Iraq if it means abandoning their tribe or family.

Based on what I saw from the Triad experiment, the hypothesis that once Iraq is secure and peaceful it will sprout cooperation among the people and democratic institutions is false. I think this is because Americans apply their logic and reasoning to the situation. They assume that the Iraqi people will trust one another and choose to work with one another once the violence has ceased. But there is no historical precedent for Iraqis getting along on a national scale. Moreover, I doubt the Iraqi cultural traits of distrust, corruption, selfishness, and survivalist mentality will leave this area of the world anytime soon. Also, for the hypothesis to be true, the local sheiks and warlords who have ruled Iraq since the dawn of time must be willing to let democratic institutions flourish, knowing that this will directly degrade their power and influence over their area. The realist in me thinks this is about as likely as the pope converting to Islam.

The people in Iraq and the systems in Iraq, as they are currently established, will never become what America wants them to become. The United States came into the Iraq situation with a desire to fix the failures with American solutions. There is a problem in trying to fix Iraqi issues with American ideas: It allows the Iraqi people to blame their problems on our attempted solutions to their failed systems. What the Iraqis really need to do is be intellectually honest as to why their country is a failure. Once they realize that the faults in their system are due to a lack of initiative, lack of desire, laziness, corruption, selfishness, welfare-recipient attitude, and religious radicalism, they may be able to change from within. I do not think we can change them from outside.

Leaving Haditha

Before we departed Haditha, the area left us with a final memory. Twenty minutes before our flight we were all sleeping against the cinder blocks lining the rim of the dam when an enormous jolt went through all of our bodies. The ground shook beneath our boots. Major Gaines popped his head up over the cinder block and yelled, "What the fuck was that?" Everyone jumped to see what had happened. There had obviously been an enormous explosion in our immediate vicinity. Le Gette turned to look at me and said, "Dude, how lucky are we? We're going to die on the last day here from a fuckin' rocket attack. Amazing!" I flashed my trademark hang loose sign and replied in a sarcastic fashion, "Oh, yeeaah. Get some!"

We looked on the landscape of the Euphrates Valley for evidence of an incoming rocket attack. A thousand meters from the dam we spotted the culprit. An enormous billow of smoke was churning from the center of a road near the dam. The EOD team had conducted a controlled detonation of multiple IEDs they had found, which included five propane tanks filled with high explosives. Adams looked at everyone on the team. "Gents, let's get the fuck out of this place," he said. "Where the hell is the bird!"

The bird arrived ten minutes later. I felt like William Wallace in the movie *Braveheart*, when he triumphantly yells out "Freeeedom" just before his execution. I boarded the CH-53 Super Stallion helicopter and screamed William Wallace's final word, inaudible to anyone else because of the helicopter's engine noise. I was finally free.

We were finally in Kuwait and the nightmare was over. I will never forget the flight out of the Triad. I was able to see from the sky all the areas where we had been attacked with IEDs, all the areas we had been fired upon, all the FOBs we had visited, and all the homes of people we had visited. The place was so much smaller than I had believed it to be. The Triad had been my life. It had been the center of my world. It amazed me to think that in that little slice of the world I could experience so much and learn so many new things. In the Triad we were America's main effort. I am just now beginning to realize that Camp Ali is just another place in Iraq with two hundred hard-charging Iraqi bums trying to make a difference in a Third World land.

Being around the MiTT my last few days in Iraq made me realize something: No matter how dicked up everyone is on our team, or how idiotic or lazy people are, I still love all of them and think we had the best adviser crew Iraq has ever seen. We may not have been blessed with the most talent or that much brainpower, but we sure as hell knew how to have fun and make things happen with limited resources. For all the bitching, complaining, fighting, and hatred I had seen between the members of our team, I think circumstances brought us together as brothers in the end.

On my last day in Kuwait I focused on the beauty of McDonald's golden arches and the many women in camp. When you haven't seen a McDonald's or a woman in a long time, they do wonders for you.

Later on in the day, on our adventures around the Kuwaiti camp, Adams, Doc, Le Gette, and I went on a four-mile walk to visit the local market. We wanted to load up on pirated DVDs for the ride home and purchase gifts for family and friends. Four miles away from the main camp we tried to hitch a ride with one of the many U.S. Army or U.S. Air Force personnel that drove by. We were passed by no less than ten unloaded fifteen-person passenger vans. Nobody wanted to help the Marines. In all honesty, though, we didn't really care. We had survived hell and lived to tell the tale.

We were the few. We were the proud. We were the Marines.

APPENDIX

U.S. Marine Corps Rank Structure

Enlisted

Rank	Pay grade	Abbreviation
Private	E-1	Pvt.
Private first class	E-2	Pvt. 1st class
Lance corporal	E-3	Lance Cpl.
Corporal	E-4	Cpl.
Sergeant	E-5	Sgt.
Staff sergeant	E-6	SSgt.
Gunnery sergeant	E-7	GySgt.
First sergeant / master sergeant	E-8	1st Sgt./MSgt.
Sergeant Major	E-9	Sgt. Maj.

Officer

Rank	Pay grade	Abbreviation
Second lieutenant	O-1	2nd. Lt.
First lieutenant	O-2	1st. Lt.
Captain	O-3	Capt.
Major	O-4	Maj.
Lieutenant colonel	O-5	Lt. Col.
Colonel	O-6	Col.
Brigadier general	O-7	Brig. Gen.
Major general	O-8	Maj. Gen.
Lieutenant general	O-9	Lt. Gen.
General	O-10	Gen.

GLOSSARY

2/3. 2nd Battalion, 3rd Marines.

3/3. 3rd Battalion, 3rd Marines.

Ali Babba. Arabic term for "thief" or "robber."

berm. Large mound of dirt that acts as a protective barrier.

BIOP. Baghdad International Airport.

BOLO. Be on the lookout.

chemlight. Chemically activated light source similar to a glow stick.

CO. Commanding officer.

COC. Combat Operations Center.

comms. Short for communications.

CP. Control point; command post.

CWIED. Command-wire IED.

DoD. Department of Defense.

ECM. Electronic countermeasure.

EOD. Explosive Ordnance Disposal

FOB. Forward operating base.

GPR. Gunpowder residue test.

H&S Company. Headquarters and Service Company.

HET. Human Exploitation Team.

hooch. Living quarters; home.

HUMINT. Human intelligence.

IA. Iraqi army.

ID. Identification.

IED. Improvised explosive device.

IP. Iraqi police.

JDAM. Joint direct attack munition.

JIEDD TF. Joint IED Defeat Task Force.

jundi. Arabic for "soldier."

KBR. Kellogg, Brown and Root, a former Halliburton subsidiary.

khubbis. Iraqi homemade bread.

MEDEVAC. Medical evacuation.

MiTT. Military transition team.

mm. Millimeter.

MOD. Iraqi Ministry of Defense.

MRE. Meal, ready-to-eat.

ODA. Operational Detachment Alpha
   (reference to U.S. Army Special Forces Team).

OIF. Operation Iraqi Freedom.

OP. Observation point.

overwatch. Position from which to observe enemy activity or protect
   friendly maneuver.

PLB. Personal locater beacon.

POG. People other than grunts, a derogatory term for nonactive
   combat participants.

PPIED. Pressure-plate IED.

PT. Physical training.

PTT. Police Transition Team.

QRF. Quick reaction force.

RCIED. Radio-controlled IED.

RIP. Relief in place.

RPG. Rocket-propelled grenade.

SAPI. Small-arms protective insert.

seven-ton. Marine troop transport vehicle.

SOP. Standard operating procedure.

terps. Short for interpreter.

VBIED. Vehicle-borne IED.

wadi. Dried riverbed.

wasta. Clout, or the ability to get things done in the eyes of Arabs.

XO. Executive officer.

INDEX

ABOUT THE AUTHOR

After a four-year "sabbatical" as an active-duty U.S. Marine officer, Wesley R. Gray returned to the University of Chicago Booth School of Business to finish his Ph.D. dissertation. He also serves as a portfolio manager and managing member of Empirical Finance, LLC. In his spare time, Wes enjoys sports and manual labor.